Community
Fundamental
Education

Community Fundamental Education

A Nonformal Educational Strategy
for Development

David Harman

Lexington Books
D.C. Heath and Company
Lexington, Massachusetts
Toronto   London

Library of Congress Cataloging in Publication Data

Harman, David.
    Community fundamental education.

    Originally presented as the author's thesis.
    Bibliography: p.
    1. Fundamental education.   2. Illiteracy.
3. Under developed areas–Education. I. Title.
LC5161.H37 1974   370.19'4   73–18235
ISBN 0–669–91850–4

Published simultaneously in Canada.

Printed in the United States of America.

International Standard Book Number: 0–669–91850–4

Library of Congress Catalog Card Number: 73–18235

For My Parents

Contents

Preface

The creation of a viable system of education for illiterate societies in the underdeveloped regions of the world must surely rank among education's greatest challenges. Mass illiteracy is but a symptom of a vicious cycle of underdevelopment, also typified by poverty, disease, malnutrition and, above all, by traditionalism and resistance to change. This book is an attempt to grapple with the educational context of development and is offered as an effort proposing a nonformal educational strategy aimed at inducing development and fostering change.

Originally written as a doctoral thesis at Harvard University, the ideas developed in the book began germinating during my association with the Israel literacy campaign eight years ago. Since that time I have had the benefit of association with the Adult Basic Education program of the United States Office of Education and the adult education activities of the Thailand Ministry of Education. I have also been able to visit activities in several other countries and meet with many people engaged in various levels of adult and literacy education. All of these contacts have helped shape my thinking and have contributed, in their own way, to the current volume. I owe a debt of gratitude to a great many people—program directors, teachers, supervisors, curriculum developers, organizers, and program participants. A collective acknowledgment must suffice as the list of names would be too lengthy to enumerate.

Professors Jerome Bruner, Adam Curle, and Manuel Zymelman of Harvard University served as members of my original thesis committee. They each read through several drafts of the book, offered sage advice, and devoted many hours of long and thoughtful conversation during which much of my thinking was clarified. For this, as well as their constant encouragement and warm friendship, I am greatly indebted. The late Zalman Aranne, Dr. Shlomo Kodesh, and Moshe Arnon, all of Israel, were of great assistance and encouragement during the beginning phases of my involvement with literacy and adult education work. Paul Delker, Tom Keehn, and Professor Jack Mezirow of the United States have provided both opportunities for involvement with additional programs and provocative feedback to many of the ideas presented here. Dr. Kowit Vorapipatana of Thailand has been a thorough interpreter of his country as well as a most valuable associate. Professor Paulo Freire of Brazil in many lengthy conversations has aided in the critique and analysis of many of the issues raised in the book. It is with a keen sense of indebtedness that I acknowledge the warm friendship and assistance of them all.

Dorothy, my wife, has helped in countless ways. Many hours that were rightfully hers and my daugher Danna's went into researching and writing this book. Without her understanding and constant companionship it would not have been completed.

Part I
On the Role of Education
in Development

1 Introduction

Among the foremost means being utilized in the furious race for development is education in its broadest sense. Education understood in this sense encompasses what is commonly called formal and nonformal education. Hence, any perceived experience resulting in or leading towards behavior change, either involving physical action or mental processes, is considered.[1] Such an experience consists of "the process of remaking, or reconstituting experience, so as to give it a more socialized content, through the medium of increase of control of experience." [2] While this definition lies at the root of this book it goes far beyond what is often the conception of education in educational policy making bodies in both developed and developing countries. Further clarification is, therefore, necessary.

The observation that most developed countries have highly developed systems of education has been widely interpreted as an indication of the requisite nature of education to development.[3] As the importance of the human factor in development becomes increasingly evident, so the desire for the proliferation of education becomes more urgent. Low illiteracy rates and high school enrollment figures, commonly found in developed countries, have become, together with measures of gross national product and per capita income, indices of development.[4] As a result the development of systems of education is included in most countries in overall plans of national development.

It has become a fairly academic question whether the developed state of the developing nations was achieved due to advanced systems of education or whether these resulted from development. Some people have pointed out that schools, until recently, were institutions for an elite not slated for hard work; and indeed that formal education was not a prerequisite for many occupations.[5] Others have shown that many people who centuries ago occupied positions that today would necessitate high levels of education were barely literate.[6] There is mounting evidence that increased expenditure on education is a result of economic development rather than a prerequisite to it.[7] Despite these assertions few would argue that substantial development can be achieved without the existence of a certain degree of education and training in a population.

Economists have given the arguments favoring massive investment in education added impetus in recent years. Since economic growth is the quintessence of most development schemes [8] this discovery of education by economists is of significance. It was not until the latter part of the 1950s that economists started focusing attention on education.[9] Humans were seen as an important component of economic growth, and as such warranted a portion of a nation's investment capital. Arguments were forwarded showing the nexus between investment in "human capital" or "human resources" and national growth.[10] These arguments have served to legitimize investments in education from an economic standpoint and may have occasioned an increased effort in educational development in some areas.[11]

As the manpower requirements of the modern state are legion, so the forms of educational experience need be varied. While primary education may be sufficient for some purposes, various forms of secondary and tertiary educational institutions are necessary for others. The latter two are dependent upon a flow of candidates from the former, forcing, in the first instance, the establishment of a large system of primary schooling. Coupled with the economic validity of this reasoning is the more social objective of insuring, for all citizens of a country, at least that minimum level of education. Indeed, this is today an accepted inalienable human right.[12] Certainly, the growth of secondary and tertiary systems of education is largely contingent upon a prior development at the primary level. If one accepts Jan Tinbergen's assertion, made in 1962, that, in view of the needs of developing countries, university enrollments should be "somewhere near" the European levels,[13] the necessity for expansion of formal systems of education becomes acute.

This approach to the role of education in development is largely quantitative. Underlying it is a tendency to equate a certain number of years of formal schooling with the capacity to perform set functions. Both C.E. Beeby and Adam Curle, among others, have cautioned against this tendency and have pointed to qualitative aspects of education,[14] arguing that the mere existence of schools does not insure levels of attainment. Attainment is, indeed, largely a function of many factors, most of which are not derived from the purely physical aspects of education as manifest in the existence of schools. Heeding these warnings, the logic underlying the argument for education as a prime factor in the development of manpower, and hence in economic growth, is nevertheless overpowering. One can raise many points pertaining to the implementation of educational growth but would be at a loss in trying to refute the basic contentions.

Many of the needs of the developing areas of the world cannot be expressed in solely economic terms. Hunger, malnutrition, and disease, while definitely having economic implications, are of themselves, for reasons of social and humanitarian concern, in need of eradication. The often cited vicious circle of poverty and underdevelopment must be broken if development is to proceed. As the role of education in this context is the prime concern of this study, a more detailed view of these problems that confront developing countries is warranted. Since illiteracy is commonly considered to be the educational manifestation of these ills its role in development will also be scrutinized.

2 Literacy and Development

Illiteracy and underdevelopment are usually linked in the minds of men. Indeed, wherever underdevelopment exists high rates of illiteracy are found. It is a common practice to associate illiteracy with the existence of other societal ills in developing areas. Nutritional, agricultural, population, and health problems, for example, are typically related by experts in those fields with a high incidence of illiteracy. The view expressed by Gunnar Myrdal that "Obviously, advances in literacy and advances in economic development are interconnected" [1] would elicit widespread agreement. Myrdal goes on however, to say, "In the total absence of any intensive research on the value of literacy for development, the argument must be cast for the time being in general and common sense terms." [2] Although Myrdal is incorrect in his assertion that there is a total lack of research into the questions of literacy and development, his statement pertaining to the common-sense nature of the arguments for literacy as a tool of development aptly explains the source of many similar insinuations.

Arguments such as the one quoted from Myrdal are largely predicated upon the assumption that illiteracy and literacy are clearly defined universal terms. In fact they are not, and a great deal of confusion exists as to their fundamental meanings. A look at some of the definitions extant is revealing.

Illiteracy is most commonly understood as describing a state of "being cut off from the written word, that is, being unable to read and write." [3] Literacy, therefore, as the opposite state, connotes the ability to read and write. Understood at its most elementary level, this set of definitions could mean that a person who can read and write his name has crossed the threshold of illiteracy and can be considered literate. Indeed, in many countries demonstration of this ability has been the criterion for qualifying as being a literate person.[4] Obviously, literacy at this rudimentary level can serve no practical purpose. Lacking from such a definition is a theory of literacy. What are the uses of literacy, and what are its societal functions?

Literacy as it is commonly understood is basically an extension of spoken language. It is that process by which a spoken language is reduced to a system of symbols that convey to people who speak the same language a constant rendition of a spoken letter, word, or phrase. Language is primarily a mode of communication, a medium through which a mutually understood set of sounds—words— are used by one person to convey a thought to another. "Language," wrote Edward Sapir, "is a purely human and non-instinctive method of communicating ideas, emotions and desires by means of a system of voluntarily produced symbols." [5] Literacy, therefore, is a mechanism for committing language into a form whereby the idea or thought being expressed is preserved and can be proliferated. To be literate one should be able to both read what has been written and write his own thoughts. A person can be considered fully literate only if he is able to perform both ends of the literacy schema, i.e., if he can receive and transmit through a written medium. Those who are able to read but not write have often been considered semiliterate. [6]

These basic understandings occasioned a series of attempts to define a level of mastery over written symbols that could be considered a baseline for qualifying literates from illiterates. While the mere ability to read and write one's name does prove a certain level of literacy skill, that level is too elementary for one to utilize his skills for purposes of wider communication. The United Nations Population Commission proposed, in 1948, that the "ability to read and write a simple message in any language" [7] be the threshold level of literacy. This definition was made somewhat more explicit in 1951 by an international "Expert Committee on Standardization of Educational Statistics," which proposed that to "both read with understanding and write a simple statement on [one's] everyday life" [8] become the basic criterion. While clarifying the phrase "simple message" in the earlier definition, the new recommendation raised several new questions. On the practical level, the message had become a "simple statement on everyday life." This was still insufficiently explicit—"I ate" would be such a statement and yet not be proof of any significant level of either reading or writing. On the conceptual level the term "understanding" was introduced, indicating that the technical skill alone was not a sufficient criterion.

During the mid-1950s, apparently in an attempt to get away from further polemics on level of literacy and content of literacy, a differentiation was proposed between a "literate" and a "functionally literate" person. "A person is functionally literate when he has acquired the knowledge and skills in reading and writing which enable him to engage effectively in all those activities in which literacy is normally assumed in his culture or group," proposed William Gray. [9] Had Gray's definition been accepted with the proviso that each "culture or group" determine for itself what level of literacy was requisite, much subsequent confusion would have been averted. UNESCO, however, adopted the following definition in 1962:

> A person is literate when he has acquired the essential knowledge and skills which enable him to engage in all those activities in which literacy is required for effective functioning in his group and community, and whose attainments in reading, writing and arithmetic make it possible for him to continue to use these skills towards his own and the community's development. [10]

This definition was further qualified: "In quantitative terms, the standard of attainment in functional literacy may be equated to the skills of reading, writing and arithmetic achieved after a set number of years of primary or elementary schooling." [11] Thus Gray's original definition was broadened practically by the addition of numeracy skills to those of literacy, the implication of a certain basic knowledge requirement, and conceptually by the proviso that these skills be applied to individual and community development in order to functionalize them. Functional literacy was, by this definition, given an active element. Confounding the definition, however, is the quantitative addendum. It serves an evaluative function of placing a primary-school level of attainment as the basic level of literacy and numeracy skills needed as a normative functional level. While some may interpret this as an attempt to achieve functional levels of these skills at the primary-school level, the more obvious result was that existing primary-school levels were adopted as norms. This definition thus took the element of self-determination of functional literacy skills from the individual society into the international realm. Fourth- or fifth-grade equivalents were adopted by most countries and became the quantitative definition of functional literacy.[12] In this respect the UNESCO definition ignored differences existing between different societies and cultures and, in an attempt at international standardization, created a sweeping determination of level of literacy irrespective of national and cultural needs. Nevertheless, this definition was formally endorsed in 1965 by the World Conference of Ministers of Education on the Eradication of Illiteracy as the accepted definition of functional literacy.[13]

Among the cultures ignored in the UNESCO definitions are those that are nonliterate, where literacy plays no role whatsoever in communication patterns. A definition forwarded by Paulo Freire takes cognizance of these groups:

> Learning to read and write ought to be an opportunity for men to know what speaking the word really means: a human act implying reflection and action. As such it is a primordial human right and not the privilege of a few. Speaking the word is not a true act if it is not at the same time associated with the right of expression, of creating and recreating, of deciding and choosing and ultimately participating in society's historical process.[14]

Freire argues that reading and writing cannot be construed merely as technical skills, but that they imply a prior act of conceptualization of the ultimate power and application of the skills. This conceptualization precedes the actual acquisition of the skills themselves and is applicable at the societal as well as the individual level. Non-literate or preliterate cultures need undergo a cultural metamorphosis of "literalization" entailing the internalization of a literacy consciousness prior to the adoption of the relatively simpler process of "alpha-betization" of the language. Then, and only then, will the UNESCO standards of functional literacy have any meaning. Literacy is thus seen as a three-stage process entailing the conceptualization of literacy as a tool of communication, the technical aspects of skill acquisition and, in order to transform literacy into a functional tool, the application of those skills to actual communication uses.[15]

For purposes of this study it is further stipulated that level of literacy accepted as functional can only be determined in the context of the particular society and culture in which literacy is utilized. The determinants of that level are a composite of the types of written communication extant and fostered in that particular society. The overall UNESCO stipulation of level is not accepted as a part of the basic definition of functional literacy.[16]

A UNESCO document prepared as background material for the World Conference of Ministers of Education on the Eradication of Illiteracy states, "Illiteracy is simply the manifestation at the educational level of a complex series of economic, political, social, psychological and cultural factors which has prevented entire groups of human beings from participating in the process of development going on around them."[17] This statement implies a correlation between illiteracy and other factors of underdevelopment. An analysis of the literature pertaining to this question would be of aid in either substantiating or refuting this contention.

One approach taken to demonstrate the role of literacy in development has been the examination of the rise of literacy in the developed countries of the West. C. Arnold Anderson concludes that data reviewed in this light shows that an approximate literacy level of 40 percent is a precondition for economic development.[18] Indeed, mideighteenth-century England seems to have had an adult literacy level of around 50 percent.[19] In the American colonies fragmentary evidence seems to point to a similar rate of literacy somewhat earlier than England.[20] By the midnineteenth century, Carlo Cipolla estimates that for the whole of Europe adult illiteracy was approximately at the 50 percent level.[21] The less developed countries predictably had high rates of illiteracy (Italy, Spain, and the Russian Empire), while the industrialized countries had literacy rates of between 50 and 90 percent. Significantly, however, those countries with the highest literacy rates (Prussia, Scotland, and Sweden) were not the most developed industrially.[22] Herbert Passin estimates that on the eve of the Meiji period in Japan adult male literacy was between 40 and 50 percent.[23] Clearly, in all of the industrializing societies rapid urbanization was also characteristic of the preindustrialization and industrialization periods. Surprisingly however, a comparison between literacy rates and degree of urbanization yields no correlation.[24] Nevertheless, for each of the countries mentioned literacy rates were always higher in urban areas and significantly lower in the rural zones.[25] As this lack of statistical correlation is for figures pertaining to 1850, one could hypothesize that beyond a certain point the two variables cease to correlate and that that point may have been reached a century or more earlier. There are some data available to support this contention.[26] While these data do support Anderson's conclusion, they do not imply a cause-effect relationship between literacy and economic development. Furthermore, as Cipolla points out, the data used in this analysis are incomplete, poorly collected, and often based on criteria such as signatures on marriage registers, hardly sufficient to show any substantial level of literacy. Anderson, too, is aware of this difficulty, but does not seem perturbed by its reflection on his conclusion.[27]

Anderson's conclusions from the historical development of literacy and economic growth are best questioned by another study of Anderson's, in collaboration with Mary Jean Bowman.[28] Correlating literacy rates for 1950 from ninety-three countries with per capita income for 1955, they found a definite relationship between literacy and income only where literacy rates were below 30 percent or above 70 percent. No correlations were found between the two variables in the twenty-seven countries in which literacy rates were in the range of 30 to 70 percent. Despite the argument forwarded by Anderson and Bowman that a 30-percent literacy rate is the threshold figure requisite for economic development, one cannot but agree with Mark Blaug's assessment that the most that can be concluded is that "while literacy may not always cure poverty, affluence always eradicates illiteracy."[29] In fact, Blaug finds the study useful only "in refuting the popular notion that literacy is the sure way to attain development."[30] This conclusion seems applicable also to Anderson's other contention that a 40-percent literacy level is necessary for economic development to occur.

Recent empirical inquiry into the question of effects of literacy on economic development expressed in terms of individual economic status does not clarify the issue. Peter Wright, for example, in an evaluation of relative economic status among 120 Guatemalan peasants concluded that "net worth" of the individual did not correlate significantly with functional literacy scores.[31] Similarly, Rose Goldsen and Max Ralis, studying acceptance of innovations in a Thai village, arrived at the same conclusion, i.e., that there is no significant correlation between literacy and economic status.[32] A somewhat different finding, however, emerged from a study conducted by Alfredo Mendez and Frederick Waisanen among Guatemalan communities.[33] They found a highly significant correlation (.005 level) between functional literacy scores and income level. Relating income level to literacy, however, is a different proposition, and a number of studies in developing countries have arrived at similar conclusions. Blaug's contention in this respect, that only a portion of income differential attributed to literacy can actually be ascribed to literacy, holds true for most of these.[34] The studies that have been cited, limited in scope and inconclusive, cannot be forcefully utilized in arguing that literacy and economic development, on either the macro or micro level, are associated in a cause–effect relationship. While literacy and economic development may have some connection, to argue that the former is in any way, independently of other factors, a precondition for the latter would be grossly misleading and insubstantial.

A number of attempts have been made to show the relation of literacy to other aspects of development. The capacity to incorporate change in both attitudes and behavior, or innovativeness, is one such aspect. Among rural communities in developing countries Everett Rogers and William Herzog, studying the correlates of functional literacy in Columbia,[35] Mendez and Waisanen in Guatemala, Goldsen and Ralis in Thailand, Howard Schuman, Alex Inkeles, and David Smith investigating the effects of literacy in East Pakistan,[36] and Wright and others working among Ladino peasant communities in Guatemala [37] all concluded that, in varying degrees, literacy and innovativeness are related. Schuman, Inkeles, and Smith confirmed their results for urban as well as rural populations. Despite the variations in degree of correlation these findings tend to support an assumption that, other factors being equal, literacy attainment is associated with a willingness to consider and adopt innovations. It is clear, however, that literacy alone is insufficient and must be supplemented by exposure to sources of information. It is the application of functional-level literacy skills to available sources of information that bridges the willingness to consider an innovation and ultimate adoption.

Exposure to sources of information as they are manifest in the mass media and literacy as independent variables has also been the subject of some empirical studies. Findings from these studies are significant, as they reflect on innovativeness, besides other factors. Rogers and Herzog, Mendez and Waisanen, Schuman, Inkeles, and Smith, Wright, and others all found significant correlations between literacy and media participation. These findings tend to validate their conclusions relating to innovativeness. Herzog, in a study of Brazilian rural communities,[38] and Frederick Fliegel, in a study among farmers in southern Brazil,[39] both concluded that literacy and mass media participation are not significantly related. While it is interesting that both of these negative results were obtained in independent studies in Brazil whereas the collective results of the other studies represent a much wider geographic spread, Herzog and Fliegel serve an important function in dampening the enthusiasm over this aspect of literacy attainment. Indeed, one of the primary objectives of literacy in modern society is to facilitate the utilization of mass media. Daniel Lerner has stipulated that media exposure and literacy are interrelated, in that literacy produces media consumers who, in turn, stimulate media production.[40] Using data from seventy-three countries, he found high correlations between literacy and all aspects of media exposure. Unfortunately, the data Lerner utilized for the purposes of his correlations is to a large extent highly suspect in its accuracy,[41] and thus diminishes the significance of his results. Furthermore, beyond his initial stipulations, Lerner's own empirical investigations failed to substantiate his assertions. While literacy is clearly a necessary tool for certain types of media participation, and seemingly fosters participation in other forms of mass media that do not require literacy as a precondition (radio, television, movies, etc.), the available evidence does not single literacy out as the one most significant factor in media participation. On the basis of this research one is led to conclude that literacy is a significant factor in media exposure but does not act independently of other factors.

Empathy, defined by Lerner as the "inner mechanism which enables newly mobile persons to operate efficiently in a changing world,"[42] is considered a major component of the characteristics of modern man. Once again, currently available research on its connection with literacy is inconclusive.[43] Similarly, attempts to find significant correlations between literacy and political participation, achievement motivation, cosmopoliteness, productivity, various health factors, and birth control have all produced conflicting results that do not lend themselves to the formulation of any definite conclusions pertaining to the actual effects of literacy on the various indices of development.[44]

Lacking from most of the research cited is any indication of the direction of causation. Thus, even in cases where correlations between literacy and certain of the other variables proved positive, we remain in the dark as to which variable occasioned the appearance of the other. One is left to conclude, upon reviewing these various studies, that the empirical evidence available is totally inadequate in answering any of the basic questions relating to literacy and development. Furthermore, one cannot infer whether literacy is a precondition for development or vice versa, or, indeed, whether the question of preconditions is applicable at all.

A very plausible clue to some of the answers pertaining to literacy can be found in another portion of Lerner's work.[45] Correlating data on degree of urbanization and literacy, Lerner concludes that "only after a country reaches ten percent of urbanization does its literacy rate begin to rise significantly." Between a 10-percent level of urbanization and 25-percent level he demonstrates that literacy and urbanization tend to increase in a direct relationship. Beyond a 25-percent rate of urbanization there appears to be no correlation between the two factors. Lerner calls this point the "critical optimum" of urbanization, and the 10-percent level the "critical minimum." While the actual points determined may not be completely accurate, due to faulty data concerning literacy, the existence of such points and the close relationship between literacy and urbanization within their limits seems to be highly acceptable. Lerner interprets the relationship as one of interdependence. Logically, however, it would seem to be one of dependence, with literacy being the dependent variable. As Lerner points out, "only cities require a largely literate population to function properly." [46] It stands to reason that the rise of cities preceded the spread of literacy and served as an initiator of widespread attainment of literacy skills.

How does this argument reflect upon literacy in rural areas? Is mass literacy preordained an urban phenomenon? The answers lie, perhaps, in an analysis of the reasons for the spread of literacy in a country after it has reached the "critical maximum" of urbanization. Assuming that increased urbanization brings about increased contact between urban and rural areas and causes increased interdependence between them, one can assert that rural literacy, too, is a function of urbanization. Just as literacy becomes a major tool of communication within a city so, too, does it become a necessary tool of communication with the city. Thus, the "critical minimum" of urbanization becomes a precondition for an initial rise in literacy rates in a country (primarily confined to urban areas), and the "critical maximum" becomes the precondition for a significant rise in rural literacy.

Other factors are also related to this argument. Nationalism and central government, the spread of technology, industrialization, and advances in transportation are all closely associated both with urbanization and economic growth. [47] While some degree of literacy does seem to be a precondition to all of these, mass literacy is more likely conditional. While the UNESCO statement quoted above thus seems substantiated, it appears to be an oversimplification of the cause-and-effect aspects of illiteracy, and is completely lacking in any conception of stages.

A blueprint for illiteracy eradication in a country, it follows, would stress the urban illiteracy situation first and then, after a certain "critical maximum" of urbanization has been achieved, should shift its emphasis to the eradication of rural illiteracy. It will, in fact, be shown hereafter that attempts at achieving mass literacy in rural areas, without the existence of the factors associated with urbanization, are largely unsuccessful. It should at this point be stressed that the possible role of education in areas such as nutrition, agriculture, health, and population growth is not conceived of as consisting predominantly of literacy education.

So far in this analysis literacy has been treated as an absolute factor. One is either literate or illiterate. This conflicts, of course, with the earlier stipulation recognizing different levels of literacy. It is assumed that as countries become more complex in their economic growth as manifest in the urbanization syndrome, the level of literacy necessary to cope with the changing life patterns also becomes more complex. Thus, the level of literacy requisite at the beginning of the process (at the "critical minumum") would be less than the levels required during subsequent stages (at the level of "critical maximum" and beyond). Literacy becomes, in this proposition, a dynamic rather than a static factor, and requires reevaluation at each stage. One could argue further that the level of literacy requisite in urban areas will always exceed that required of rural populations, although it would seem that at some point in the growth continuum a "critical optimum" of literacy requirements would be reached for the entire population. It is primarily for this reason that the establishment of universal literacy levels applicable to all societies at all stages of overall development is not acceptable.

Notwithstanding this contention, a brief look at what is considered to be the state of illiteracy in the world is instructive. Figures pertaining to illiteracy for most countries have been collected and published by UNESCO on several occasions.[48] The main feature of these data, when summed up for all countries reported upon, is the fact that while the illiteracy rate is decreasing the absolute number of illiterate adults (age fifteen and above) is increasing. Thus, in 1950 an estimated 700 million illiterates comprised 44.3 percent of the adult population, in 1960 the corresponding estimated figures were 740 million and 39.3 percent and in 1970, assuming a constant rate of decrease, 810 million and 34.8 percent.[49] When broken down by geographical region Africa, Asia, and Latin America all have adult illiteracy rates above the fiftieth percentile, with many countries having rates of 80 percent and over.[50]

The inaccuracy of these data is evidenced by data collection procedures in many of the reporting countries, in particular those with the highest illiteracy rates. Literacy is determined in census taking on the basis of a question or series of questions asked by the enumerator.[51] Tests are rarely, if ever, administered. In many of the newly independent countries gross estimates of total population size must suffice until census apparatus is sufficiently developed. Illiteracy rates are derived by taking estimates from estimates. Finally, the definitions of illiteracy vary from country to country, and while many have accepted the UNESCO standard of ability to read and write "a simple message in any language," many others have adopted different standards.[52] It should be noted that the UNESCO statistics relate only to "absolute", not functional, literacy. Any attempt at assessing the latter would be pure guess-work.[53]

Despite these inaccuracies some trends can be seen in these figures. The major areas of illiteracy correspond to the major areas of urban underdevelopment. Although urban populations are growing in these areas, the degree of growth is diminished due to the large overall rates of population growth. Finally, the figures offer adequate evidence that literacy rates are not independent of other factors affecting development and should not be considered separately.

Insofar as literacy is to be fostered, it is primarily incumbent upon various forms of education to be its agents. Literacy cannot, however, be considered as a precondition for other elements of development, but rather must be considered in conjunction with them. A further proposition forwarded in this study is that in some cases education aimed at objectives other than literacy takes precedence over literacy education, and that, indeed, literacy cannot be isolated from either the state of societies and other manifestations of underdevelopment.

3 Some Aspects of Underdevelopment

Malnutrition, poor health conditions, overpopulation, and inadequate agricultural output are all manifestations of underdevelopment. Although specific conditions prevailing in different countries and areas of the world may differ, differences are only of degree. Each of these factors must be looked at separately, for each is in need of specific activities for improvement. Taken together, however, they portray a grim picture of underdevelopment.

Malnutrition [1]

According to estimates derived by the Food and Agriculture Organization of the United Nations (FAO), between 10 and 15 percent of the population of the World are undernourished, while as many as half of the population suffer from some degree of malnutrition.[2] Problems of malnutrition are predominantly evident in developing regions around the globe where they affect large segments of the population.[3] Malnutrition is by no means entirely confined to these areas. Besides pockets of populations suffering from symptoms similar to those found in the developing countries, a form of malnutrition resulting from overeating appears in developed countries, although its incidence is relatively lower.[4] Children, particularly preschool age children, are the primary victims of malnutrition. It has been estimated that as many as 70 percent of all preschool-age children in developing countries are malnourished.[5] While there may be some disagreement as to the estimates and even the application of the term "protein-calorie malnutrition,"[6] none would dispute the World Health Organization's (WHO) assertion that malnutrition or protein-calorie deficiency is the foremost public health problem in the world today.[7]

The effects of malnutrition are dramatic. Infant mortality in developing countries is approximately four times as high as in most developed countries, while early childhood mortality is as much as forty times higher.[8] Most of these early deaths are directly attributable to malnutrition although many may be recorded as resulting from a variety of other causes.[9] Kwashiorkor, a disease principally due to a diet low in protein and primarily affecting children of the ages of one to three, is the classical form of extreme malnourishment. Its symptoms of swelling, growth retardation, weakness, and misery are all too well known. Nutritional Marasmus, directly resulting from protein and calorie

15

deficiencies, is increasing in many portions of the developing world. The sight of children with wasted bodies and expressions of old men, symptomatic of this disease, is haunting.[10] While these may be the more glaring examples of the effects of malnourishment, they represent but a fraction of the diseases and infirmities directly caused by it.

Recent investigations into problems of malnourishment indicate that physical retardation due to protein and calorie deficiencies interacts with impaired mental development, much of which is irreversible.[11] The future development of many countries is severely compromised due to the effects of malnutrition in children.

Malnutrition also takes its toll of adults. By weakening the body it impairs their capacity for work and hence affects productivity. Many illnesses, some of which may be fatal, are more prevalent in undernourished persons.[12] Nutrition of mothers is a particularly important aspect of the problem, as it affects not only their capacity to function but also the health and development of their children, if they are either pregnant or breast feeding.[13]

Two main causes are cited as portents of malnourishment; lack of foods and improper utilization of available nutrients.[14] While one obvious means of combatting malnutrition consists in increasing the supply of food, another lies in the improvement of food utilization. The role that education can play in the latter endeavor seems quite apparent, as much of what is involved consists of attitude and behavior change. Education can also play a role in the former undertaking, that of increasing the supply of food.

Population Increase

Aggravating the fundamental problems posed by malnutrition are those resulting from the demographic explosion occurring in the developing world. Insofar as malnutrition is attributable to a lack of basic foods to feed the existing population, it is easy to see how any increase in population works against alleviation of this problem. It is not uncommon to see the population-growth problem as a race between people and food.[15] Significant as the problems of feeding a vastly increased population may be, the total effects of this increase are far more overpowering. The implications of the population explosion for economic growth in general, employment, urbanization, health, and education are far reaching.[16]

The world population in 1970 was approximately 3.5 billion, and increasing steadily at an approximate rate of 2 percent annually. By the end of the century, therefore, the overall population will be in the region of six billion.[17] Most of this increase will occur in those regions least able to cope with their present population levels, the developing regions. It is estimated that 85 percent of the increase will be in Asia, Africa, and Latin America. Thus, by the end of the century nearly four-fifths of the entire global population will be found in these three continents.[18]

The current rate of growth of the developing countries averages 2.2 percent annually and is expected to remain constant.[19] This fact would perhaps, be less alarming if food production, public health, and general economic levels were increasing at much higher levels than they in fact are. Consequently many of the advances being made are not having the impact they could on raising basic living standards and correcting existing ills, as they are being rapidly absorbed by the additional population.

A wide variety of programs is being conducted aimed at lowering the rate of population increase. Since ultimately population growth depends on the attitudes and behavior of individuals, education has a significant role to play in this area.

Agriculture

Closely related to problems of malnutrition and population growth are those of agricultural production. Agriculture must, first and foremost, produce food. In order to keep abreast of the population explosion around the world at present levels of feeding, therefore, agricultural production must expand by 2 percent per year.[20] However, it is precisely present food consumption levels in many countries that result in malnutrition. Thus, agricultural production must increase much more than 2 percent if malnutrition is to be alleviated, at least as it is a function of insufficient food. The income elasticity of demand for food in developing countries is between 0.5 and 0.8. Assuming an average annual growth of 3 to 4 percent in per capita incomes in developing countries, the demand generated for additional agricultural produce will be from 2 to 4 percent.[21]

Agriculture also serves industry. Many industries are dependent upon its produce for raw materials. In developing countries alone, it has been estimated, [22] industries dependent upon agricultural raw materials accounted for 51 percent of value added to the gross national product. This, of course, places an added burden on the overall picture of agricultural needs.

Despite bleak pronouncements from the FAO that the average agricultural output per capita in developing countries has barely been able to keep abreast of the basic food requirements of their populations,[23] some experts see cause for optimism.[24] New varieties of rice, wheat, grain sorghum, and corn are available that could potentially more than double current yields. These figures and projections reflect the macro aspects of agriculture. In order to comprehend the scope of the problem more fully it is necessary to examine the effects of agriculture on the individual and the impact of the individual on agriculture.

Roughly two thirds of the populations of developing countries are employed in agriculture.[25] Between 70 and 90 percent of these populations are sequestered in rural areas where agriculture is the major occupation and largely the sole source of livelihood. Subsistence farming is more often the rule than the exception. In many parts of the world farmers are tenants on lands owned by absentee landlords, and are forced to pay high rents.[26] When the sole occupation of large population segments consists of subsistence farming, cash returns, if any, are small. Consequently, those groups become tied to the land and their vocations in a Gordian knot.

Farming methods are generally antiquated, utilizing age-old farming implements and traditions. In addition, land holdings are usually too small for modern technology to be fully applied or higher yields to be fully realized. As the margins for experimentation are extremely small, many farmers prefer the continued use of the well-known strands and methodologies.[27] Traditional agriculture is a most serious impediment to any major changes in agricultural production. In fact, continuation of traditional approaches and farming methods, coupled with the increasing pressures placed on the land due to population increases, can only serve to aggravate the agricultural problem of the developing countries.

Numerous programs are being conducted by international and national organizations, all aimed at alleviating the "agriculture problem." Crucial to the outcome of many of these programs are the attitudes and actions of the many farmers in the developing countries. Here, too, education has a significant role to play.

Health

Life expectancy in most of the developing countries is about half that of developed countries.[28] This figure, not entirely surprising, is primarily due to a combination of factors that are considered the "health problem." The statistics of the problem are overpowering. Over half of the deaths in developing countries occur in children under the age of five, mostly as a result of malnutrition and a group of communicable diseases that have long been conquered in the developed world. These diseases, which affect hundreds of millions of people, include diphtheria, tetanus, whooping cough, cholera, tuberculosis, leprosy, various childhood diarrhoeas, malaria, bilharzia, and others.[29]

This situation is seen as a composite of malnutrition, high incidence of communicable disease, and general unsanitary conditions. There is, obviously, a cause–effect relationship among these factors, and alleviating one would contribute to alleviation, if not the eradication, of the others.[30] Many hygienic measures such as cleanliness, ventilation, destruction of vermin, personal care, and care of soil and water, to mention just a few, if introduced and accepted, would help change the health picture considerably. As in the cases of the previous problems cited, attitudes, understanding, and behavior of individuals are prerequisites to any major changes in this area. Education, once again, has a significant contribution to make.

Education's role in development is as complex as it is crucial. At its minimum level it will hereafter be called fundamental, and it is at that level that it will be further explored.

Part II
Fundamental Education:
Theory and Practice

4 A Theory of Fundamental Education

The term "fundamental education" enjoyed an all too brief currency. It was first brought into use in 1947 by UNESCO connoting basic education.[1] There were two main thrusts inherent in the UNESCO usage of the term. First, a universal minimum quantum of education was stipulated. Second, a qualitative assay of content was proposed, including both basic skills and knowledge.[2] These last were to consist of skills and knowledge considered universally essential, such as literacy skills and skills and knowledge deemed requisite in different cultural situations and applicable only to them. The overall objective of fundamental education was to integrate the use of all educational agencies in developing countries in a concerted attack on social and economic problems.[3]

Fundamental education was considered by UNESCO to be an emergency measure. The emergency was dictated, on the one hand, by the need to provide "minimum knowledge and skills which are an essential condition for attaining an adequate standard of living; a prerequisite to the full effectiveness of work in health, agriculture and similar skilled services." On the other hand the emergency had a stop-gap aspect, as fundamental education was concerned with "children for whom there is no adequate system of primary schooling and with adults deprived of educational opportunity." [4] The attainment of universal primary schooling in itself became one of the aims of fundamental education. Theoretically, once primary education for all was satisfactorily instituted in a country emphasis would shift to adults who had not had primary education backgrounds.

It is not surprising that fundamental education became increasingly identified with adult education. Indeed, by 1952 UNESCO had added the words "adult education" to its publications dealing with fundamental education.[5] As fundamental education for adults was typically conceived of as consisting of literacy education and community development, usage of the term was further narrowed. Finally, in 1961, UNESCO completely dropped the term "fundamental education" and substituted "adult education" in its stead.[6]

Unfortunately, discontinuance of the term was accompanied by a discontinuity of some of the ideas inherent in it. Fundamental education was concerned with all segments of the community, whereas its successors focus on adult populations. This different vantage point also occasioned a change of strategy. Literacy education stresses the acquisition of a set of particular skills, while community development is aimed at mobilizing communities for self-help.

Community development was a stipulated objective of fundamental education, but the medium was the individual, not the community, and the skills and knowledge perceived were not limited to literacy. Perhaps most unfortunate was the segmentation of the integrated effort envisioned by the articulators of UNESCO's fundamental education. At least in theory, coordination of various programs and approaches was implicit in the UNESCO articulation. In this sphere, perhaps more than in others, fundamental education had great potential.

The objective here is not to revive a forgotten term, let alone all of its conceptual underpinnings. However, in presenting a theory of fundamental education not totally different from UNESCO's an understanding of its initial use and connotations is useful.

At all levels of human development the act of living requires of the individual a certain set of skills and knowledge. Many of these are self acquired, a function of growth and environment. Many others are not. They are learned through a variety of means, depending upon the particular culture. Common to all cultures, however, is the existence of a system designed to transmit these skills and knowledge from one generation to the next. In static or unchanging societies such systems are primarily concerned with the perpetuation of certain life styles and behaviors. Transfer of skills and knowledge is quite literal. The underlying concept is one of growth and gradual assumption of adult roles and tasks. In dynamic or changing societies emphasis is placed upon change rather than growth. Margaret Mead sees this difference between nonchanging and changing societies as a dichotomy of "what is done to people rather than . . . what people do".[7] Thus, in the dynamic situation the object is to transfer skills and knowledge as a basis for change rather than as a means of perpetuation. Perpetuity in the static situation, however, is largely contingent upon the maintenance of an unchanging set of circumstances. As long as all other factors affecting life patterns remain unchanged the system can remain successful. Any change in any aspect of the environment serves to force change and necessitate modification in the skills and knowledge requisite and the means of transferring them. In the eventuality of any such change the static society is transformed into a dynamic one and, as in the latter case, the existing skills and knowledge become the basis for change.

Man's environment throughout the world is in a state of flux. Demographic, economic, geographical, and political realities combine to create this state. Traditional knowledge and skills passed down through the generations are no longer sufficient to enable man to cope with his new circumstances. Traditional transmittal systems are inadequate, as they were not designed to incorporate change. Once change has been introduced to a static society it is no longer static, and the static–dynamic dichotomy is no longer valid. The degree of modification necessary in both the skills and knowledge and the means of transmitting them becomes contingent upon the nature of the change. As such change is, in the terms of this study, development, the nature of the change can be understood as the degree of development.

The skills and knowledge required for coping with one's environment are here considered fundamental skills and knowledge. The ways and means by which these are imparted are fundamental education. Any system, formal or informal, aimed at imparting these skills and knowledge is considered a system of fundamental education.

The precise content of fundamental education in this definition is determined by each specific situation. However, insofar as it is possible to detect a direction of development it is also possible to forecast what set of skills and knowledge will become requisite. In this respect developing societies are fortunate in being able to learn from the trials and errors of the more developed ones and incorporate into their fundamental education frameworks sets of skills and knowledge that, while perhaps not immediately applicable, could in due course become so. Fundamental education in developing societies thus becomes not only a means for maintaining the pace of development but also, in itself, an agent of change.

In the preceding chapter several impediments to change and development were discussed. The existence of these impediments in many countries is a hindrance to development. Solution of these problems becomes a precondition for development in situations where other developmental objectives are envisioned and a prime goal of development in other situations. In both cases fundamental education must deal with the problems and devise effective means of transmitting the needed sets of skills and knowledge.

The nature of some of the problems described is such that skills and knowledge alone would be insufficient tools, in some areas, for overcoming them. Awareness of the problems becomes a prior condition that must exist if the subsequently transferred capacities for dealing with the problems are to be effectively applied. Awareness in this sense also, therefore, becomes an aspect of fundamental education.

It is not implicit in this theory that the strategy of fundamental education is through groups or individuals or by integrated action or otherwise. These can only be determined on the basis of each specific situation. Insofar as situations have common elements the strategies may be similar, but as situations differ so the strategies employed can be disparate. Later in this study certain common modalities will be pointed out and a strategy developed and proposed. Neither those commonalities nor the strategy are, however, conceptually a part of this theory of fundamental education. Any framework that provides fundamental education, through whatever strategy it chooses to employ, "qualifies" as a system of fundamental education.

Literacy in Fundamental Education

Thus far the role and place of literacy in fundamental education is unclear. Is literacy, as Lerner contends, the "basic personal skill that underlies the whole modernizing sequence,"[8] and hence axiomatically a major component of fundamental education as it is conceived in this study, or is literacy a set of skills whose inclusion as an element within fundamental education must be assessed anew in each different environmental situation? Earlier it was shown that the various studies correlating literacy with developmental variables are inconclusive in their evidence that literacy is indeed the "basic personal skill" required. In setting forth a theory of literacy it is necessary, therefore, to rely to a large extent on nonempirically derived arguments.

Literacy has often been considered much more than the simple ability to read and write. Hortense Powdermaker asserts that "literacy is not just learning how to read but is concerned with comprehending a form of reality beyond immediate experience."[9] Lerner, too, holds that "with literacy people acquire more than the simple skill of reading," and argues that "the very act of achieving distance and control over a formal language gives people access to the world of vicarious experience and trains them to use the complicated mechanism of empathy which is needed to cope with this world."[10] Similarly, David Riesman contends that illiterate people "are led by folk tales and songs to identify with the tribe as it has been and will be, or possibly with a legendary golden age, but they are not incited to imagine themselves outside its comforts and coherence."[11] Literacy, therefore, according to Riesman, helps to liberate the individual from his group and environment. Common to all of these assertions are two basic assumptions; first, that literacy skills are sufficiently developed such that they enable their possessor to put them to use at a fairly high level, and second, that the literate person have access to a fairly large range of written materials. The skills associated with literacy alone are insufficient to extend an individual's horizons, but rather the skills applied bring about the described results. Literacy is, thus, a composite of the skill of reading and the act of reading.

The literate person, by utilizing his reading skills becomes a "media participator." In terms of media participation Lerner shows that literacy has a "snowball" effect. "Those who read newspapers also tend to be the heaviest consumers of movies, broadcasts, and all other media products." Assuming, again, that these media products are present and available, Lerner conceives literacy as being the key to a whole new world that transcends the printed message. One is led to wonder why it is that literacy rather than, say, exposure to radio broadcasts initiates this chain of events. Is there inherent in literacy a factor that is especially suited to enabling an individual to become an active media participator?

Gray observes that "reading is a highly complex activity including various important aspects such as recognizing symbols quickly and accurately, apprehending clearly and with discrimination the meanings implied by the author, reacting to . . . ideas . . . and integrating them into definite thought and action patterns."[12] Charles Fries saw this complex of activities as being divisible into three distinct stages. The first stage is the "transfer stage," during which "the process of learning to read in one's native language is the process of transfer from the auditory signs for language signals (which have already been learned) to the new visual signs for the same signals."[13] The second stage is the "productive stage," during which response to the visual symbols becomes unconscious. Finally, at the third or "imaginative stage," the decipherment of the written symbols becomes as simple and automatic as speaking a language and "reading is used equally with or even more than live language in the acquiring and developing of experience."[14] Both Gray and Fries observe that symbol recognition is a major factor of reading. Since the written word is primarily a code symbolizing the spoken word, symbol recognition becomes a process of decoding. Indeed, Jeanne Chall points out that most linguists agree that decoding should be the emphasis in beginning reading.[15] A letter symbol is, however, no more than a code for a given sound and, in itself, has no meaning. It is only when several separate sounds are combined and a word is formed that meaning is introduced. Thus, Fries's third stage is contingent upon a reader being able to decode whole words and phrases. The essence of reading becomes the ability to decode symbols with a fair amount of agility and literacy, a process of decoding and encoding. The act of reading entails more than the mere ability to break a code. One must be able to abstract meaning from the deciphered code in order to complete the process.

This process of encoding, decoding, and abstraction of meaning contains another significant aspect—that of divorcing the message from its sender. Herzog suggests, therefore, that the literacy process alters the "individual's perceptions of the symbol–referent relationship."[16] In an illiterate or predominantly oral culture the message is transmitted from one person to another in face-to-face contact. The basic notion of literacy is that a message can be transmitted independently of such a relationship between sender and recipient. This cognitive apperception is considered, in this study, to be the fundamental aspect of literacy education. The conceptualization of literacy as a tool that can serve to expand one's reality through communication that is not based on direct, face-to-face contact is here considered to be a fundamental skill requisite for any change to occur. In this sense, too, I agree with Lerner that literacy is necessary for wider media participation. As in reading so, too, does media participation in its other forms necessitate an ability to separate the message from its source and internalize it for its content.

This leads to a further observation. Literacy is conceived of here in a very broad sense. Based on the understanding that literacy is a process of encoding, decoding, and abstraction of meaning from the code, the commonly accepted notion that literacy is the ability to read and write is extended to subsume also the ability to represent any three-dimensional reality on a two-dimensional surface. With considerable license I would term this "visual literacy," as opposed to "written literacy." Thus the ability to perceive and interpret pictures, photographs, diagrams, maps, charts, etc. is also considered to be literacy of a sort. Literacy is conceived of as the basic communication skill that enables the individual to extend the range of his contact well beyond his immediate environment. It is the skill necessary not only to become the recipient of information, ideas, and thoughts emanating from outside the immediate environment, but also to become a sender of such communications to that "outside" world. Fundamental to this two-way communication is an awareness of the existence of an extended environment and of the benefits of communication with it. Whether or not literacy in the sense of the written word is to be the tool of communication must be determined in each societal situation on the basis of its own criteria. While written communication seems the most expedient way of fostering this exchange, it is not the only way. As an ultimate communication skill literacy seems irreplaceable. However, in some situations it could conceivably be preceded by visual or audio communication. With these clarifications Lerner's contention cited earlier that literacy is "the basic personal skill that underlies the whole modernizing sequence" is accepted.

In the following pages three strategies, all of which purport to provide fundamental education as defined above—primary education, community development programs, and literacy programs for adults—will be examined and their effectiveness as instruments of fundamental education analyzed. Emphasis will be laid on their manifestation in rural areas in developing countries—the primary focus of concern in this study.

5 Primary Schooling as Fundamental Education

Among the nebulous goals of primary education is that of providing its recipients with a set of fundamental skills and knowledge.[1] Indeed, primary schooling is usually considered the backbone of fundamental education. The original UNESCO approach to fundamental education, whereby the attainment of universal primary schooling was in itself a prime aim of fundamental education, is quite common. Certainly a major portion of educational development in developing nations has been devoted to the expansion of primary-school systems.

Among the targets of the first United Nations Development Decade set forth in December 1961, large increases in primary-school enrollments were stipulated. By the end of the decade it was intended that 70 percent of all children between the ages of six and twelve in Africa should be enrolled in primary schools, 50 percent in Asia, and 100 percent in Latin America.[2] During the 1960s most of the developing nations spent unprecedented sums of money on this expansion of primary education. For the majority of countries in these regions expenditures on primary education accounted for approximately half of the total expenditure on education.[3] The ultimate objective of this drive is the establishment of universal primary schooling well before the end of the century.

The quantitative expansion of primary education in most developing countries during the 1960s has been extensive.[4] Although many countries have not reached the precise quantitative goals set in regional and national plans at the outset of the decade, the large majority have been making significant strides.[5]

Most of the available statistics do not differentiate between primary-school expansion in urban and rural areas but, rather, give national figures. However, since the majority of the populations in developing countries are rural it stands to reason that a major part of the development of primary education has taken place in rural areas. It seems evident that the institution of primary schools at the rural level is considered essential as a prime means of providing fundamental education.

In assessing the success of primary schools as agents of fundamental education in rural areas, one is severely hampered by a dearth of field evaluations and must resort to drawing conclusions from a variety of quantitative and qualitative information. The following analysis will draw upon this information in an

29

attempt to show that primary education in rural areas of developing nations is, generally, not achieving any significant role in the fundamental education of its client population.

The primary school being instituted throughout the developing world is a familiar one. From both an organizational and curricular point of view it does not differ from its counterpart in the developed nations. It is, in fact, a poor copy at best. Unfortunately, the stress laid upon quantitative expansion of primary education has tended to gloss over the qualitative aspects of primary schooling.[6]

Quality of education itself can be adjudged from different points of view. On the one hand there are a set of internal criteria by which a school can assess how well it is educating its pupils. These criteria must, therefore, be based on a conception of what the school is supposed to teach. Assuming that such a conception exists, the degree of success of a school in teaching specified material can be measured with relative ease. On the other hand, the question of what a school should teach arises as a qualitative problem. Thus, the query is aimed at the conception of what is to be taught rather than how well specific material is taught. This external criterion is primarily a question of fitness and relevance of educational content to specific needs and environments.[7] R.S. Peters has referred to these two aspects of quality in education as "quality of the product" and "quality of the process."[8] It seems that quality of a system is comprised of both of these. A determination of what is to be taught is a precondition for evaluating how well it has been taught. Thus, in ordering the questions one must first pose the problem of process or relevance. Torsten Husen's statement that "the criteria of quality . . . relate to the objectives which explicitly are guiding the operations of a given type of school within a given socio-cultural framework"[9] is a good starting point.

In practice it appears that the quantitative objective of primary-school expansion has served to make the mere existence of a school the main objective, rather than attempting to give the school specified directions. What the school should be doing has become a less important question. A model of primary schooling has emerged, and seemingly been universally accepted, that views this institution as a place where reading, writing, and numeracy skills are taught, along with a smattering of information on various subjects such as history, geography, civics, and the like.[10] The format of primary schooling is also virtually universal. Children sitting in rows facing a teacher standing in front of a blackboard is the typical situation, labeled by Philip Coombs the "monk's cell of the educational process."[11] Little has been done to adapt the primary school to the specific needs and situations of rural communities. A comparative study of seventy-two countries published in 1958 shows that, with only a few minor exceptions, no special provision had been made either in organization or content for rural primary schools.[12] The few exceptions cited were all attempts to add some instruction in agriculture to the regular syllabus. Little has changed in this respect since publication of this study. Nicholas Bennett paints a picture of the primary-school experience of the typical rural child:

> Typically, at the age of 5, 6, or 7 (legal age) the child will enroll in a primary school. It is likely that this school will be some distance from his home, and that he will spend one hour each way every day travelling to and from school. Each day he will spend about seven hours in school, most of the time sitting in a crowded, hot, ill-lit building. He will be taught by a teacher with not much more than primary school education himself. At least half the time will be spent on reading (reciting after the teacher), writing (copying from the board) and arithmetic (copying and reciting). In many countries a large proportion of the remaining time will be spent on learning (by drill) a language other than the mother tongue. There might also be some work on a school garden, and lectures and recitation in geography, history, general science and religion.[13]

The first problem raised by this description is one of facilities. In most of the developing nations the construction of adequate school facilities in the rural areas poses a nearly insurmountable problem. The costs of providing buildings and school furnishings for such large segments of the population are staggering. All of the countries participating in the Karachi Plan, for example, with the sole exception of Japan, quote the lack of adequate facilities as one of the main obstacles to reaching the Plan's goal of full enrollment by 1980.[14] Rather than construct fewer but more substantial schools, most countries have tended to provide poor facilities for large portions of the population, with the result that few of the installations are conducive to learning. Experiments such as those conducted in Cambodia in which classes were held outdoors [15] are probably healthier approaches than cramming children into the cramped, dark rooms Bennett describes.

The second point Bennett raises is that of teachers. It stands to reason that good teachers could to a large extent compensate for inadequate facilities. However, the problem of teachers stands out as one of the most serious afflictions of primary education in rural developing areas. There are manifold aspects to the teacher problem. Education, Coombs points out, is a labor intensive industry largely dependent upon its ability to hire large numbers of its products.[16] These products can only be as good as the system that produces them. A poor system of education will obviously only recycle poor teachers. Being labor intensive, educational systems require large numbers of teachers. Since few developing countries have yet succeeded in graduating large numbers of secondary and higher educated manpower, standards are often compromised with and primary school graduates are being pressed into service as primary-school teachers. This situation is further compounded by the fact that education is not the only industry competing for the better qualified personnel.

Since salaries of teachers are typically low [17] the better of the graduates
of secondary and tertiary institutions are hired away from careers in education.
One can assume that of those who do take up teaching as a profession few
are keen on being posted to rural areas.

Bennett also implies criticism of the curricula and teaching methodologies
extant in the primary schools. Beeby points out that one would "have no
difficulty in finding in Africa and Asia scores of examples of curricula and
educational objectives more suited to England and France half a century ago
than to the crying needs of an emergent tropical country today."[18] There are
many explanations as to why this is the case. Most stem from the observation
that economically advanced Western countries all seem to offer similar curricula
in their primary schools. Christopher Cox, speaking in 1956 about one group
of developing nations, observed that "the general practice all over British
Africa, despite its many remaining backward areas, is today increasingly one on
which the Africans have set their hearts, with an impatient fervour that it is
hard for us to realize, upon a complete Western education as they believe it to
be."[19] Even in situations in which educational policy bodies recognize
the fallacy in this mode of thinking, popular demand for the "Western" model
of education serves as an obstacle to the introduction of change.[20] One
result of this demand is the fairly consistent failure of attempts to give an agricultural bias to primary schools in agricultural countries. However, while
popular demand for education no doubt exists in many areas of the developing
world and is steadily increasing, in many rural areas where educational traditions are completely lacking and contact with the outer world is minimal it
seems fair to assume that this demand is minimal, perhaps even nonexistent.
Moreover, one wonders where notions of "Western" education emanated from.
A likely explanation seems to be that demand for a particular form of education
exists more in urban areas or areas with a certain amount of urban contact
and areas in which some form of Western education, perhaps mission schools,
has already been established.

Paul Mort has shown in a series of studies that "the average American
school lags twenty-five years behind the best practice."[21] If this is true of
American schools it would certainly be true of rural primary schools in developing countries, which suffer the added disadvantages of underfunding and
poorly qualified teachers. It comes as no surprise, therefore, that instructional
methodologies are outmoded and revolve upon rote learning. Beeby aptly
explains the plight of the underqualified teachers thus: "Their only way to get
safely through the day without revealing the gaps in their knowledge is to stick
to the textbook and encourage no one in the classroom, besides themselves,
to ask questions."[22] Obviously, change in teaching methodologies is needed.
The corollary with American education can again be evoked: If conservatism in
educational techniques exists in the relatively well-endowed schools of the
United States among relatively highly qualified teachers, then it can surely be
taken for granted in rural, developing areas.

Further compounding this already sorry picture of primary education in rural areas is the factor of retention. There are a number of different aspects to this issue, all of which argue that the little that is taught in the schools is soon forgotten by the bulk of the students. Most obvious of these aspects is that of wastage, defined as both early dropping out and grade repetition. Bennett estimates that in the developing world, approximately 15 percent of all children entering the first grade will drop out at the end of the first year, and at least an additional 10 percent will drop out after the second. Moreover, between 10 to 30 percent of all children in any particular year of school will have to repeat that year.[23] In country after country these estimates are borne out. In India it was calculated in 1967 that 65.3 percent of all primary-school enrollees drop out by grade five and 78.36 percent by grade eight, with about half of the wastage occurring during and immediately after the first year.[24] In the countries of French-speaking Africa, with the sole exception of Senegal, 50 percent or more drop out by the end of grade four.[25] It has been calculated that in the Latin American countries 50 percent of primary school entrants drop out by the third grade;[26] the wastage rate for the countries of South-East Asia, with the exception of Ceylon and Malasia, for the cohort enrolling in 1957–58 was between 60 and 85 percent over an average of five years of schooling.[27] While there are reservations as to the accuracy of these statistics,[28] it is clearly evident that the wastage in primary education is inordinately high. Moreover, wastage figures pertain only to those children enrolled in schools. Adding these figures to those of the children not enrolled in any grade gives an indication of the size of the population that received little or no primary schooling.

Another aspect of the retention factor is the question of what is retained by primary-school graduates. Since the major part of the curriculum in the early years of primary schooling is concerned with the instruction of literacy skills, an appropriate measure of retention would be the degree to which these skills are maintained and utilized upon completion of primary-school education. Earlier it was noted that most countries have adopted a fourth- or fifth-grade equivalence as a standard of functional literacy. This determination has a double meaning; on the one hand, a fourth- or fifth-grade reading level is stipulated as a minimum for coping with the type of written material with which an adult will be confronted, and on the other, attaining a fourth- or fifth-grade level is a precondition for subsequent retention of literacy skills. Both contentions are questionable. The only materials that can be read with a fourth- or fifth-grade reading level are those written at those levels. Any materials requiring higher reading levels would be beyond the scope of the fourth- or fifth-grade graduate, assuming, of course, that he receives no further instruction upon graduation. (The problem of reading materials will be discussed at greater length later.) G. Flores studied the number of years of schooling necessary in order to retain a level of functional literacy fifteen years after graduation in the Philippines, and concluded that at least five years are required.[29] It is difficult, however, to infer from this that four or five years are the universal requirement, as there are major differences between various languages and the quality of instruction is far from being uniform. Indeed, how can one compare the achievement of a Thai rural child who learned his literacy skills in a crowded, ill-lit room from an underqualified teacher by a rote recitation method with a child who received individualized attention from a well-qualified teacher in a proper learning environment in Australia? The Thai child is not only at a disadvantage due to learning situation, he must also master a language that consists of forty-four consonants, twenty-three vowels and five different tones, while his Australian counterpart has the seemingly simpler task of learning an alphabet with only twenty-six symbols. Retention of literacy skills is more a function of quality of teaching, learning environment, and specific linguistic structures than a mere calculation of number of years spent in school.

Further complicating this picture is the factor of adequate supporting systems. These consist of a series of separate but interdependent components. Since the adult populations of most of the rural areas in the developing countries are illiterate, literacy plays little or no part in their daily life. Ithiel de Sola Pool observes that in traditional societies "word-of-mouth is more trusted than the written word, that word-of-mouth everywhere is an essential stimulus to action, that it is more adaptable to the variations in style and manner which are so particularly important in a dual and transitional society."[30] This reliance upon oral communication does not stem from a rejection of written forms of communication, but rather has deep cultural roots. J.C. Carothers, for instance, in comparing modes of communication in rural Africa with those inherent in West European cultures, maintains that "rural Africans live largely in a world of sound—a world loaded with direct personal significance for the hearer—whereas the Western European lives much more in a visual world which is on the whole indifferent to him."[31] Similar observations pertaining to other aspects of traditional culture and their comparison with Western societies have been made by others. W.D. Wall notes that "the early teaching of arithmetic depends upon concepts of number, quantity, weight and the division of space which are acquired incidentally by children in . . . Western cultures, but such concepts are only imperfectly, if at all, present in some others."[32] Along the same lines Francis Dart points out that "in Nepal, as in most of Asia and Africa, children grow to adulthood in a world that is saturated not with science but with non-science—with a deep running view of nature that is essentially non-rational, non-objective."[33] Daily life in the large majority of developing rural areas consists of farming with traditional methods handed down from generation to generation, and getting along with family, neighbors, and community. These pursuits do not require literacy skills and there is no premium attached to their acquisition. Thus a weighty coalition of factors militates against the usage of the barely acquired literacy skills of the primary-school leavers. The adults in their communities are themselves illiterate and perceive no use for literacy skills: literacy is not required for any of the daily pursuits of life and the concepts contained in literacy skills or implied by them are foreign.

One could argue that, while the foregoing is true, the primary-school leavers will serve as agents of change and that, eventually, literacy will have its effect. However, in this too the systems are nonsupportive. Most primary-school leavers are ten or eleven years of age at most (those that complete the typical four- or five-year cycle of primary schooling available). There is typically little possibility in the traditional rural social structure for these children to assert their newly gained skills. Children are pressed into traditional social patterns in which age is the significant criterion in determining with whom decision-making powers and wisdom reside. Despite the many different patterns of family structure extant in various parts of the developing world, the dominance of elders seems virtually universal.[34] Whatever "outside wisdom" could potentially result from utilization of literacy skills is likely to be discouraged by the ruling elders. In many traditional cultures the assertion of individuality itself is discouraged. Carothers, for example, states that in Africa "a man comes to regard himself as a rather insignificant part of a much larger organism—the family and the clan—and not as an independent and self-reliant unit; personal initiative and ambition are permitted little outlet; and a meaningful integration of a man's experience on individual, personal lines is not achieved."[35] Aggravating this situation still further is the pragmatic factor of the dearth of appropriate reading material in most rural areas. The problem of reading matter is complex. It begins, perhaps, with the fact that in many parts of the developing world paper is scarce. At a United Nations sponsored conference on Pulp and Paper Prospects in Asia and the Far East convened in 1960, for instance, it was concluded that "there is a serious danger that current educational programs will be jeopardized, the creation of an informed citizenry retarded, antiquated distribution systems retained, and industrial progress hampered" due to the situation pertaining in the paper industry.[36] Statistics on the increase of newsprint consumption and the number of volumes in public libraries in developing countries throughout the developing world are depressingly low.[37] The distribution problem is further complicated by poor communications and systems for the delivery of materials to remote areas. Even where materials are made available they must usually be read during the day, as few of the rural areas in developing countries have electricity. Since children are usually employed alongside the adults in physically exacting agricultural labor in the daytime, the amount of time available for reading is further diminished. Finally, for materials to be functional they must be written at levels necessitating no more than fourth- or fifth-grade literacy skills. This in itself poses severe problems in many countries, where complete literatures need be created to serve rural populations. Materials need be geared to the interests and needs of the target groups as well as to appropriate reading levels.[38] Reading materials are not only necessary as a source of information; they also serve to reinforce the actual reading skills which, like most acquired skills, can easily be forgotten through lack of use. Indeed, individual reading of materials other than those taught in school both during and after the initial instructional period are considered essential for maintaining reading proficiency.[39] The combination of traditional social patterns and the sorry state of availability of reading matter not only serve to inhibit the use of literacy skills by primary-school leavers but also cause regression to a state of illiteracy.

Whether or not all of the elements described exist uniformly in all rural areas in developing countries is not crucial to the argument that there is little chance for utilizing or retaining either the literacy or numeracy skills learned in the primary school. Obviously, there will be variations in these factors in different situations. Only a few of the conditions need exist for the skills to fall by the wayside.

In addition to literacy and numeracy skills, curricula of primary schools usually include other subjects such as history, geography, general science, religion, a second language and, occasionally some instruction in agriculture and hygiene. Instruction in these areas fares certainly no better and probably worse than instruction in literacy skills. Little time is devoted to these subjects. The teachers are probably less qualified to teach them than they are literacy skills; the predominant instructional methodology is most commonly recitation by the teacher of the contents of a primer, and whatever facts are actually retained by the pupils are of little practical value and soon forgotten. Agriculture lessons typically consist of working in a small school garden utilizing techniques similar to those the children see their parents using.[40] Even if attempts were made to teach some agricultural practice innovations, chances of their being introduced by the young children into actual usage are indeed slim. Clifton Wharton, in a detailed study of the relationship between level of education and changes in output and technological efficiency in two Brazilian villages, concluded that there was no relationship between agricultural performance and years of schooling completed.[41] This conclusion is supported by a study conducted by Gordon Pierson in which data from fifty-one countries was analyzed.[42] In view of these facts one can but agree with Wharton's conclusion that "agriculture as an applied science cannot be taught at the primary level." The contribution of primary education to agricultural development is usually seen in terms of creating a literacy base that can serve as a useful tool in promoting change in agriculture in later years.[43] The net result, then, is that neither agriculture nor skills deemed necessary for agricultural development are learned in the typical rural primary school. The few sessions devoted to health and hygiene in the several countries in which these are offered suffer a similar fate. Prodipto Roy and Joseph Kivlin, for example, in a study of the correlates of health innovation in eight Indian villages, found that the education of children correlated with the acceptance of health innovations only very slightly and then only in families in which parents had accepted innovations.[44] The rural primary school cannot boast of significant achievements, one is led to conclude, in any areas of its curriculum.

Any assessment of primary education's role in fundamental education or its potential as an agent of fundamental education must also take cognizance of the mounting evidence relating to the detrimental effects of infant and early childhood malnutrition on learning. C. Woodruff suggests the existence of a critical period during the first months of life during which advanced malnutrition acts permanently upon both physical and psychological development.[45] There is substantial evidence that children from economically depressed populations where malnutrition is rife experience severe retardation in motor development.[46] In a study conducted among rural children in Guatemala, Joaquin Cravioto and Elsa De Licardie found that malnutrition had definite derogatory effects on intersensory development of school-age children. They see the delayed development of intersensory functioning as related to conditioned reflex formation necessary for much of early learning and the acquisition of certain academic skills such as reading.[47] Mavis Stoch and P.M. Smythe found "cumulative and impressive [evidence] that severe undernutrition during the first two years of life, when brain growth is most active, results in a permanent reduction of brain size and a restricted intellectual development."[48] Malnutrition, of course, is only one facet of a general social and economic situation where the solution of problems is, to a large extent, an interdependent process. Thus, the problem of malnutrition cannot be solved without parallel action on other issues. Moreover, in charting activities such as primary education the influence of such factors as malnutrition should definitely be taken into account. It seems quite clear that the effects of malnutrition, most prevalent in rural areas in developing nations, seriously impede the implementation of effective primary schooling.

An interesting approach to the school as an agent of modernization has been forwarded by Alex Inkeles. In the course of a six-country study on the causes and consequences of individual change, he concluded that the modernizing effects of the school do not derive from its curriculum "but rather, from its informal, implicit, and often unconscious program for dealing with its young charges."[49] This program, Inkeles claims, is inherent in the school as an organization. Thus, by merely spending time in a school the student is influenced positively in regards to his propensity for modernization. Testing this contention empirically in the six countries Inkeles found that "on the average, for every additional year a man spent in school he gains somewhere between two and three additional points on a scale of modernity scored from zero to one-hundred."[50] This finding supported the conclusion that education is "perhaps the most important of the influences moving men away from traditionalism toward modernity in developing countries."[51] Elsewhere, however, Inkeles qualifies this finding with the following reservation:

In many countries, the weakness of the nation's resources permits
schooling to be only of very poor quality, and the pressures on the
poorer people force the children to be quite irregular in their attendance. In a number of countries it has been observed that if children
can obtain only two or three years of schooling, and especially if they
do so under conditions where the environment does not particularly
reinforce or support the school, there the effects of education on
modernization will be very modest indeed. Similarly, the degree of
traditionalism of the school itself plays some role. Little or no change
toward modernity is evident in the more traditional schools that devote
themselves mainly to passing on religious practices or to inculcating
and preserving traditional lore and skills.[52]

Certainly the primary schools extant in rural areas of developing countries fit the
description contained in this statement. However significant education seems
to be as a tool of modernization, rural primary schools tend to be exceptions to
the rule.

One final point must be made. In some societies in rural areas education in
the form of formal schooling is considered a valuable commodity. Its value,
however, is not perceived in terms of the contributions that the educated individual can make to the community, but rather as a means for leaving the community, as a passport to a life totally different from that in the rural village. In a
sense, the educated villager becomes a deviant, estranged from his society
and environment, going on to a different life experience. The village remains
unchanged.

I would conclude that the primary school as it currently exists in the large
majority of rural areas in developing countries is not serving as an agent of
fundamental education, and indeed is not geared to serve as such. Furthermore,
it does not seem likely that anything less than radical reconceptualization and
reform of primary education in this context will make it a valid agent of
fundamental education.

6 Community Development as Fundamental Education

Community development programs are, in general, defined as programs or processes "by which the efforts of the people themselves are united with those of governmental authorities to improve the economic, social and cultural conditions of communities, to integrate these communities into the life of the nation, and to enable them to contribute fully to national progress."[1] Under this broad umbrella are included myriad types of programs which Peter du Sautoy has attempted to classify into four main categories:

Adult literacy and basic social education
Specialized work among women and youth
Self-help construction projects
Extension education work in various "nation building" fields[2]

Fundamental education as defined in this study is implicit in the general definition and explicitly stated in at least two of these categories. Indeed, the United Nations concept of the community development process emphasizes that it is "essentially both . . . educational and . . . organizational."[3] Whether or not fundamental education is, in fact, imparted in any particular community development program is, of course, a function of that program.

Different agencies have emphasized different aspects of the community development movement. Thus, the United Nations stresses that the educational component is primarily "concerned with changing such attitudes and practices as are obstacles to social and economic improvements, engendering particular attitudes which are conducive to these improvements and, more generally, promoting a greater receptivity to change."[4] Such attitude change is viewed as a more significant achievement than "a series of episodes resulting in concrete achievements," as its main objective is to "increase the continuing capacity of the people to help themselves."[5] Community development programs, therefore, should aim at self-perpetuation even after withdrawal of the outside agency worker or catalyst. Many definitions of community development emphasize community initiative as a prime ingredient. The United States International Cooperation Administration (predecessor of the current Agency for International Development), for example, adopted a definition of community development as a

> process of social action in which the people of a community organize
> themselves for planning and action: define their common and individual
> needs and problems: make group and individual plans to meet these
> needs and solve their problems: execute these plans with a maximum
> reliance upon community resources; and supplement these resources
> when necessary with services and materials from governmental and non-
> governmental agencies outside the community.[6]

This approach exhibits a bias carried over from community development work in
the United States, where the organization of local bodies for purposes of
developing and activating local initiative were considered the main objectives.[7]
A widely used British definition takes a different view of local initiative:

> Community development is a movement designed to promote better
> living for the whole community with the active participation and, if
> possible, on the initiative of the community, but if this initiative is not
> forthcoming spontaneously, by the use of techniques for arousing and
> stimulating it in order to secure the active and enthusiastic response
> to the movement.[8]

Here local initiative is considered desirable as a precondition to a program,
but not requisite. Indeed, if local initiative is lacking its stimulation becomes
one of the aims of a specific program. Active participation of members of a
community in any particular program is deemed necessary. T.R. Batten sees the
main objective of community development as the creation of local initiative.

> Should not one of the prime tests—the prime test in fact—of community
> development be the emergence of local leaders willing to take initiative
> and able to exercise responsibility, and the emergence of groups, clubs
> and committees which local people control and through which they
> act to achieve purposes of their own?[9]

An extension of the local initiative emphasis is that placed upon "felt
needs." Du Sautoy, for instance, considers "attention to people's 'felt
needs'"[10] to be a major characteristic of a community development program. He goes as far as stating that any program not taking cognizance of such
needs cannot be considered a community development program in the strict
sense of the word. In practice, however, despite these qualifications and injunctions, community development has come to mean "any action taken by any
agency and primarily designed to benefit the community."[11]
     Some of the incongruity between the various definitions of community
development results, it seems, from the lack of a clear dichotomy between the
role and method of community development in developed and developing
societies. Community development in the West is a logical outcrop of Western
democratic traditions. As early as 1835 Alexis de Tocqueville described what
today would be considered an ideal community development process:

These Americans are the most peculiar people in the World. You'll not believe it when I tell you how they behave. In a local community in their country a citizen may conceive of some need which is not being met. What does he do? He goes across the street and discusses it with his neighbor. Then what happens? A committee comes into existence and then the committee begins functioning on behalf of that need, and you won't believe it but it's true. All of this is done without reference to any bureaucrat. All of this is done by the private citizens on their own initiative.[12]

Conceptually, little has changed from this formulation. A community development worker may be installed in a community in order to elicit such community initiative and get a movement aimed at betterment on its way, but basically the onus of the process falls upon the members of the community as individuals acting in aggregation. This approach takes the existence of a number of preconditional factors for granted. Members of a community who can act or be prodded to act in the fashion described by Tocqueville must first be aware of alternatives to whatever facet of their lives they are dissatisfied with. Thus, they must have a certain amount of communication with communities other than their own. They must believe or be brought to believe that they are capable of bringing about change. Indeed, attitudes favoring change are a prerequisite for any form of action. These preconditions cannot be taken for granted in rural developing situations. Charles Erasmus remarks,

Much of the talk about self-help and self-determination and "leading" the people to formulate their own objectives for self-improvement is actually as unrealistic as it sounds. Negative and even coercive controls are to some extent unavoidable in the internal development of pre-industrial areas.[13]

Coercion is certainly a concept foreign to what is considered to be the community development process. While coercive means may bring about change that will be beneficial to the developing rural community, they certainly do not take cognizance of "felt needs" and "local initiative."

The bridge between these two distinctly different approaches to community development is suggested by the United Nations emphasis on attitude change. Adam Curle sees community development in the developing country context essentially as a

method of stimulating communities to manage their own affairs constructively, an operational training ground for democracy that has real and cogent meaning for people since the decisions they have to make do not concern ideological issues which may seem remote, but practical matters of immediate importance to themselves.[14]

A dual role for community development in the development context emerges.

On the one hand, there is an initial task of providing fundamental education, and on the other of initiating projects aimed at bringing about fairly immediate change. Since the latter can neither depend upon existence of the former nor be delayed until favorable attitudes are fostered, recourse to methods considered strictly nonorthodox in community development theory is often necessary. The test of the validity of community development in rural areas in developing countries as an agent of fundamental education is thus twofold: Do these programs succeed in their direct fundamental education function? Do the operational projects have an indirect fundamental education function and affect?

The more formal educative role of community development takes place in a number of different frameworks. Most common of these is the adult literacy program extant in a great many communities throughout the developing world. (Since this form of program is considered to play a major role in the fundamental education of rural adults, it will be analyzed in detail in chapter 7.) The village school is also often considered to be an agent of fundamental education.[15] Such schools are usually primary schools of the type described in the previous chapter. A third institutionalized framework aimed at imparting fundamental education is that known as the community school. Community schools have been described as institutions "in which children are taught, and well taught, during what are normally regarded as 'school hours'" and that at the same time "offer to adolescents and adults the education, training and even recreation for which they are asking or for which they can often be so easily stimulated to ask."[16] Underlying the concept of the community school are two main ideas. The first, expressed by the phrase "well taught," relates to both the curriculum and teaching methodologies of the primary school. The primary school itself is to be maintained but its curriculum and instruction are to become more "relevant."[17] The second idea relates to the use of the facility in "non-school hours" and basically lays a blueprint for a fairly elaborate system of adult education, including recreational activities. The idea of the community school as a framework within which fundamental education can be imparted is certainly an improvement over the primary school. Conceptually it takes cognizance of the fact that the potential of the primary school for success in developing rural communities is, to a large extent, dependent upon a supportive system among the adults. Thus, by incorporating adult educational activities in its overall program a framework is established wherein adults can also participate in an educational endeavor. A framework alone cannot be an agent of any type of education. Whether or not the community school is an agent of fundamental education is more a function of the curricula, instructors, and methodologies employed. Under present conditions in rural developing areas the primary-school aspect of the community institution does not seem far different from independent primary schools. Similarly, the adult activities would suffer from the same maladies that afflict noncommunity school adult programs. This conclusion is predicated upon several observations. First, a clear dichotomy between the "formal" and "non-formal" educative role of the community school is strictly observed in the fact that the primary school and adult programs are conceived of as separate activities to be conducted at different times. It seems unlikely that the provision of primary education in the same facility as adult education itself would be cause for improvement of the former. In fact, in many rural communities where adult education is conducted, primary-school facilities are utilized without any effects on either primary or adult education. Second, while curricular and instructional improvements are implied in the community school concept, there is no reason to assume that they will result from the mere idea of joint use of a facility. Third, the main programmatic responsibility in the community school is placed upon the primary school teacher.[18] Thus, the ill-qualified primary-school teacher is essentially being asked to expand his activities into the realm of adult education, for which he is, at best, no better prepared.

Jack Mezirow includes institutions such as local councils, cooperatives, advisory boards, and community centers in the list of frameworks primarily concerned, in the community development context, with the provision of educational experiences.[19] With the exception of community centers all of these frameworks are essentially administrative. The notion thus implied is that of "administration as 'directive education.'"[20] B.B. Schaffer, writing from the point of view of a development administrator, sees this use of administrative frameworks as a positive direction. "Administration is not politics and it is wrong if it seeks to recruit support by ideology. It is rather part of a response to demands, but there is no reason why its response should not be made more comprehensible by education."[21] Schaffer's advocacy of the use of such frameworks for educative purposes apparently results, in part, from his criticism of their use as administrative tools. Indeed, he makes the assertion that the entire approach employed by community developers is "political, not administrative." Moreover, he aptly points out that "the [community development] approach assumes an appropriate fit, a harmony and absence of conflict between the central and the local community and the list of what each wants and provides." Since he holds that "the poorer the community the less its cooperative resources," one can assume that discord rather than harmony would be the rule and that, as a result, this "may reinforce factional conflict rather than strengthen coherence."[22] Add to these arguments Mezirow's injunction that "some degree of organizational success in meeting the needs and expectations of members is . . . a condition for continued participation," [23] and all the ingredients for a dysfunctional system of fundamental education are present. The frameworks cited by Mezirow (community centers excepted) are organized for the avowed purpose of serving an administrative function, though their instigators may have a purely educational motive.

Since they cannot, it seems, perform their administrative function, membership drop-out occurs. Furthermore, the educational content is based upon the administrative function. Thus, lack of success in the administrative venture would only serve to disprove all that is attempted to be taught. The end result may well be that participants learn that the mode of operation advocated by the community developer is dysfunctional and wrong—the opposite of what they were supposed to have learned. Such a result is unquestionably more negative than no result at all. Admittedly, there have been instances in which the use of such administrative frameworks for educative purposes has been deemed successful.[24] The arguments against this approach, however, rule out its adoption as a model for fundamental education. Surely it is unreasonable to expect a generalized model of fundamental education to be contingent upon the broad administrative and material accomplishments of a community development effort.

Much of the discussion about the educative role of community development has centered on the function of the community development worker. Batten comments:

> Agencies which aim at promoting changes in peasant agriculture, in diet, in health practices, or in child care in the home, equally with those which aim at influencing people's attitudes and behavior towards each other, must primarily depend on the skill of their workers in educating, influencing, and stimulating people to act.[25]

According to this statement the local level community worker is largely reliant upon his own resources in promoting his mission. He is thus charged with the dual role of implementing the specific program or project for which he has been stationed in a community, and serving as a purveyor of fundamental education. These roles are complementary and, indeed, a form of educational activity is often requisite before a specific project can be implemented. V.L. Griffiths points out some of the fallacies of placing too much emphasis upon the educative role of the field worker.[26] Lack of training, lack of direction in his educative role, lack of enthusiasm for being stationed in a village, and lack of a framework within which he can function combine to make the field worker an improbable agent of fundamental education. The many examples of failure of community development workers to form the relationships necessary for fostering fundamental education and actually providing any permanent educational stimulus are ample evidence of Griffith's reservations.[27] The exception to this situation would normally occur, Griffiths holds, under conditions of a "project covering a limited, perhaps experimental area, where the total number of field staff is more concentrated, and where the salaries of individual workers need not be kept down to the minimum."[28] It follows that the community development worker cannot be viewed as an institutionalized agent of fundamental education and replication of a particular success on a wide basis is extremely dubious.

In order to complete this assessment of community development as fundamental education it remains to be seen to what extent various projects labeled community development projects or programs have an indirect fundamental education function. Such a function would result from the demonstrative effects of a project. Once initiated, and if successful, it stands to reason that perceptions of villagers relating to the specific innovation introduced would change. A certain amount of receptivity to change could enable the introduction of future changes and projects. Thus while an "imposed public works" [29] type of project may seem objectionable to the orthodox community developer, it could be argued that the spin-off effect resulting from it is in itself an important educative objective. Leonard Doob observes that a project can "facilitate learning since people who are so predisposed (toward a particular undertaking) are likely to expose themselves to instruction, to evaluate favorably what they perceive and learn, and then to be both willing and able to behave appropriately." [30] Examples of this effect abound. A not atypical instance is the following statement from a village medical worker:

> You can go into a community were they have forty percent yaws and you give them a shot of penicillin and come back a week later and it's all cleared up and you can do anything you want after you have established this respect—you must do something dramatic.[31]

Conversely, there are an ample number of examples where the initial incursion into a community for purposes of promoting a certain aspect of development were failures and had the result of creating suspicion of any future attempts. Margaret Mead cites a case where "actual harm was done when cultivators in Burma were persuaded to weed their rubber plantations and found that this reduced the sap; and when they were persuaded to do deep ploughing in the rice fields and thus broke the pan that held the water." [32] Individual projects, through the material good that they produce, can create an atmosphere conducive to the introduction of fundamental education. Often this potential is lost as a result of the withdrawal of the field worker upon completion of a project. The project approach to much of community development work underscores any attempts at instituting an orderly and systematic program of fundamental education. Thus while various projects have amassed an impressive roster of achievements, these tend to be primarily of a material, not educational, nature.[33] It should be noted that some projects, albeit very few, have also educated in a very fundamental sense. These however, constitute rare exceptions.

The community development approach does appear to carry great potential as an aid to fundamental education. Relating actual activities to a systematic educational input the duration of which is determined on the basis of the educational rather than project needs seems to be a viable fundamental education situation. As currently conducted, however, the community development effort that can claim success in the realm of fundamental education is rare.

7

Adult Literacy Programs: The Record

Adult literacy programs encompass all educational endeavors whose explicit concern is the teaching of the fundamental skills of reading and writing to illiterate adults.[1] As an educational framework they have two significant characteristics: first, they are entirely aimed at a target population that is considered "disadvantaged"; and second, they are predominantly engaged in fundamental education. These characteristics combine to make adult literacy programs a unique educational framework designed for fundamental education in the sense of this study. Indeed, while primary education and community development programs in certain contexts also cope with problems of disadvantaged groups and fundamental education, these are not their sole or even main concerns. It is therefore not surprising that fundamental education and adult literacy programs have become virtually synonymous terms.

There is a distinct dichotomy between the approaches to adult literacy education in developed countries, where universal compulsory primary education has long been a feature of the society, and in developing countries, where this has not been the case. In the former, adult literacy programs are largely considered remedial in nature and are offered primarily as a "second chance" to adults who for some reason did not benefit from primary education when they were of school-going age.[2] Adult illiteracy has been dealt with either as a passing problem, as in the case of the relatively few adults who did not go through primary schooling (e.g. new immigrants to a country as in the United States), or as a problem to be coped with at the primary-school level. Assuming that the efficacy of primary schooling determines the degree of literacy or illiteracy of future generations, and that all children of primary school age will in fact attend school, it follows that, in global terms, adult illiteracy is related to primary education in a cause–effect relationship. As a result the main thrust of reading-improvement programs, as in the American "Right-to-Read" effort, has been aimed at the primary level.[3] Adult literacy education has been relegated to a position that is, in the words of James Allen, "peripheral and secondary."[4] Not so in developing countries. There adult literacy programs are theoretically a first exposure to formalized education aimed at a population that did not have the "first chance." The numbers of adults having completed primary schooling is low as it was not available when they were at the appropriate ages. Furthermore, the spread of primary schooling is such that considerable numbers of children will grow to maturity without having been through primary schools. Whereas in developed nations problems of adult illiterate segments of the population are considered marginal, in the developing world they become integral and central. This major difference becomes more sharply focused when one considers the fact that developed countries tend to be highly literate societies, in the sense that literacy skills are an important "commodity," so that the social system is supportive of all literacy efforts at the primary level regardless of whether the parent generation is literate or not. Neither the literacy tradition nor the supporting systems are generally as well developed in the developing world (certainly not in rural areas), so the mere existence of primary schooling does not, in itself, solve the problem of future adult illiteracy. The policy implications for developing countries are clear: adult literacy programs should be accorded a high priority in educational policy. Julius Nyerere has stated this bluntly: "We must educate our adults. Our children will not have an impact on our economic development for five, ten or even twenty years. The attitude of our adults, on the other hand, will have an impact now."[5] Alas, this is not generally the situation. Literacy and fundamental education for adults in most developing nations are as low on the priority lists as they are in developed countries.[6] This state of affairs may be partially a result of the emulation of educational systems of the developed countries, where primary, secondary, and higher education are understandably higher on the totem pole. The effect of this attitude toward adult literacy programs has been a general underfunding and under-staffing of activities.[7] Nevertheless, some form of adult literacy work is extant in over one hundred countries.[8]

Although the ostensible objective of literacy programs is the instruction of literacy skills, most efforts have what Benson Snyder has called, in another context, a "hidden curriculum."[9] Three such hidden curricula are discernible: literacy for religious purposes, for political purposes, and for modernization and economic progress.

The earliest adult literacy education activities had as their hidden curriculum a religious, missionary thrust. Organized and directed by various Christian churches, they were primarily aimed at enabling adult illiterates to read the Bible.[10] Literacy education was seen as a precondition to the "proper" conversion of the target groups to Christianity. Foremost among the early literacy efforts were those conducted by Protestant groups. Their activity is traced to the supreme importance attached in Protestantism to the Bible. Indeed, the earliest of the recorded formalized literacy programs were conducted in Europe and were closely related to the spread of Protestantism.[11] It was a missionary of the Congregational Church, Frank Laubach, who established the first modern institutionalized literacy programs.[12] The impact of his work is apparent in the fact that the method of instruction he first developed while an active missionary in the Philippines has been translated into 312 languages and is the most widely used method around the world.[13]

The Soviet Union originated and established the political hidden curriculum, predicated upon Lenin's assertion that "an illiterate man is non-political; first he must be taught how to read."[14] The first of the national mass literacy campaigns were organized by the Soviets. Except in methodology of organization the Soviet utilization of literacy education does not differ radically from that of the Christian missionaries; the Christian objective was conversion to the "true religion," the Communist conversion to the "new religion." Even so, the use of literacy education in the establishment of a new political order served to broaden the scope of literacy education considerably. As an underlying motif the Soviet approach of literacy for politicization has appeared in several programs. Literacy instruction was a crucial factor in Luis Muñoz Marín's strategy for forming and popularizing the *Partido Popular* in Puerto Rico, for instance.[15] The Cuban literacy campaign was also politically inspired, stipulating in its objectives that its aim was "to contribute to the strengthening of the revolutionary consciousness of our peasants."[16] Indeed, its basic text was called a "Revolutionary primer." A significant departure from the foregoing attempts to utilize literacy instruction as a means of establishing a predetermined political order is contained in the writings of Paulo Freire. His political credo is contained in the term *conscientização,* which is a composite term meaning both the perception of social, political, and economic contradictions and the action taken, as a result, against the "oppressive elements of reality."[17] Waving a banner of *conscientização* rather than of a particular political persuasion, his objective in literacy work among "Third World" peasants is to enable people to "develop their power to perceive critically the way they exist in the world with which and in which they find themselves [so that] they come to see the world not as a static reality, but as a reality in process, in transition."[18] Literacy itself, rather than a given political credo, becomes the "liberating" vehicle. UNESCO, too, has incorporated a political hidden curriculum into its agenda for literacy. Based on the belief that for political life to run smoothly "it is essential to evolve some sense of national cohesion and general agreement on a whole range of common values," it asserts that "the active and conscious participation of citizens in the political life of a modern state cannot develop harmoniously unless these citizens have crossed the threshold of modernization—and literacy is only the first step in this direction."[19]

There appear, therefore, to be two distinctly different political hidden curricula. The approach initiated by the Soviet Union and adopted by UNESCO argues that literacy is necessary for the attainment of political unity around an established order. Freire, on the other hand, approaches literacy as a tool for inciting revolution. Both approaches, it is interesting to note, find support in studies of different social scientists. Seymour Martin Lipset generally supports the contention that literacy is necessary for fostering stability, while Samuel Huntington argues that literacy actually increases *in*stability.[20] In considering these two conflicting arguments cognizance should be taken of the differences between the proponents of the two hidden curricula. The

Soviets, the Cubans, and UNESCO all represent established political orders primarily interested in the securing of regimes, while Marín and Freire are both individuals interested in instigating political upheaval—in the former case the upheaval preceded the literacy or stabilizing efforts, while in the latter it is considered to be conditional upon a prior state of mass literacy. If one accepts the contention that literacy fosters political awareness, it stands to reason that the direction the awareness may take is unpredictable, and both approaches could prove counterproductive. Thus, while the immediate objectives of these two aspects of the political hidden curriculum are in conflict the assumptions underlying both are the same—the awakening of political consciousness.

The third hidden curriculum, that of modernization and economic progress, derives in the main from a similar assumption that literacy extends an individual's awareness beyond his immediate environment and results in cognitive stimuli that occasion behavioral change. This curriculum differs from the political one in that the realm of desired change is that of modernization and economic development rather than political participation. First articulated during and immediately after World War II, the third hidden curriculum is directly related to the emergence of newly independent political entities in the developing areas of the world. Its origins, indeed, are embedded in a political "hidden curriculum" and are associated with political independence. The following statement of the British Advisory Committee on Education in the Colonies from 1943 is illustrative of the beginnings of this phase in literacy programs:

> A man may be healthy though illiterate. He may be prosperous without without being learned. He may, while still almost ignorant of wider duties of a citizen, live, and indeed, enjoy life under a government which provides him with security and justice. All these things may, in a measure, be true, but it is far truer that the general health of the whole community, its general well-being and prosperity, can only be secured and maintained if the whole mass of the people has a real share in education and some understanding of its meaning and purpose. It is equally true that without such general share in education and such understanding true democracy cannot function, and the rising hope of self government will inevitably suffer frustration.[21]

The "real share in education" on the adult level was considered to be literacy education. The notion contained in this statement and the need for initiating literacy programs gained wide acceptance in the developing world. Mahatma Gandhi, for example, soon after India's independence, expressed it as follows: "Mass illiteracy is India's sin and shame and must be liquidated; but the literacy campaign must not end with knowledge of the alphabet, it must go hand in hand with the spread of useful knowledge."[22] Underlying this approach

to literacy was the unqualified assertion that "illiteracy acts as a brake upon
the advance both of individual countries and of human society as a whole
along the path of economic and social progress."[23] It was not until the
1960s that this assertion was given substance and amplified. In proposing that
adult literacy campaigns be considered an essential component of the educational strategy incorporated in the United Nations Development Decade,
UNESCO elaborated upon the "hidden curriculum" aspects of literacy. Based
on the differentiation between literacy and functional literacy, it argued that
adult literacy was a pre-requisite "for raising the standards of living for all
throughout the world."[24] Specifically, adult literacy was deemed necessary
for the successful spread of universal primary schooling by serving as a safe-
guard against wastage. "In the long run," it was argued," . . . the progress of
universal schooling will put an end to adult illiteracy. The success of any
adult literacy campaign is accordingly no temporary objective; it is rather the
necessary adjunct to a program for total schooling."[25] Furthermore, adult
literacy would have more immediate effects on the society and the economy
of nations by bringing about a "rationalization of behaviors" called for in any
attempt at modernization and development. Another UNESCO document
further amplified this line of argument by asserting that "the extension of
literacy is a pre-requisite for the successful implementation of national plans
for economic and social development."[26] Further clarification of the role
of literacy education in modernization and economic development was proposed
by UNESCO at the World Conference of Ministers of Education on the Eradication of Illiteracy (1965). It was suggested that literacy would enable the
individual to "extend the range of his mental processes and gain the knowledge
which makes the world around him intelligible and manageable."[27] Following from this suggestion UNESCO proposed that "there are five [areas] in
respect of which literacy work seems capable of playing a particularly vital
role: modification of economic and social structures, economic diversification,
industrialization, rural development and the achievement of higher productivity."
In each of these areas the specific effects of literacy would be to "ensure the
dissemination of the basic knowledge permitting wide and more effective
participation in the development process and the acquisition of further knowledge, while promoting a change in mental attitudes and the creation of new
behavior patterns posited by social and economic transformations."[28] Literacy
programs in this approach are conceived of as a form of functional education
optimally intended to show fairly rapid returns to a country's social and economic development. To some extent literacy is considered as an adjunct to
what might be seen as a form of vocational education. Literacy is a fundamental
element of this form of education and is considered a crucial factor in its
ultimate success. Of the three hidden curricula this last one of literacy for
modernization and economic progress has, in recent years, become the most
widespread.

One could argue that the different dimensions of literacy programs outlined above as "hidden curricula" are not really "hidden" but appear to be as explicit as the literacy component itself. As far as the explicit objectives of program organizers and policy-makers are concerned this observation would, no doubt, be true. The curricula are hidden, however, from the program participants who, in each case, are presented with a fairly similar fare of literacy instruction. Thus, the "hidden" aspects of each of the approaches are basically manifestations of reflections regarding the outcomes of literacy and the character of a society in which mass literacy is a reality. There is no substantial empirical evidence that could lend unqualified support to any of the three agendas. It is thus not entirely clear whether literacy is, in fact, positively correlated with any of the three hidden curricula, nor to what degree it is required for their attainment. From this point of view too, these three approaches are hidden curricula.

In terms of fundamental education a further distinction need be noted among the various approaches to literacy. This distinction could be labeled the "literacy-as-an-end" vs. "literacy-as-a-means" dichotomy. The difference between the two is methodological rather than conceptual, for clearly each of the approaches to literacy education discussed considers literacy skills as a necessary condition to attain a given end objective. Methodologically, however, while some programs consider the mere attainment of literacy skills a sufficient condition for achieving the hidden objectives, others feel the need to explicitly relate literacy skills to these objectives within the program. One result of this methodological distinction has been the erroneous observation made by many of the programs in the former category that their "sole aim had been the eradication of illiteracy, considered as constituting an end in itself."[29] Gray explains the source of this misunderstanding: "Unfortunately, little or no effort has been made in [literacy programs] to relate the skills acquired to the practical uses they should serve."[30] While it seems that if there was a literacy program organized solely for the purpose of illiteracy eradication without having a hidden curriculum it was the rare exception, the illusion created was the root cause of the establishment of the literacy-as-a-means movement. (The fact that many programs projected an image of being interested solely in illiteracy eradication is further evidence that the "hidden" aspects of the curriculum are indeed hidden—not only to the participants in the programs). Typical of the literacy-as-a-means movement is the exhortation contained in the proposals for action for the United Nations Development Decade (1962): "They [the illiterates] must not only learn how to read and write, but must be taught to make effective use of these skills."[31] UNESCO later elaborated upon this "new approach" to literacy programs:

> The essential elements of the new approach to literacy are the following: a) literacy programs should be incorporated into and correlated with economic and social development plans; b) the eradication of

illiteracy should start within the categories of the population which are
highly motivated and which need literacy for their own and country's
benefit; c) literacy programs should preferably be linked with economic priorities and carried out in areas undergoing economic expansion; d) literacy programs must impart not only reading and writing,
but also professional and technical knowledge, thereby leading to a
fuller participation of adults in economic and civic life; e) literacy must
be an integral part of the overall education plan and educational system of each country.[32]

Clearly, the literacy-as-a-means approach is closely associated with the modernization and economic development hidden curriculum. It contains several
implications for literacy education. Methodologically it implies a need for
greater specificity in program curricula regarding the ultimate uses of literacy.
To some extent this can be understood as an attempt to elaborate on the
meaning of "functional literacy." Earlier it was seen that functional literacy
related to a level of functioning with literacy skills such that they could be
applied to a certain level of reading material. The implication here is that
attaining that level is not, in itself, a sufficient condition for being considered
functionally literate. Literacy skills need be actually used for literacy to be
considered functional. This contention parallels the assertion made earlier that
literacy is a composite of the skill of reading and the act of reading. Organizationally the UNESCO statement implies criticism of the efficacy of mass
literacy education, and suggests, as an alternative strategy, a more selective
approach to program dissemination. By planning for programs in "areas
undergoing economic expansion" a dual effect is being sought; on the one
hand, the demand created by economic expansion for skilled and semiskilled
manpower will, it is believed, provide a motivational force for adult illiterates
to participate in programs, and on the other hand, the existence of new literates
will facilitate the particular developmental activity. Thus, literacy-as-a-means
can be seen as a methodological and organizational adjunct to the third of the
hidden curricula in literacy programs.

One of the problems brought to the fore by the literacy-as-a-means
propositions is that of the scope of literacy program activity. This problem can
be basically seen in terms of a mass literacy campaign versus limited, selective
activity. As the term suggests, a literacy campaign is conceived of as a one-time
assault on adult illiteracy, aiming, as it were, at its eradication in one fell
swoop. The Soviet and Cuban literacy campaigns cited above are examples of
this approach. UNESCO, originally adopting this approach, proposed to the
General Assembly of the United Nations in 1963 the launching of a "World
Campaign for Universal Literacy" aimed at its initial phase at making "literate,
within the Development Decade, two-thirds of the five-hundred million adults
now presumed to be illiterate in the Member States of UNESCO in Asia, Africa
and Latin America, namely a total of three-hundred million persons between

the ages of fifteen and fifty years."[33] This onslaught strategy evoked a wide range of criticism. Curle suggests that "to launch a world-wide campaign in the hopes that literacy *per se* will have, at least within a decade, an appreciable economic impact could lead, ironically, to the most uneconomical wastage of very large resources."[34] The Chairman of the Expert Committee on Literacy, reporting to the General Conference of UNESCO that adopted the campaign resolution, cautioned that

> a campaign against illiteracy should not be something isolated, but should be integrated into a program of continuing adult education and into the total educational program; it should also be integrated with the development programs of the countries concerned, since it is closely linked both to productivity and to the process of adaptation to a changing world.[35]

The source of these objections is explained by Curle:

> We are still exploring the complex interrelations of education and economic growth. Nevertheless, we do know that some forms of education may have only the most peripheral impact on the economy: they may be of extremely low quality; they may inculcate skills having no practical application; they may not be accompanied by opportunities for practice, and so may wither; they may foster both ambitions which cannot be satisfied and distaste for necessary types of work. Approaching from the point of view of the individual, we know that the adult needs some special incentive to volunteer for and remain in literacy classes. . . . A program which has not deep roots in socio-economic reality will not, in fact, attract students in the numbers needed either to affect the economy, or to achieve the goal of approaching universality.[36]

One further objection must be recorded: literacy campaigns of the type described have not, as a rule, been successful in inculcating functional literacy skills to broad segments of a population. Indeed, their success has been quite limited at best. Although this factor is clearly implied in the foregoing arguments, it is not adequately stressed. One could argue that this assertion is too broad and has been disproved by several literacy campaigns, notably those of the Soviet Union and Cuba.

The literacy campaign conducted in the Soviet Union between 1919 and 1939 is often considered the apex of achievement in literacy education.[37] Officially published Soviet government statistics certainly indicate immense success: from a literacy rate of 51.1 percent for the population of the age of nine and over in 1926, the Soviets recorded a rate of 81.2 percent in early 1939, an increase of 30.1 percent.[38] In 1950 a literacy rate of between 90 and 95 percent was reported for the population of the age of fifteen upwards.[39]

The success recorded for the rural sector is even more impressive: the literacy rate climbed from 19.6 percent in 1897 to 76.8 percent in 1939.[40] Much of this increase in overall literacy rates is ascribed to the success of the literacy campaign which, claim the Soviets, instructed over forty million people. Unfortunately, no independent evaluations of the Soviet literacy efforts seem to exist. Other than an admission that, during the early years of the campaign, instruction was rather sketchy and relapse to illiteracy among participants common, great emphasis is placed in Soviet sources on the instructional success of the program.[41] Nevertheless, some light can be shed on the efficacy of the literacy campaign. Literacy rates among male army recruits, largely reflecting rural literacy, increased from 20 percent in 1874 to 56 percent in 1904 and 68 percent in 1913.[42] During roughly the same period primary-school enrollment in rural Russia increased significantly—from 1,754,000 in 1885 to over 7,000,000 in 1914.[43] In 1959 it was reported that the entire population from the age of twenty-five upward had had some formal schooling—70.3 percent of this group had up to seven years of primary schooling while 29.8 percent had more than seven full years of primary education.[44] It is clear from these data that both the adult literacy rate and primary-school enrollments had increased quite significantly prior to the Russian Revolution (1917) and, hence, prior to the concerted literacy education activities. The educational attainment figures cited for the population in 1959 clearly indicate that the majority of those who in 1959 were over twenty-five years of age had attended primary school prior to 1939. Further, it seems evident that many of those reported as illiterate in the early post-Revolution period had, by 1939, been replaced in the population by people who had attended primary schools. During the same years in which the literacy campaign was "waged" the Soviet Union also experienced rapid industrial advances which generated a demand for large numbers of skilled and semiskilled personnel.[45] It thus appears that a combination of the spread of primary schooling and rapid industrialization made a major contribution to the eradication of illiteracy in the Soviet Union, and can perhaps account for that eradication more than the literacy campaign can. Indeed, the elimination of illiteracy from a country over a period of twenty to twenty-five years is not an isolated phenomenon. In Meiji-era Japan illiteracy was virtually eliminated over a similar period of years directly as a result of the dissemination of primary schooling and industrialization, without benefit of an adult literacy effort.[46] These data and arguments do not invalidate the Soviet claims to having conducted a highly successful and effective literacy campaign, but they do cast some doubts upon them.

Cuba, too, has laid claim to having eradicated illiteracy by means of a highly successful literacy campaign. Following a brief campaign during which actual instruction was conducted during only one year (1961) Cuba declared itself a "territory free from illiteracy."[47] No criteria were adopted by the campaign regarding a requisite level of literacy for qualification of a literate person.[48] Nonetheless an instructional objective of a first-grade reading level attainment was established.[49] This level is substantially below the UNESCO determination of a fourth-grade level as a minimal criterion for functional literacy. Some evidence, albeit scanty, suggests that a minimum of a fourth-grade literacy level is necessary for literacy to become permanent. [50] (The emphatic rejection earlier in this study of the utilization of primary school grade equivalents referred to their use in defining levels of functional literacy, not as indicators of minimal reading level necessary for literacy retention). Even though the evidence is based upon studies conducted in languages other than Spanish, the language of instruction in the Cuban campaign— and though the permanence of literacy skills is as much a function of such factors as method of instruction, availability and use of written and printed materials, the particular language taught, and a broad range of social and psychological elements as it is of level of instruction attained—it seems clear that a certain minimum of instruction is necessary for the proper inculcation of literacy skills. It furthermore seems evident that a first-grade reading level is insufficient for an individual to be able to read materials written at a higher level. Most materials for adults, it stands to reason, are written at a level higher than first grade. Therefore, assuming that a first-grade reading level was attained in the Cuban campaign (an assumption that gives the Cubans the benefit of the doubt), it seems hardly likely that the literacy skills learned will either be long retained or put to the test of practical usage. While Cuba, partly in realization of this, has planned postliteracy "follow-up" courses, these have not gotten off to a good start and are currently insufficient to enable all those who participated in the literacy campaign to continue receiving instruction.[51] In view of this, serious doubt can be cast upon the Cuban claims of success.

Mexico is another country that has experimented with mass literacy campaigns. The most extensive of these, launched in 1944 with a "Federal Literacy Law," was in operation for fifteen years.[52] The Mexican Ministry of Education, in charge of the campaign, claimed in 1959 that over four and a half million people had learned to read and write in the program. It admitted, however, that at least a third of thos had by that date forgotten what they had learned.[53] Neither of the two figures was arrived at by administering tests to the participants. Despite the campaign an overall illiteracy rate of 50 percent was reported for Mexico in 1959.

Mass literacy campaigns of the type conducted in the Soviet Union, Cuba, and Mexico are extant in a number of countries around the world.[54] However, a trend has emerged in recent years to abandon this mass approach in favor of a more selective strategy. Curle suggests that "adult literacy will have the greatest effect if concentrated on persons having some definable skill, however simple, which could be improved."[55] He notes that "this would apply to most categories of industrial workers," which form "a relatively small

proportion of the population of most developing societies." The International
Committee of Experts on Literacy also espoused a selective approach, arguing
that it "may be more rational and more effective, and that it is reasonable
to launch the literacy campaign in more organized sections of the economy,
in particular in sections of the population where people are employed and
need literacy for their regular work." [56] Accordingly it proposed "potentially
profitable starting points such as: public or private businesses, cooperatives,
trade unions and specific organizations in the villages." In adopting this selective
strategy UNESCO also took cognizance of several other factors. First, it
recommended that programs should not be undertaken unless adequate "provision is made for effective continuing programs through the mass media of
communication . . . continuing education . . . and appropriate follow-up
reading material." [57] Second, it realized that the planning of adult literacy
programs necessitated close coordination with the planning of primary education. [58] Finally, the selective strategy was predicated upon the understanding
that literacy programs must, of necessity, be coordinated with "other elements of social and economic development," [59] and could not be conducted
in a vacuum. Substituting the term "literacy program" for "literacy campaign,"
UNESCO defined the difference as "a strategy of intensive projects rather
than of extensive campaigns." [60] J.D.N. Versluys points to a relationship
between functional literacy and the selective approach, stating that "functional
literacy is selective since it does not direct itself to the whole population but
only to those who require literacy. It is also selective in another sense: different
groups of people should receive different programs according to their needs."
[61] Literacy programs were not to be maintained, in the selective approach,
merely for the instruction of reading and writing skills. Rather they were
to be utilized as a "means of training and a method of development." [62]
In this sense the new approach did signify a radical change in the basic role of
literacy education. Literacy programs were no longer conceived of as frameworks for reading and writing instruction alone, albeit with a "hidden curriculum," but rather as frameworks for training of a type that transcended literacy
skills.

    As part of its selective strategy UNESCO undertook to conduct a five-year
"experimental world literacy program" aimed at developing, implementing,
and evaluating methods for the new approach. The ultimate objective of this
program was to "pave the way for the eventual launching of a world campaign
in this field." [63] The projects in the experimental program were to be "work
oriented"; clearly associated with the occupations or planned occupations of
the participants. Twelve pilot projects and eight "micro-experiments" in
eighteen countries were undertaken as part of the program. [64] A look at these
programs would shed further light on the selective approach and its rami-
fications.

    In Algeria pilot projects in which literacy education and vocational training were to be combined were designed in three different areas: a particularly fertile farming area, where a large number of farmers worked on self-managed farming units; an industrial area, in which chemical and oil industries are major employers; and another industrial area, in which an iron and a steel complex were in the process of being completed.[65] The original plans for the project called for the establishment of functional literacy classes in each of these contexts in which specially designed curricula would be offered to an estimated target group of 100,000 participants.[66] Two years after the project was initiated only 1400 persons were reported actually enrolled in classes.[67] After three years enrollment had increased by only 600.[68] Most of the efforts of the Algerian project were in the production of materials for the programs. These consisted primarily of a variety of film-strips, movies, and reading cards. Although no evaluations of the project are available some indication of its lack of success can be gleaned from a recommendation of a UNESCO mission that visited it in 1970: a possible "solution" to the situation created by the project was to terminate it and "resume cooperative relations with the Algerian government in a few years time when conditions will have changed and additional resources will be made available for combatting illiteracy."[69]

Mali, too, conducted a project in two different types of situation; agricultural and industrial. In the agricultural areas the program was designed to stress farming techniques, in particular the use of fertilizer, so that ultimately the rice and cotton crops in those areas would improve. In the industrial sector the program was to incorporate vocational training for employees of a wide variety of governmental enterprises. In both situations the project was planned to be manifest in formalized classroom instruction to groups of forty in which instruction was to be given by unpaid instructors, who in turn would be supervised by primary-school teachers. These instructors were to receive two months of training prior to beginning their work.[70] As in Algeria, films, film-strips, and reading cards were the methodological innovations. Of 110,000 estimated participants, only 20,140 had actually enrolled three years after the project's inception.[71]

In Tanzania a project was planned for a vast cotton-growing region in which literacy instruction was to be combined with practical training in all aspects and phases of cotton-growing. Participants spent six months studying a specially written primer and viewing classroom demonstrations by extension workers on cotton-growing, then six months actively engaged in cotton cultivation in the fields. During this period practical demonstrations were offered in special plots of land by the agricultural extension workers. A final six-month period provided for further classroom instruction, the curriculum consisting of a number of supplementary readers on such topics as arithmetic, health, cooperatives, budgeting, civics, and others. In this fashion it was intended that the curriculum be integrated with the main preoccupation of the participants— cotton-growing.[72] Participation, originally intended to reach 250,000 people was in fact only 4680 strong three years after the project started.[73] H.S. Bhola concluded, on the basis of a literacy test administered to a sample of the teachers participating in the program, that over half of them were themselves not sufficiently literate to be teaching in the program.[74] It also appears from Bhola's report that the project experienced a severe participant drop-out rate.

An experimental project in Ethiopia intended to provide functional literacy instruction to 100,000 people in three agricultural development areas and one industrial development sector.[75] Although all instruction was to be in Amharic, only 20 percent of the target group in the agricultural areas originally chosen spoke the language. As a result areas other than those originally intended were chosen as project sites. These new areas were not agricultural development zones, thus causing a compromise with one of the basic precepts of the program.[76] The program consisted primarily of the preparation of materials, training of teachers, and organization of formalized classes. Due to the lack of availability of instructors with adequate educational backgrounds, local farmers were selected to serve as instructors and given three-to four-day training sessions. It seems hardly likely that these farmer-instructors were sufficiently qualified to teach classes. Indeed, the few clues available as to the success of the program are not encouraging. A UNESCO-sponsored evaluation asserted that its "entire effort is now considered to be a waste."[77] Actual participation in the program a year after its inception was only 2250.[78] The directors of the project characterized their efforts as follows: "We are, of course, hit and miss—so was the work leading to the discovery of radium and penicillin."[79]

One of the projects in the program, a micro-experiment conducted in Nigeria, has been concluded. The program was aimed at teaching basic literacy skills to tobacco-growers and curers who had been formed into cooperative bodies under the aegis of the Nigerian Tobacco Company.[80] Second-grade primary-school teachers were recruited, given five days of initial training, and assigned to classes in twenty-one centers. The curriculum consisted of a series of fourteen primers and readers mostly related to various aspects of tobacco-growing. A global approach was utilized for reading instruction. In addition to instruction of literacy skills, the program was designed to increase the knowledge of participants on the various aspects of tobacco-growing. Actual instruction took place over a twenty-month period instead of the nine and a half months initially planned. Enrollment in the classes fluctuated widely, reaching 564 at the peak and dipping to 251 at the end of the course, despite attendance incentives of prizes.[81] A final examination was administered to the 251 participants who remained in the classes through the end. Only 157 participants (62.55 percent) passed with a grade of 35 percent and over, while 94 (37.45 percent) failed. Even these figures, however, do not indicate the success of the program, as 313 people had dropped out from the peak registration and it can be assumed that they did not learn much, if anything. Viewed from the vantage point of the entire venture, only 36 percent of its total participants were able to pass the final examinations. Knowledge of tobacco-growing among the final 251 participants increased only marginally— 9.4 percent, as compared to a 6.6 percent increase among a control group that had not participated in classes.[82] Considering these results one finds difficulty in accepting the assessment of the project's director, who suggests that the project was most successful.[83]

The experimental projects being conducted in Iran are considered exemplary by UNESCO. Iran is conducting two separate projects, one in the predominantly agricultural Greater Dez Irrigation Area, and the other in the industrial urban area of Isfahan. In both areas the functional literacy projects were planned to be tied in with general developmental activities.[84] Accordingly, the programs in the project are concerned with the relation of literacy to both industrial development and rural agricultural development. In addition to these two emphases a third program, primarily concerned with the fundamental education of women, has been designed. Included in this program is instruction pertaining to health and hygiene, nutrition and the diet, and elementary aspects of family planning.[85] The theme underlying the approach of the Iranian experiment is to instruct reading and writing skills through texts that relate to the occupational needs and interests of participants. Thus, a program on irrigation and crop rotation will present simple texts on the topic which will be utilized to teach participants both new words and letters of the alphabet.[86] Twenty-one sets of curricula relating to a similar number of topics in the five broad areas of agriculture, industry, prevocational training, handicrafts, and health and home economics are in various stages of preparation. [87] The instructional methods adopted were uniform for the entire project without any provision for differentiation.[88] Teachers for the programs are recruited from various sources: foremen, supervisors, and technicians from the industries involved, agricultural extension workers, and primary-school teachers. Originally planned to incorporate 100,000 participants, after two years the two experiments had enrolled only 8000.[89] The drop-out rate between the three cycles of each of the programs appears to be quite high—between 30 and 50 percent. In addition, the Iranian efforts have been beset with other problems: lack of coordination with the agencies directly concerned with industrial and agricultural development, lack of experimentation with different methodologies of instruction, and dissatisfaction with much of the actual classroom instruction.[90] It does not appear from the currently available reports on the experimental efforts being conducted in Iran that they signify any significant departure from the norm of adult literacy programs.

The Farmers' Training and Functional Literacy Project being conducted in India is the largest undertaking in the experimental program, aimed at enrolling 750,000 illiterate farmers. Conceived of as part of India's "Green

Revolution," the project is designed to be the literacy component of a broad program of farmer training in areas in which high-yielding seed varieties are being introduced.[91] The objective of the project is to teach reading, writing, and arithmetic skills solely, as technical training is undertaken by agricultural extension workers in a different framework. Materials in the literacy classes are based upon different aspects of farm life.[92] One interesting aspect of the program is its coordination with specially designed radio broadcasts. Each class is supplied with a radio and classes are timed to coincide with the broadcasts. Planned as a five-year venture, the project succeeded in enrolling only 18,000 participants during its first year of operation.[93] There was also quite a bit of dissatisfaction with other elements of the program: coordination with the technical training of the farmers was minimal, little support was given the literacy work by the organizations running the general training programs, lack of adequate preliminary preparation occasioned errors in the choice of methodologies of instruction, materials, and teachers, and no provision was made for follow-up work upon completion of the initial literacy stage, thus opening a door to relapse into illiteracy for those who had completed the initial phases of instruction.[94]

Other programs included in the "experimental world literacy program" are similar to those described in their close association with technical or occupational training and in attempts to coordinate the projects with specialized developmental programs.[95] In each of the programs the main innovation seems to be the connection drawn between literacy training and vocational training and the choice of contentual material for literacy instruction from the general topics of training. Indeed, in practice, these two elements seem to be the main features of UNESCO's selective strategy. The main difference that emerges between the selective strategy and the mass campaign is that while the latter considers literacy skills a sufficient condition for attaining the hidden curricula, the former recognizes that literacy instruction must be associated with a more explicit rendition of the hidden curriculum in the guise of a training or development program. Literacy programs in this approach should occur concurrently with other development programs, not in advance of them. It is in this proviso that the selectivity of the approach lies. The question of scope of literacy, mass campaign versus the selective strategy, is, therefore, both an administrative and methodological one.[96]

Although it is too soon to assess the efficacy of UNESCO's work-oriented functional-literacy program, the initial data emanating from them and cited above do not indicate that they are significantly more successful than programs undertaken under the literacy-campaign approach. Several scattered evaluations of programs conducted along lines similar to those adopted by the UNESCO-sponsored strategy lend support to this conclusion.

A functional-literacy program conducted in Maharashtra, India and generally considered to be successful was evaluated both immediately after instruction and again after a lapse of one and two years. Fifty percent of the program's enrollees were literate at the time of the termination of participation, but only 44 percent of these proved to have retained their literacy after a lapse of one and two years. In addition, there was a 50 percent drop-out during the program.[97]

Evaluating a literacy program in Tunisia, John Simmons and James Allman found that only one out of every forty-five program enrollees attained "simple literacy," defined as "the ability to read simple sentences and sub-newspaper level texts.[98] They also calculated that due to the low rate of attainment the economic cost of producing a "simple literate" was a staggering $1530, or approximately three times as much as it cost to graduate a youngster from primary school. Although participants who attained this minimal level of literacy also consistently scored higher on scales of modernization, efficacy (productivity), and national awareness, Simmons concludes that this is more a function of the "traits of Tunisian men who have the perseverance to follow such a course rather than any effects which education may have inculcated."[99] In all aspects of the study, in particular in the gains made on the modernization, efficacy, and national-awareness scales, program participants in rural areas scored consistently and significantly lower than those in urban areas.

A study of the effects of literacy training over time conducted by Simmons and Allman in the Tunisian village of Tazerka is even more discouraging. The participants in this pilot functional-literacy project were tested in 1965 after nine months of instruction. At that time 50 percent received passing grades. When retested in 1968 only 22 percent were able to receive passing grades, a decline of 45 percent in retention. This finding is all the more disturbing in view of the fact that after the first test in 1965 the majority of participants had an additional period of instruction of one to two years' duration. The actual decline in retention can therefore be assumed to be much higher than the 45 percent calculated.[100] Further limiting the actual program results is the contention of the authors that their 1968 sample was constructed such that an upward bias was reflected in their overall assessment of literacy retention.

Prodipto Roy and J.M. Kapoor compared literacy retention among primary-school and literacy-program graduates in the state of Uttar Pradesh in India. [101] Seventy percent of those tested who had attended literacy classes showed low literacy retention, as opposed to only 33 percent low retention for primary-school graduates. Within the sample of literacy-program participants rural adults showed significantly more relapse into illiteracy than did the urban group. Compounding these results is the fact that the rural samples were drawn from villages in which literacy programs had been conducted by Literacy House, a private organization situated in Lucknow, and not by the government. Roy writes of the differences between the two programs: "This [Literacy House] rural literacy training is probably the most competent and effective training in India. The government programs are far less effective and not researchable." [102] It should also be noted that the literacy retention scores obtained in this study reflect retention only among those who completed literacy programs, and does not account for in-program drop-out. A separate study conducted by T.R. Singh of Literacy House in two villages in which functional literacy programs were conducted in the Lucknow area utilized a case-study approach to assessing the effects of literacy training on participants. Singh's conclusions parallel those of the Roy–Kapoor study, showing that 40 percent of the participants graduating in 1966 had completely relapsed into a state of illiteracy by 1969, while an additional 35 percent had a partial relapse and could no longer be considered functionally literate. The 1966 graduates, in turn, represented only 25 percent of the total number of enrollees in the program. [103]

In Israel a survey was conducted in 1968 in eighty-six villages in which literacy programs had been in operation for at least one year, and in most cases for as many as six years. All adults in each of these villages were individually tested to ascertain their reading capabilities. When compared with census data from the 1960 national census the overall level of illiteracy in each village as determined by the 1968 tests showed little if any decrease. In only seven of the villages were literacy rates lower than they had been in 1960. In some of the villages it was found that illiteracy rates had actually increased.[104]

Joanna Landy-Tolwinska, studying literacy retention among literacy program participants in Poland, found that by 1963-64 60 percent of those who had participated in literacy programs during 1949-51 had relapsed to illiteracy. The relapse was particularly pronounced among craftsmen, unskilled workers, and farmers in rural areas. Ninety percent of the program participants were unable to write or wrote very poorly.[105]

There appears to be mounting evidence that literacy programs are, at best, only minimally effective in inculcating literacy skills. The few retention studies available indicate that even where literacy skills were attained during the course of a program they rapidly dissipated. Furthermore, most of the empirical studies thus far conducted clearly and significantly conclude that rural literacy efforts, when compared with urban ventures, are far less successful. The few studies undertaken in which literacy has been correlated with various modernization variables (see chapter 2), inconclusive as they are, all show literacy itself, and not the attendance in literacy programs, to be the variable that correlates with factors of change and modernization. It thus stands to reason that gains in factors such as mass media exposure, productivity, introduction of innovations in agriculture, nutrition, and health, and empathy cannot be attributed to the success of literacy programs. These have proven, on the whole, to be ineffective vehicles of fundamental education.

Lack of motivation to attend literacy classes and attain literacy skills is the cause most often cited for program failures. "Personal motivation," claims du Sautoy, "is a key factor in all adult literacy work." [106] Indeed, unless adults are motivated to attend classes they will not become program participants, and once enrolled in programs unless they are motivated to continue instruction they will drop out. Consequently, an analysis of the motivational factors associated with literacy program participation may shed light on the reasons for program failures.

Cyril Houle has differentiated three categories of adult motivation: extrinsic factors, such that attendance in programs is seen as a means to achieving another objective: social factors, such that attendance in programs is a means of socializing: and intrinsic factors, such that learning is pursued for its own sake.[107] The first of these categories can be seen as a form of achievement motivation. David McClelland notes that in developing nations the "achievement sequence more often dwells on obstacles to success and specific means of overcoming them, rather than on the goal itself, the desire for it, and the emotions surrounding attaining it or failing to attain it."[108] Surely illiteracy is such an obstacle and attendance in literacy programs conceived of as a means of overcoming it.

Two distinct phases can be discerned in motivation related to attendance in literacy programs. The first or "initial motivation" is that which results in enrollment in a program. The second or "subsequent motivation" is that which causes an individual to remain in a program throughout its duration. In rural developing areas, where literacy skills are of little if any consequence, it stands to reason that initial motivation is not predicated upon a particular desire to attain them. A combination of factors including the notion that literacy is an obstacle to attaining another, preconceived objective, the desire for social diversion and curiosity, can more aptly explain initial enrollment. M. Bazany and H. Kaufman, in a study of motivation in four Iranian villages, found, through interviewing program participants, nonparticipants, and drop-outs, that only a small minority were motivated to enroll in classes due to a desire to become literate—the majority of enrollees saw in the program a means for the attainment of some other objective.[109] Ora Grabelsky found, in a similar study in Israel, that a social motive was of considerable importance. [110] It thus appears that initial enrollment in literacy programs occurs largely due to motivational factors that have little relation to the actual curriculum offering—literacy attainment.

Once enrolled in programs adults need to sustain their motivation in order to maintain attendance. The program itself bears the onus of creating this continuing motivation. The extraordinarily high rate of attrition in most literacy programs is, to a large extent, an indication of the failure of programs to sustain the interest of their participants. Indeed, "lack of interest" is often cited by exparticipants as the cause of their dropping out from programs.[111]

A number of factors contribute to the failure of programs to sustain interest. Foremost is a combination of the methodologies of instruction, content of the curriculum, and materials used. Most literacy programs are primarily concerned with the inculcation of literacy skills and hence emphasize reading instruction rather than any specific content. Several methods or combinations of methods are in most common use. All of these derive from either a "synthetic" or "sound-syllabic" approach, or a "global" one. The "synthetic" approach is based upon the recognition of letters of the alphabet and the sounds associated with them. Letters are then formed into syllables and words are derived from different combinations of these.[112] Typical of the application of this method to literacy programs is that employed by Laubach. The "Laubach Method," applied to literacy programs in 312 languages, consists of a series of charts in which letters are superimposed upon drawings of objects, so that each letter is identified by the shape of an object and the sound associated with it. Combinations of letters into syllables (without meaning) follow the instruction of the individual letters. Finally, words are derived.[113] Although proponents of the synthetic approach claim that initial alphabet instruction is swift, the few lessons devoted to it tend to be spent in enunciating nonsensical sounds quite meaningless to learners at the critical stage when their interest must be held.

The global or "analytic" approach is based on the recognition of words or phrases with their meaning. By weaving words into stories or paragraphs with meaning and constantly repeating them it is assumed that the learner will begin to associate written words with the objects or verbs they represent.[114] While no time is spent, consequently, reading or, rather, reciting, lists of syllables, users of this method find it to be lengthy in application and a strain on learners.[115]

Gray had developed a third approach in which he derived a synthesis between the synthetic and analytic methods, combining various aspects of each. Known as the "eclectic" or "analytic-synthetic" method, it "entails the selection of carefully graded words, sentences and simple passages which the children analyse, compare, and synthetize more or less simultaneously right from the beginning, and in doing so become acquainted with the elements of language, in the desired order, while learning the mechanics of reading."[116]

Whatever method is utilized, the extent of the vocabulary introduced is usually quite limited. Gray, for example, contends that no more than three hundred words should be introduced. Laubach asserts that a vocabulary of between one and three hundred words should be used, depending on the particular language. Program participants, as a result of these methods and approaches, tend to spend hours acquiring limited vocabularies, reciting syllables and words without being able to clearly perceive either substantial gains or the potential pragmatic uses of what they are learning. The instructional methods used, originally developed for the teaching of reading to children, are not, in the main, geared to sustain adult interest.

The primer, typically the mode in which materials are presented in adult literacy programs, is also not geared to the needs of adult instruction. Primers, present in most literacy programs, are teaching aids in the form of one or more books or booklets used during the initial stages of instruction, serving as "the main instrument in the stage of learning to read and write when the adult pupil is "learning the mechanics of reading."[117] Since learning is difficult and advancement slow the primer format often discourages adults from continuing instruction. Recognizing this, Gray has suggested that primers be printed in series of short pamphlets each of which could be taught in short periods of time, so that learners would become "more keenly aware of the progress they are making, and thus acquire confidence in their ability to learn."[118] Even this compromise does not completely solve the basic problem inherent in the primer. Evidence from a number of programs indicate that drop-out from programs occurs at a much greater rate during the initial phases of instruction than later on. In Israel, for example, it was found that in programs where a short primer based on the Laubach method was used attrition tended to be highest between the third and tenth lessons.[119]

Attempts to vary the methodology of instruction have not proven successful. Robert Barnes and Andrew Henrickson, for instance, report that in a program in which programmed learning materials were used, 70 percent of the participants dropped out as a result of boredom.[120] In a program in Nigeria in which compulsion was used to force adults to attend classes, only 50 percent of the participants were able to pass a rudimentary literacy test following one year of instruction, and of those 25 percent had relapsed to illiteracy two years later.[121]

While some programs terminate instruction immediately following the primer phase on the assumption that literacy skills have been learned, most incorporate a continuation phase during which specially written readers are introduced. Recognizing that the primer phase of instruction is geared towards the attainment of literacy skills and not functional literacy, and that program participants upon completion of the first stage of instruction are "neo-literates" who need be made into "functional literates," it was emphatically recommended by the Conference of African States on the Development of Education in Africa that "adult literacy campaigns should not be launched until there is an adequate and continuing output of attractive and interesting reading matter available for those who have learnt to read and have attained different levels of literacy."[122] In many programs such readers have been written and circulated. [123] However, since these materials are typically circulated for use after the primer stage, only a small proportion of participants read them. Furthermore, they are written at fairly low levels of reading requirements, so that while in optimum situations they serve to retrench basic reading skills, they fall short of enabling new literates to transfer their skills to general reading materials published for adults. Due to the general lack of availability of appropriate reading materials in developing rural areas, once an individual has exhausted the usually meager supply of supplementary readers there is little if any material he can turn to for additional reading. The supplementary readers thus become the sole appropriate reading matter available and after one or several readings are set aside, and the literacy skills attained are dissipated through disuse.

Quality of teaching in literacy programs presents a further problem. "Because of the shortage of funds, those responsible for literacy work have often been tempted to teach people to read and write by makeshift means, using only the services of unpaid or poorly paid teachers, or of volunteers drawn from the educated sections of the population," charges UNESCO.[124] Volunteer teachers, usually unqualified, have often been pressed into service as literacy teachers. Indeed, in some cases this was done by fiat.[125] Mass-literacy campaigns in particular have made use of volunteers. Laubach's "Each-One-Teach-One" approach to literacy programs is based on the notion that literate volunteer adults become the main corps of teachers in programs. In practice, however, quite apart from the fact that most volunteers are not qualified, they are also found, in the main, to be unreliable for tasks that necessitate a sustained and intensive effort. Drop-out among volunteers has at times been greater than among learners. Primary-school teachers are also a favorite source of teachers for literacy programs. It is quite common practice to hire primary-school teachers for instruction in literacy programs in the evenings. Teachers, sorely underpaid, usually welcome this extra income.[126] While some primary-school teachers are capable adult teachers, the majority tend to repeat the classroom practices and approaches they use when teaching young children in their adult classes.[127] This, too, is a cause of attrition from programs. The problem of teachers is particularly acute in rural areas, where primary-school teachers are typically the sole source of instructors. Poorly qualified for instruction in primary schools , these teachers also function poorly in adult classes. Tired after a full day's work, poorly paid, and with an attitude that adult classes are of marginal importance, many teachers attend their classes sporadically. In some programs this, too, is reported to be cause of participant attrition.[128]

Inadequate classroom facilities add to the problem of literacy programs. Typically conducted in the evenings for several hours each week, classes are most often held in local school buildings.[129] Compounding the fact that these buildings are inadequate to begin with is the usual lack of electricity, which makes learning by candlelight or lantern more the rule than the exception. Makeshift classrooms in places of work, public facilities, and fields are also usually inconvenient for instruction.

In many developing countries, in addition to one or more national and official languages, a great number of vernacular languages are in use. Most of these are oral languages only and do not have a written form. For example, in the former British colonies of Africa alone 369 languages have been listed, and in Latin America there are at least 558 known languages.[130] The existence of these myriad tongues complicates any adult education efforts, of course. On the one hand, provision of programs in vernacular languages presents a most difficult administrative task, while on the other, utilization of only one or two languages for instruction often creates a situation whereby illiterate adults are being taught how to read and write concurrently with learning a second language. The problems created by this situation transcend purely educational considerations. For instance, when it was decided by the educational authorities of the former French colonies in Africa that "vernacular languages are to be used in fundamental education programs with adults who do not understand French," there was opposition by learners themselves, who feared that "this would be the beginning of a policy of segregation" and preferred to learn French.[131] Similarly, it is reported that "among Africans who become literate in English there has been certain opposition to the use of vernacular languages in education on the grounds that their use will prevent the spread of Western ideas and culture, will impede the progress of the African and his integration into the modern world and is, in fact, a retrograde step."[132] While it is generally recognized that instruction of adult illiterates in their mother tongue is more effective,[133] implementation of this is often extremely difficult. In the cases of nonwritten languages orthographies must be prepared, word lists and grammar organized, and appropriate texts written. In addition teachers must be trained in the use of the new language. No doubt, political considerations and the desire of countries to establish a lingua franca are also important factors in the determination of language of instruction. Indeed, Jyotirindra das Gupta points out that language is often considered an important unifying factor in countries composed of many linguistic groups in which "the natural tie of the people to their segmental groups is often valued more highly than their civil ties with the nation."[134] Consequently, literacy programs are usually conducted in the official language or languages and many adult illiterates are forced to learn a second language which has no apparent use or application to their daily lives. In rural areas where contact with the lingua franca is much more limited than in urban areas, often totally nonexistent, the language problem becomes even more acute.

As adult literacy programs are typically held during the evenings, their participants are often fatigued after a day's work in the fields or other occupations requiring physical exertion. Added to this is the fact that many suffer effects of malnutrition and disease. Illness is an often-quoted reason for drop-out from programs.[135] Poor eyesight caused by malnutrition and disease is a common condition that greatly inhibits an individual's capacity for reading. Injunctions such as those stated by Charles Richards and Gray that large type be used in printing materials only partly compensate for this.[136] In Israel, for instance, it was found that despite large print many adults were not able to see the characters on a page and were in need of ophthalmic care. None of these conditions, of course, are conducive to proper learning.

One area of particular significance to the efficacy of adult literacy programs as fundamental education is that of the access of women to literacy. Wherever illiteracy prevails, without exception, the numbers of illiterate women exceed those of illiterate men.[137] In cognizance of this fact the World Conference of Ministers of Education on the Eradication of Illiteracy recommended "that special attention be paid to the problem of making women literate, in view of the high rate of female illiteracy and the woman's role in the education of the family and in society."[138] The importance of promoting literacy programs for women is widely accepted. UNESCO contends that "the existence of a special problem of female illiteracy can have very serious consequences, for it creates a considerable gap between men and women and precludes the harmonious development of society as a whole."[139] The International Council of Women emphatically declared that "only with the full participation of women can standards in such vitally important domains as health, hygiene, child care, food production and nutrition be improved; and if, for development, a community needs the comprehension and collaboration of its women, for such comprehension women need the tool of literacy."[140] A recent UNESCO survey on the access of women to literacy programs is enlightening.[141] Participation of women in programs resembles a normal curve, with approximately half of the reporting countries having underrepresentation of women and the other half representation that approximates the proportion of women in the population. Overrepresentation, however, is reported for a very small minority of countries. Indeed, most countries report having special curricula for women participants in which various aspects of the domestic sciences are stressed. Unfortunately, adequate information on drop-out of women from courses is not given. Most of the countries participating in the survey, however, noted significant differences between the ability of women to attend classes in urban and rural areas.

A statement made at the Meeting of Experts on the Access of Girls and Women to Education in Rural Areas in Asia aptly describes the plight of the rural woman:

> The experts noted that in all countries of the region the obstacles to the access of women to education in rural areas were primarily connected with family circumstances. In the country-side women not only had to take care of the home and the children, but also worked in the fields and usually did not have any domestic help. These obstacles were all the more serious as the economic level was lower. The lack of premises where women could meet for community activities and the absence of day nurseries where they could leave their children also contributed to shutting them off from educational opportunities.[142]

To this is added the prejudice existing in many areas of the world against the education of women and their participation in activities of any sort outside the home which take them away from their "destined" chores. A study conducted in Iran in nine villages clearly points to the traditional disadvantages of women as compared to men as a prime cause for low participation, and high attrition from programs.[143] A further difficulty in programs for women is the time factor. Evenings, during which most programs are conducted, are often taken up by chores or require the woman's presence to care for her younger children. During the day household chores generally rule out participation. It seems quite evident that throughout the world women are at a definite disadvantage regarding their access to education. This situation appears to be increasingly aggravated in rural areas.

There are, without doubt, a small number of programs that have been more successful agents of fundamental education than others. UNESCO's work-oriented literacy programs hold some promise. However, adult literacy programs as currently conducted in the large majority of countries have not proven themselves to be successful in inculcating literacy skills or in the provision of fundamental education. The hidden curricula of adult literacy programs, to the extent that they have been attained, cannot in most cases ascribe that attainment to the programs sponsored under their aegis. Indeed, the picture that emerges from a survey of adult literacy programs as fundamental education is one of a rather chaotic and ill-planned venture. The need for the infusion of new ideas and directions is evident.

Part III
A System of Community-Based
Fundamental Education—
A Model

8 An Alternative Approach to Fundamental Education: Precepts of a Model

Primary schooling, community development programs, and adult literacy programs are the most prevalent approaches to the spread of fundamental education. In the previous chapters the performance of each of these as they are manifest in rural areas of developing countries was discussed. On the basis of their record, none of these approaches offers a valid, workable, and generalizable model for fundamental education. The need for an alternative approach is evident. In this section of the study such an alternative will be presented.

"Instruction," writes Jerome Bruner, "is, after all, an effort to assist or to shape growth." [1] Growth in fundamental education is conceptually a community notion, where the primary objective is to facilitate growth of all segments of the community. Indeed, if fundamental change is to result from fundamental education its effects will permeate the entire community and its membership. Change and growth are complementary concepts in fundamental education, as the major objective is to "assist or shape" growth in the direction of change. It is, of course, the individual who, through his growth, can become an agent of change. It is the collective growth of many individuals in all stations of society that can, by acting in concert, bring change to a community. In this sense, it is contended, fundamental education must be community based. It is incumbent upon the planner of fundamental education to view both the community as a whole and the community as individuals. One can compartmentalize a community by dividing its membership into various categories conforming to given criteria, but at the same time one must realize that these compartments are not self-contained. Like a mosaic floor each of the compartments joins together to form an integrated picture—the community.

The approach to fundamental education forwarded in this study is predicated upon three main precepts. In the following chapter each of these will be discussed. In the final chapter a model of fundamental education in the form of a blueprint will be presented. The emphasis in this presentation will not be on the details of the model but rather in the delineation of its main precepts, framework, and strategies. Details, it is asserted, cannot be designed in a strategy that is intended to be generalizable. They must be determined independently and specifically for each separate situation.

First among the precepts is the notion that an educational endeavor undertaking to provide fundamental education to a community cannot be narrowly focused on just one segment of that community. Primary schooling and adult literacy programs, by definition, have a segmentalized approach in that their target audiences are either children of known age or adults of known station. Consequently, in neither framework can more than one segment of society become actively participant. The cake, as it were, is cut into slices largely on the basis of an age criterion in disregard of actual "real life" interage interaction. The slices are taken out of a coherent context by assigning to each a self-contained learning experience. In contrast, the present approach predicates that community fundamental education must take the form of an integrated and coherent educational effort involving all segments of society in frameworks that approximate the naturally formed interactive groupings.

The second precept contends that man and his environment exist in harmony, each with the other. The environment molds man's attitudes and behaviors just as man has the capacity to shape the environment. Hence, an educational program that attempts to divorce the one from the other is not only dysfunctional but also self-destructive. Sowing an environment-independent system of fundamental education will yield a failing crop. The second predication, then, is that fundamental education should be environment-bound.

Last among the precepts is a theory relating to the role of literacy in society. Not only, as will be argued, is literacy a much broader concept than traditionally accepted but it, too, is situation bound. As a tool of communication it derives its definitions from the specific conditions prevailing in each society rather than from an absolute set of criteria. The type and level of literacy required by a society need be commensurate with the status of a society. Therefore, an individual in a modern, sophisticated urban area will be in need of a different order of literacy skills than one living in an underdeveloped rural environment. Furthermore, it is contended that the definitions of literacy cannot be static and final. As a society advances in its development literacy requirements, too, will change so that a constant process of redefinition is called for. Determinants of that definition are the nature of literacy-based communication requisites prevailing. As tasks performed by members of a society become more complex the types of written materials needed to cope with them will demand higher order literacy competencies. Literacy is, therefore, a functional concept not only in the sense of the UNESCO formulation of associating literacy with occupational tasks but in the more fundamental sense that the very definitions and determinations of the nature and level of literacy derive from the broad environment. Furthermore, it is asserted that underlying all literacy inculcation, and indeed preconditional to it, is a "literacy consciousness," the conceptualization of the essence of the tool. That essense is the notion of symbol notation as a means of communication that enables one to communicate beyond his immediate environment and interpersonal contacts. In nonliterate societies it is that awareness that need be established prior to the actual introduction and instruction of literacy skills. Moreover, the model proposed contends, the existing "vicious circle" of illiteracy must be breached through a process that consists of the establishment of such awareness, the introduction of an appropriate system of literacy, and the creation of an adequate supportive system that would sustain permanent literacy. Throughout, literacy is considered a means toward attaining certain clearly defined ends, never an end in itself. The final predication, then, is that literacy as a means of communication is a flexible notion that must be introduced into nonliterate societies gradually and be redefined according to specific needs, as determined by the type and level of literacy-based requisites of societies at different stages of development.

On the basis of these three precepts, the theory of fundamental education expounded earlier, and the experiences of the three current approaches to fundamental education, an alternative strategy will be presented.

Socialization, Group Interaction, and the Model

Throughout one's life the nature of the relationships formed and the inter- actions occurring within these relationships affect one's attitudes and behavior. The significance of relationships and interactions between and among individuals in a society in forging patterns of development and growth is widely acknowl- edged. The nature of society is, indeed, such that these relationships largely govern the course of human behavior within the specific societal context.

Bruner has identified two ways in which learning "serves the future."[2] The first is the "specific transfer of training . . . the extension of habits or associations." The second way is through "nonspecific transfer or, more accu- rately, the transfer of principles and attitudes." In sociological parlance, the result of this process of learning is that the individual is "socialized" into a frame- work consisting of behavioral and attitudinal norms. Orville Brim explains the socialization process thus: "The individual learns the behavior appropriate to his position in a group through interaction with others who hold normative beliefs about what his role should be, and who reward or punish him for correct or incorrect actions."[3] In a sense one can view society as being comprised of socializers and those being socialized, with each individual exchanging roles in different situations. Brim asserts in this respect that "in the life of every person, there are a number of people directly involved in socialization, who have great influence because of their frequency of contact, their primacy and their control over rewards and punishment."[4] Raymond Hunt conceives of the socialization syndrome as being structurally a complex of interlocking positions. "These posi- tions represent the functional divisions of labor deemed useful to achievement of the system's goals and are populated by a collection of particular individuals each of whom occupies at least one but commonly more than one of them."[5] Each such position can also be seen as an interactive framework in which learn- ing, as defined by Bruner, occurs. As an individual advances through life his social position or membership in interactive groups broadens so that he simultaneously belongs to several.

The primary interactive group into which an individual is initiated is that of the nuclear family, consisting of parents and siblings.[6] Normal Bell and Ezra Vogel distinguish between nuclear and extended families, arguing that "even in . . . relatively undifferentiated societies the nuclear family is never completely fused with other groups; in some circumstances and for some purposes, the nuclear family is quite distinct and 'walls of privacy' separate it from others." [7] George Murdock, on the basis of a survey of 250 societies, concluded that a definite nuclear family arrangement existed in all.[8] This finding lends support to Robert Lowie's emphatic assertion:

> It does not matter whether marital relations are permanent or temporary; whether there is polygyny or polyandry or sexual license; whether conditions are complicated by the addition of members not included in our family circle: the one fact stands out beyond all others that everywhere the husband, wife and immature children constitute a unit apart from the remainder of the community.[9]

Moreover, there appears to be a fairly constant differentiation of roles between the adult members of the nuclear family. Morris Zelditch Jr. has shown, in a study of fifty-six societies, that the father generally assumes the role of "instrumental" leader while the mother is the "expressive" leader.[10] The instrumental leadership role is basically one of task leadership and the expressive role is associated with the "expression of emotions, supportive behavior to others, the desire to please and be liked and a more generalized liking for other members." [11] The contention, then, that the nuclear family, and a fairly constant role differentiation within that family, are virtually universal is relatively well established.

Within the nuclear family Murdock has identified eight different interactive subsystems: "husband–wife, father–son, father–daughter, mother–son, mother–daughter, brother–brother, sister–sister, and brother–sister." [12] The core interactive grouping within the family is that of the mother and child. Talcott Parsons contends that "the very young child does not participate in, is not fully a 'member' of his whole family, but only of a sub-system of it, the mother–child sub-system." [13] He sees the mother–child subsystem or the mother–child identity as being "in its essentials . . . a product of learning." [14] Through interaction with the mother the child is initiated into a family and learns some of its basic motivations, skills, and behaviors.

The process of learning at the initial mother–infant interactive phase is primarily one of identification. As defined by Jerome Kagan, identification is "an acquired, cognitive response within a person (the infant). The content of this response is that some of the attributes, motives, characteristics, and affective states of a model (the mother) are part of (the child's) psychological organization."[15] The effects upon the child of this early interaction are seen as crucial. Both Roger Brown and Courtney Cazden, for example, explain early language development in the child as being largely resultant from the mother–child relationship.[16] Although there is some disagreement among various researchers as to the exact nature of language acquisition, most agree that the mother–child relationship plays a most significant role in it.[17] Similarly, the important influence mothers have on the development of the child's intelligence has been shown by many.[18] The learning of motivations, sex roles, behaviors, and attitudes are all traceable to early parent–child interaction.[19] There is, indeed, widespread agreement as to the formulative significance upon the growing child of early mother–child and familial relationships. That the effects of these early interactions within the nuclear family determine much of later adult behaviors of the individual has been convincingly shown in many studies.[20] It also appears that, as Brim states, "the effectiveness of childhood socialization certainly is greater in relatively unchanging societies."[21]

Socialization within the core family is not only unidirectional, acting solely between the adult members and their children. Although some studies imply that there is very little in parent-role performance that cannot be explained as the playing out of unconscious desires acquired in childhood,[22] it seems evident that there is a multidirectional socialization process going on within the nuclear family, which for the children is the family of orientation and for the parents is the family of procreation. Thus, husbands socialize wives through interaction into their marital roles, wives socialize husbands, siblings interact and socialize each other, and the adult members of the family are socialized into their roles as parents by their children. While much of role differentiation in the family of procreation is determined by prior experience in the families of orientation of the parents, it is clear that children contribute to the socialization of their parents by directly exerting influence upon specific activities and actual role performance. Yonina Talmon has referred to these interactions as informal, as opposed to the more formalized interaction between parents and infants.[23] Brim sees the adult learning process in the procreational family setting as being one of trial and error, as opposed to the more clearly regulated learning of infants and children in the family of orientation.[24]

Little recognition has been given in child psychology to the fact that the behavior of children influences that of their parents. Lois Stolz, however, found that such influence is of major importance, and concluded that "the interaction between a child and parent . . . becomes circular: child behavior instigates parent behavior; the parent behavior in turn influences the child; and then the cycle may begin again." Indeed, she asserts, it is "often difficult to tell whether child or parent is the initiator of the sequence."[25] Similarly, Stolz found that fathers play an important socialization role in respect to both mothers and children, and are in turn influenced by them.[26] The role of the father in child rearing and in the overall socialization process in the family has been recognized in several other studies as well.[27] It should be mentioned, however, that in some matrilineal societies the socialization function of the father is relegated to male members of the mother's family of orientation.[28]

The role of the nuclear family in socializing its members seems quite evident and well established. The interactions between the members of that family have a crucial influence on the behavior, motivations, and attitudes of its members. It is also clear that interactions within the nuclear family do not exist independently of other, external, interactions. Thus, Parsons contends:

> The nuclear family is never . . . but a small differentiated sub-system of a society. This fact is crucially relevant to our interests at two points. First, the parents, as socializing agents, occupy not merely their familial roles, but these articulate, i.e., interpenetrate, with their roles in other structures of the society, and this fact is a necessary condition . . . of their functioning as parents at all. Secondly, the child is never socialized only for and into his family of orientation, but into structures which extend beyond this family, through interpenetrating with it."[29]

In addition to interaction within the nuclear family people have recourse to a variety of reference groups. A reference group, as defined by Tamotsu Shibutani, "is that group whose outlook is used by the actor as the frame of reference in the organization of his perceptual field. All kinds of groupings, with great variations in size, composition, and structure, may become reference groups." [30] Thus reference groups might include the extended family, various peer-group relations, and occupation-related groupings, as well as groups with which the individual need not necessarily maintain direct contact and membership, such as religious orders. Each of these reference groups has a bearing on social-ization of the individual, either directly or as manifest in the influencing of individual behaviors in other group associations. N. Ackerman, for example, points out that values, as formed by the norms of a society and transmitted through a variety of reference groups, become the regulating force that helps a parent perform his socialization role in the nuclear family.[31] Stolz, in this regard, contends that "in a relatively static, homogeneous culture, a parent's behavior is habitualized, and closely follows that of other parents in the group." [32] One can conclude that, while perhaps the major socialization roles and certainly the primary responsibility for socialization are incumbent upon the family, wider group participation and interaction have definite and important socialization effects.

Peer groups are the most common manifestation of the reference group. For the young child the extrafamilial peer group is the first contact with the larger society, bringing him into initial contact with other nuclear family systems. Bernard Barber remarks that the child

> associates to some extent with his age peers in school and at play, but usually under the more direct supervision of adults, such as parents or

teachers or play-group directors. The growing child's first real independence from adults comes in his adolescent peer groups, which are important socializing agencies transitional between the family and adult groups.[33]

Nonetheless, as Jesse Pitts indicates, the earlier peer-group associations play an important role in socialization through their "pattern-maintenance" functions, which are geared to provide "a steady supply of socialized motivation."[34]

Adult peer groupings, whether centered around occupations, religious affiliations, or social intercourse, also have an important socializing role. Herbert Kelman delineates three processes by which adult peer groupings influence their members: compliance which "can be said to occur when an individual accepts influence from another person or from a group because he hopes to achieve a favorable reaction from the other," identification "when an individual adopts behavior derived from another person or group because this behavior is associated with a satisfying self-defining relationship to this person or group," and internalization "when an individual accepts influence because the induced behavior is congruent with his value system."[35] Thus the adult peer group associations both reinforce existent behaviors and values and influence them. According to Pitts "a very high level of learning can be assimilated by the individual (through the peer group), all the more since the peer group operates as a permanent public, permissive but omnipresent."[36]

The various interactive associations formed by the individual during his life span can be seen as a series of interlocking circles wherein each, although self-contained, exerts influence on the others. Beginning with interaction in the nuclear family framework, one's attitudes and behavior are largely determined through a network of interactive associations which tend to exert influence and provide reinforcement. Each grouping is basically but a subgroup of the total societal framework, so that a coherent overall interactive structure must account for all subgroupings and the relationships among them.

The socialization functions of schools have been widely recognized.[37] Similarly, it can be posited that groupings formed by community development programs and adult literacy programs also perform a socialization function. These groupings would, in fact, be virtually congruent to other peer groupings in existence. However, both the groupings formed by schools and those formed by the various adult activities have the effect of isolating one interactive set from the overall interlocking interactive pattern. Consequently, unless there is close coordination between the programs delivered in each of the settings, so that they complement each other, the socialization functions will be only minimally effective. The child returning home from school might encounter opposition in the family to notions gleaned in school that deviate from the norm. The mother, returning from an adult-literacy program with which her husband has no contact, might well encounter opposition from him if she attempts to introduce changes into the normal patterns.

A system of fundamental education aimed at the introduction of change into community life styles must be cognizant of interactive patterns and processes of socialization. Instructional groupings, therefore, should approximate the extant interactive groupings in their membership. Furthermore, instructional groupings should encompass a number of the different subgroupings within the social structure, so that the socializing effects of one group association receive reinforcement through the activities of another. This would be especially warranted in the relatively static and homogeneous type of society typical of rural underdeveloped areas, where value and behavior norms are relatively rigid. It can also be argued that in rural primary schools and formal adult programs, groupings are of marginal importance, due to the relatively short span of time spent in them and the generally poor quality of instruction. The model proposed is predicated upon the contention that the optimum strategy for introduction of change is through the existing interactive structure of society. In effect, this approach attempts to introduce change through the naturally found socialization channels by encompassing several of them in a uniform system that must, in consequence, envelop a large range of interactive frameworks. Rather than impose new social structures taken out of context of the coherent social interactive system, the model proposes to superimpose a system of fundamental education on that structure, thus maintaining the basic patterns of interaction and socialization.

Man, the Environment, and the Model

"Environment" can have different connotations in different contexts. One may refer to a social environment, a cultural environment, and a physical environment, each having a separate set of meanings and implications. In the current discussion environmental factors will be examined as they relate to the formation of occupational patterns within a community. Emphasis will be laid on the nature and significance of occupations within a society, role differentiation in the performance of tasks related to occupations, and factors concerning time schedules and location associated with the various occupations and tasks. Underlying this discussion is a basic contention that occupational demands to a large extent dictate the nature of man's concerns, life styles, and schedules. Ecological factors as they relate to occupational patterns are major contributors to the fundamental characteristics of social systems, and hence need be taken into account in the process of charting educational endeavors.

"In classical peasant culture," Parsons and Neil Smelser point out, "the household and the productive unit are a single undifferentiated collectivity." [38] In this peasant societies differ from industrial ones, in which "the bulk of economic production is carried out in the functionally specialized organizations we call firms, which are sharply differentiated from the households of which 'workers' in the firms are members." However, despite the fact that peasant cultures do not differentiate between the household and the productive unit, these nevertheless represent two distinct functions that are performed by members of the household. Accordingly, there appears to be a fairly constant role differentiation between members of the household, so that the adult males typically assume overall responsibility for the production functions or the agricultural occupations (although women may participate in the performance of specific tasks), while household-related occupations are the domain of the adult females.[39] Indeed, role differentiation according to sex seems to be so rigidly established in rural nonliterate societies that individuals are locked into specified roles and tasks by cultural fiat.[40]

The central difference between the "classical peasant culture" and modern industrial society is in that the former, to a large extent, consumes what it produces and little else, while the latter, using monetary rewards earned through membership in production organizations, can consume a wide variety of commodities regardless of the specific commodity the individual helped produce. Consequently, a far greater onus of production falls upon the peasant subsistence culture as it need produce varied commodities according to its consumption requisites. Since the household and productive units are nondifferentiated, the bulk of production tasks falls upon members of the household. Central to peasant production, of course, is agriculture. Even the few items that are purchased rather than produced are dependent upon the agricultural crop. Indeed, the primary concern of rural populations focuses on agriculture and the various tasks associated with crop production.

The significance of agriculture in rural areas has several consequences that are of concern in this analysis. Since agricultural activities and tasks are determined by a variety of environmental conditions (e.g. climate), the work calendar of the rural household is determined by these same conditions. During certain periods in the year agricultural activity intensifies, while during others it all but dies out. In essence man and his fields exist in a symbiotic relationship. The first consequence, then, is that work schedules parallel farming needs. In addition, due to the fact that in the majority of rural areas in developing countries traditional, labor intensive-farming techniques are employed, these schedules are determined for all available farmhands, not only the adult males. Women and children actively participate in the performance of many farming tasks. Farming, as an activity, is also linked to a specific place—the fields. Most of the tasks of agriculture take place in the fields, thus determining the location of laborers at given times.

Women, it has been seen, are charged with the performance of household tasks. These too, are largely time-bound, in that certain tasks need be performed at specified times (e.g., cooking, laundering, cleaning). They are also location-bound, performed in known areas: the household compound, water source, etc.

This clear differentiation of tasks, coupled with the work schedules and task performance locations imposed by external factors beyond the immediate control of the individual, are of primary importance in the design of an educational program designed for rural communities. In some countries primary schools, in cognizance of these factors, have allowed special vacations during peak periods of agricultural activity.[41] As has been pointed out, lack of consideration of these factors has contributed to the failure of many adult education efforts.

In cognizance of the central importance of roles, of their clear differentiation, of the location and time schedule requirements of each task or set of tasks, the present model posits that the educational experience should, to the extent possible, parallel each of these factors. The educational program will be structured around the roles and tasks. In addition, locations and time schedules will be determined on the basis of the locations and schedules prevailing within a community pursuant to role performance requisites. An educational experience revolving around an agricultural task will be conducted at the time and place when the particular task is performed. Similarly, courses relating to household chores are designed to be conducted at times and places that closely approximate those in which they are normally performed. In this respect the model can be considered occupation-oriented as well as location- and time-oriented, in that it matches the normal course of events within a community. In such a manner, it is contended, people will be both motivated to attend the program and enabled to do so without serious departure from their regular schedules. As in the case of the participatory patterns stipulated, existing concerns and work patterns are not encroached upon; rather, the model is superimposed on them.

Literacy and Reading in the Model:
Icons as Precursors to Words

Although the above heading may appear to contain a redundancy in that reading is a component of literacy, it will be argued that in fact reading is but one manifestation of literacy, albeit the most common. Consequently, literacy and reading are manifest in the model in separate activities.

Earlier it was asserted that literacy is the basic communication skill that enables the individual to extend the range of his contact well beyond his immediate environment. A definition of communication proposed by Andreas Fuglesang is a helpful basis for elaborating upon this assertion: "Communication is the transportation of information coded in symbols from an individual to an individual or group of individuals—symbols that influence the latter's mental processes and behavior."[42] One could readily assume that the symbols referred to are written ones. Indeed, written symbols appear to be the most efficient forms of communication available. This efficiency stems from the fact that writing systems are inherently bidirectional, consisting of both a sending (writing) and receiving (reading) mechanism.

"Communication," notes S. Dube, "is a two way process: it involves giving as well as receiving information and direction."[43] Although there appear to be many ingenious ways in which communications media such as radio, movies, and television might be geared to serve as means of bidirectional communication, inherently they are unidirectional, aimed at transmitting a message without a built-in means for eliciting response.[44] Furthermore, each of these media is time-bound, in that the individual for whom the message is intended must be at a given place at a given time if he is to receive the transmission. Writing systems have neither of these constraints. They can be utilized by the receiver of a message as a means of reversing roles and becoming a sender, and have no time factor, in the sense stated, associated with their use.

Literacy, it has been contended in this study, is a broader concept than just systems of written symbols. Earlier it was defined as being that form of communication that represents three-dimensional reality on two-dimensional surfaces that necessitates a process of encoding, decoding, and abstraction of meaning for it to become functional. On that basis a variety of two-dimensional symbol systems are incorporated into the proposed concept of literacy. These include pictures of various kinds, charts, diagrams, maps, and the like.

The literacy process entailing encoding—the committing of a message into a code of symbols—decoding—the unravelling of the code—and abstraction of meaning from the code or the association of the symbols with a given meaning is a cognitive one. As defined by Jerome Bruner and others, a cognitive process is the "means whereby organisms achieve, retain and transform information." [45]

Consider a form of literacy that employs written symbols—that of a topographical map. These maps utilize a system of symbols to depict given geographical forms and specific permanent objects seeking to convey a precise sense of terrain. In order to be able to comprehend a topographical map one must be able to decipher each of the symbols appearing on it and associate them with the objects and forms they represent. An example of such a symbol is a little triangle with a number next to it, known as a triangulation point, which indicates a geographical landmark of significance to the geographer and its height relative to sea level. The association of the triangle symbol with a given spot and its significance would be the phase of abstracting meaning from the symbol. An individual who masters the various symbols utilized in these maps, who can encode, decode, and associate them, can be considered literate in topographical maps just as one might be considered literate in a language. Presumably, anyone who can read such a map can also draw or write one. However, the most common form of drawing topographical maps consists of translating aerial photographs into the symbol system of the maps. Reading an aerial photograph is virtually a different form of literacy, with its own rules for encoding and decoding and association. Deciphering aerial photographis is a cognitive process similar to that of reading a topographical map or any system of letter symbols, and one who is proficient in the use of these photographis can properly be considered literate in aerial photographs. That the code utilized in these photographs is not written, but pictorial does not detract from the process necessary to cope with the photographs or with the fact that they constitute a most legitimate literacy system. Indeed, a person not trained in the symbol system of aerial photographs would have great difficulty in decoding them and abstracting meaning from them.

While all systems of communication are cognitive processes, not all are literacy systems. The characteristic that differentiates a literacy system from other forms of communication is that of visual symbols or notation. Thus, audio communication transmitted through whatever medium is not a form of literacy since it lacks the notation element. Pictorial representations, on the other hand, like aerial photographs, can be considered literacy systems.

In terms of communication, literacy in the traditional sense of written language remains a more effective tool than other forms. Bound as it is with language rather than with depictable context-bound situations, the range of its potential use is far greater. Topographical maps and pictorial symbols cannot, for instance, be utilized for any purpose other than describing terrain or specific situations, whereas the limitations of written literacy are only those of language. Therefore, an end objective of the model and of fundamental education is to inculcate written literacy.

A significant distinction between oral and written language has been pointed out by Patricia Greenfield.[46] "Speakers of oral language," she observes, "rely more on context for the communication of their verbal messages . . . context-dependent speech is tied up with context dependent thought, which in turn is the opposite of abstract thought." In contrast oral speech is context-independent. Although this distinction is drawn between speakers of languages that have a written form and those that do not, it is not the fact that written symbols exist in one and not in the other that is, in the case of adult illiterates, of importance. Indeed, illiterate adults living in illiterate communities do not, for all practical purposes, possess a written language. Whether the particular language they speak is written or not, their tradition is an oral one, typified by context-dependency. Jack Goody and Ian Watt observe that in illiterate cultures

> there can be no reference to "dictionary definitions," nor can words accumulate the successive layers of historically validated meanings which they acquire in a literate culture. Instead, the meaning of each word is ratified in a succession of concrete situations, accompanied by vocal inflections and physical gestures, all of which combine to particularize both its specific denotation and its accepted connotative usages.[47]

Gray has pointed out that "the ability to understand what is read depends in large measure on the associations aroused [and] these, in turn depend on previous experiences."[48] Furthermore, as Goody and Watt indicate, "there is an intimate functional adaptation of language in nonliterate societies, which obtains not only for the relatively simple and concrete symbol-referents (relationship) but also for the more generalized 'categories of understanding' and for the cultural tradition as a whole."[49] One is led to conclude that the context-bound experiences of illiterates in illiterate societies, with the resulting context-bound language and thought, would hinder the reading process. Indeed, Bronislaw Malinowski contends that written material, by its very nature self-contained, is of necessity more abstract than oral speech.[50] It thus stands to reason that illiterate adults in illiterate societies are at a definite disadvantage from the point of view of preparation when learning how to read.

Pictorial symbols, unlike written ones, are usually context-dependent and can be presented so that they depict concrete situations. Consequently they should be more readily understandable by people with context-dependent or nonabstract thought. Julian Hochberg, for instance, reports a study of a nineteen-month-old infant who "had been taught his vocabulary solely by use of solid objects and had received no instruction or training whatever concerning pictorial meaning or content."[51] Despite this the child was able to recognize "objects portrayed by two-dimensional line drawings as well as photographs." This does not mean, however, that the ability to interpret pictorial symbols is a naturally inherent one and need not be learned. Luiz Fonseca and Bryant Kearl, in a study of pictorial communication in Brazil concluded that "the ability to interpret many kinds of pictorial symbols is a learned skill and has, in this sense, much in common with the ability to interpret verbal symbols."[52] This conclusion is supported by evidence from a number of other studies as well. W. Hudson, for example, reports that depth perception in the interpretation of pictorial symbols among various indigenous groups of South Africans is somewhat lacking.[53] Fonseca and William Lassey, in a study conducted in Costa Rica, concluded that there is a "clear difference in capacity to identify pictorial symbols between those who can read and write and those who cannot."[54] Fuglesang tested picture style preference in Zambia and found that illiterates were best able to identify photographs in which the background to the object had been blocked out, and had the most difficulty with line drawings.[55] Significantly, Fuglesang also found that the ability to abstract among illiterates was either nonexistent or not stable. While these studies clearly support the contention that pictorial symbol interpretation is a learned skill, they also indicate that certain forms of pictorial representations can be interpreted without benefit of training.

Viewing both written symbols and pictorial symbols as literacy symbols, it becomes possible to order them in terms of lower- and higher-order systems. Pictorial symbols, being context-bound, are, in a sense, lower-order literacy systems, while written symbols, being self-contained and context-independent, are higher-order literacy systems. This ordering will be of significance in the determination of a literacy strategy, as will be seen below.

In illiterate societies, Goody and Watt assert, "the whole content of the social tradition, apart from the material inheritances, is held in memory."[56]

Indeed, in illiterate cultures oral discourse is the only mode of interpersonal communication and memory is the sole means of preservation. A. Lord, for instance, remarks that in illiterate societies

> the art of narration flourishes, provided that the culture is in other respects of a sort to foster the singing of tales. . . . On the other hand, when writing is introduced and begins to be used for the same purpose as the oral narrative song, when it is employed for telling stories and is widespread enough to find an audience capable of reading, this audience seeks its entertainment and instruction in books rather than in the living songs of men, and the older art gradually disappears.[57]

Since in oral transmission memory assumes the larger part of the recording function undertaken by writing systems in the literate society, it can be assumed that, in compensation for the lack of a nonverbal mode of preservation, the capacity of the illiterate for memorization is enhanced. In some adult literacy programs conducted in rural areas where the cultures are illiterate it has been observed that participants were able to repeat entire texts from memory, although they exhibited no ability to actually read the words in the text when presented in different order.[58] Rote memorization rather than decoding was the way in which these texts had been learned, and memory, rather than a decoding process, was the way in which they were recalled.

The overall failure of adult-literacy programs to transfer to their participants permanent reading and writing skills has been reviewed in some detail. Common to all the programs discussed is a fundamental conception of literacy as consisting solely of reading and writing skills. Consequently, programs have attempted to teach these skills in a variety of ways, in complete disregard of the fact that this strategy also entails the imposition of an abstract, context-independent thought pattern on a population rooted in concrete, situation-embedded approaches. This narrow approach to literacy systems has precluded the incorporation of training in other types of literacy systems, such as that of pictorial symbols.

In effect literacy programs have thus far failed to make significant inroads to what might be considered a "vicious circle" of illiteracy. By failing to make appreciable numbers of adults literate they have also failed in introducing the basic concept of notation systems as means of communication. Despite literacy programs illiterate communities have, in the main, remained wedded to oral, context-bound modes of communication. In consequence the supporting systems necessary for literacy of the younger generations have not come into being and primary schools have been graduating new generations of illiterates. The need for new, more workable strategies is apparent.

A suggestion of a literacy strategy is contained in the various factors discussed above. The main objective of literacy instruction in the proposed model is to create a breach in the vicious circle of illiteracy, so that a workable literacy system would be introduced for usage by adults while at the same time creating an adequate supporting system that would enhance the inculcation of reading and writing skills in the younger members of the community. Context-bound pictorial representations are stipulated as the literacy system to be introduced to adult participants. Although the precise nature of these would depend, in each case, on the particular prevailing situation regarding the interpretation of pictorial symbols, photographs in which extraneous details and background are blocked out might be the most generally appropriate form. In addition to instruction in the interpretation of these pictures, adults would be introduced to written literacy symbols through the association of texts with each pictorial presentation. In such a fashion the texts also become, in a sense, context-associated, and hence easier to digest. However, in teaching the texts accompanying the photographs the adopted strategy does not propose to actually instruct participants in their reading. Instead, they should be presented orally and learned orally. Participants will acquire a capacity to interpret messages through their pictorial representation while associating an orally presented text with the concrete situation depicted by the pictorial symbol. While a literacy system that can be utilized for the transmission of messages—the pictures—will have been inculcated, an awareness of the written symbol notation literacy system will have been introduced. Thus, after a period of time, the written texts can be divorced from the pictorial symbols and taught independent of them. In the interim, until the written texts assume an independent identity, participants should be able to recall their content through their association with the context-dependent pictorial symbols.

Use of pictorial symbols has several additional advantages. Their instruction must, of necessity, be accomplished through dialogue and discussion. This represents very little, if any, departure from the traditional verbal modes of communication. Furthermore, due to the relative simplicity of the process of pictorial interpretation, a much wider range of topics can be introduced in a shorter time span than through written symbols. This flow of material can continue long after formal instruction has been terminated and thus insure continued referral to a literacy symbol.

Inculcation of a literacy consciousness, even if only through pictorial literacy systems, is a further objective of this strategy. Indeed, the lack of such support was indicated earlier as a major cause in the failure of rural primary schools to promote permanent reading and writing skills. Gray observes that "children from homes where people read have often looked at pictures and glanced through magazines as their parents have read to them. They have also experienced some of the pleasures that may be derived from reading and are keen to learn." In contrast, children from illiterate homes do not have these experiences and "much time must be spent . . . in arousing interest in learning to read in the early classes." [59]

Although there is a range of views as to what age is most appropriate for beginning formal reading instruction, there is widespread agreement among reading specialists that some prereading preparation is a requisite.[60] Omar Moore considers the abilities to sit, speak, and listen to a natural language to be the only prerequisites to beginning reading instruction.[61] Others, however, hold that a more elaborate list of essential prereading skills exist. Language attainment is the requirement most often stipulated. Gertrude Hildreth, in an analysis of thirty-seven studies that examined the relation between language capabilities and reading, found that a definite and significant correlation exists between the two.[62] Walter Loban found that "those that are high in general language ability are also high in reading ability," in a ten-year study in which kindergarten children were followed through their development.[63] Similar findings have been reported in numerous studies undertaken in a number of different languages.[64] Language development, as L. Vygotsky points out, has other significant consequences:

> Thought development is determined by language, i.e., by the linguistic tools of thought and by the sociocultural experience in the child. Essentially, the development of inner speech depends on outside factors; the development of logic in the child, as Piaget's studies have shown, is a direct function of his socialized speech. The child's intellectual growth is contingent on his mastering the social means of thought: that is language."[65]

Thought development, logic, and intellectual growth, it appears, are all related to reading capabilities.

Current research in language acquisition indicates that the child is able to distinguish speech from nonspeech sounds at about two weeks of age.[66] It has also been shown that vision, the dominant human sense, develops acuity at a very early stage in life.[67] A necessary precondition for reading appears to be the development of a capacity to associate sight and sound, words with objects, and objects with notation symbols.[68] Consequently, it would seem that activities aimed at developing such associative capabilities are of crucial importance in reading-readiness programs.

An interesting approach to prereading preparation has been adopted by the American television program *Sesame Street*.[69] In an attempt to provide prereading preparation for the decoding process and comprehension, the program elaborates a number of perceptual and cognitive prerequisites. Emphasis is also laid on the motivation of the desire to read. Specific activities have been designed to train viewers of the program in visual and auditory perception, classification and sorting, orientation to direction in progression of reading, matching of objects or pictures to varied sets of objects or pictures similar in form, size, or position, the finding of counterparts to given forms, structuring parts into meaningful wholes, concept and vocabulary development, verbal response, and letter and number identification.

Many of the reading preparation skills enumerated are likely to be provided in some illiterate societies; many are not. Indeed, surveys of child-rearing patterns and infant experiences in different communities can indicate which skills are provided and which are not. Consequently, in addition to the creation of an adult supporting system for sustaining literacy, the model proposes to undertake specific, controlled activities to enhance the preparation of infants for reading instruction. This, then, forms another facet of the literacy strategy employed in the model.

The overall strategy for the inculcation of literacy, based on the foregoing precepts, can be seen as having two major thrusts. On the one hand, a lower-order literacy system is introduced and instructed to the adult members of illiterate communities, in an attempt both to provide a workable mode of communication based on notation and to form the basis for the subsequent instruction of reading and writing skills. On the other hand, in an effort to lay solid foundations for the proper spread of reading skills among the younger generation of these communities, emphasis is laid on the creation of an adult supporting system and specific, formalized, reading-preparation activities for infants are introduced. In this manner, it is intended to break the vicious circle of illiteracy and firmly establish both reading consciousness and actual capabilities.

9 The Model: A Blueprint

Each of the precepts discussed above contributes to the design of a blueprint in which a coherent educational system is formulated. The manifestation of these precepts into a paradigm of an educational system is considered to be the essential aspect of the construct proposed. However, although operational paradigmata will also be discussed, these are not intended as a sine qua non which cannot be deviated from. Indeed, it will become apparent that there are several ways in which the basic model can be operationally modified in different situations. The following blueprint is, hence, a composite of an essential paradigm and some operational suggestions.

The fundamental underlying notion of the model is that relationships extant in society be given a formalized educational context. In traditional models of education peer groups constantly form the core educational grouping. Thus, for example, in primary schooling the entire primary school is aimed at servicing a given age group within society and, with the exception of a few experiments in nongraded groupings, classes are also stratified according to rigid age lines. While adult education frameworks are seemingly more liberal in their notion of group formation, they are nevertheless always aimed at a portion of the population above the age of fifteen or eighteen, as the case may be. In situations in which adult-education groupings are extended to include younger participants (teenagers), there is often an attempt to stratify classes by age with a resultant formation of groups of "young" adults and groups of "older" adults. Similarly, community development efforts attempt to form peer group action units, rarely mixing participants from various age and social strata. This stratification into instructional framework units, it has been seen, is to a large extent artificial, as it does not parallel the various subgroups interacting in society. Insofar as primary schooling has a direct effect on adults in a community these effects are spillover ones, not contained in the program model. Indeed, the aim of primary schooling is to provide education for children, not their parents or any other segment of society. Since most communication occurs in groups consisting of two or more age segments, and, indeed, the bulk of informal traditional education is conducted in cross-sectional rather than peer groups, a more natural educational framework would be one which also accounted for cross-sectional groupings.

Earlier a number of natural social groupings or, in the language of the sociologist, subsystems, were identified. In the current model ten of these are focused upon in a formalized educational setting. These ten groupings are:

Mothers
Fathers
Parents (mothers and fathers)
Infants and small children
School-age boys
School-age girls
Mothers–infants
Mothers–school-age girls
Fathers–school-age boys
School-age boys–school-age girls

The entire educational complex is comprised, therefore, of these ten groupings. As is evident from this listing the groupings consist of both peer groups and cross-sectional groups such that the individual, in effect, participates in two or more learning frameworks. Graphically, the system can be depicted as follows:

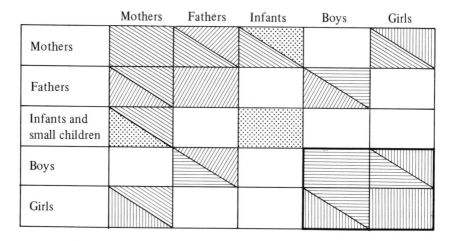

Each of the five basic peer groups (signified by the different line configurations) forms a separate instructional entity. These appear along the diagonal. Thus, mothers are grouped together, as are fathers, infants, and school-age boys and girls. Each of these instructional groups has, in the model, a specialized curriculum. In addition, there are five cross-sectional groupings in which mothers are grouped with infants, girls (daughters) and fathers (husbands); fathers are grouped with boys (sons) and boys with girls. Theoretically, of course, a further set of five groups is formed by grouping infants with mothers, girls with mothers, fathers with mothers, boys with fathers and girls with boys. These, however, are the same groups as the previously outlined five, so that the entire system consists of ten groups, not fifteen. The reason the latter are also indicated is to stress the basic intention of having both participating partners in each cross-sectional group be both donor and recipient in the newly formed instructional frameworks.

In areas in which most school-age children attend schools the four groupings indicated by the heavy black line—boys, girls, boys–girls, and girls–boys,—take place in the formalized school situation. They will, consequently, be further discussed only as the curriculum presented to them integrates with that of the entire fundamental education system.

It is evident thus far that each of the groupings requires participation of individuals already participating in at least one other group. The mothers participating in one group with their peers are the same mothers who form the learning coalition with infants, fathers, and school-age girls. The participation patterns of the model can be depicted thus:

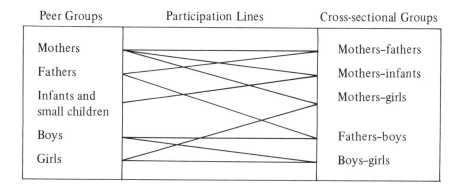

Peer Groups	Participation Lines	Cross-sectional Groups
Mothers		Mothers–fathers
Fathers		Mothers–infants
Infants and small children		Mothers–girls
Boys		Fathers–boys
Girls		Boys–girls

On the left side of this schema are listed the peer groups and on the right the cross-sectional associations. Besides the five core peer groups mothers participate in three cross-sectional groups, fathers, boys, and girls in two each, and infants and small children in one.

Although ten different and separate learning frameworks seem to have been formed this is not the case. The ten groupings mesh together to form a single, interlocking educational system. Instead of the more traditional educational network in which one progresses from a given starting point through specified age-stratified levels, this model proposes that different criteria form the basis for learning group stratification. The major stipulation is that educational subsystems be congruent with societal subgroups rather than solely an age-level specification. The resulting model is, consequently, both horizontal and vertical from the point of view of age. Emphasis is laid upon social interactive subsystems rather than age and station. However, this construct is not intended to detract from the educational coherence of the ensuing educational experience. Indeed, as will be shown, the intention is to enhance that experience through the presentation of an integrated learning experience.

Before discussing the actual educational aspects of the model, it is necessary to superimpose the precept of man's interaction with his environment onto the basic construct. Each of the groups formed is arrived at through an analysis of the role played by the individuals in that group vis à vis the environment.

The mother–infant relationship, it has been seen, remains constant in most societies. While each has a specific role to play, that role intersects at many points. The effect of the child upon the mother and her role and the crucial effect of the mother on the infant have been outlined. Clearly, these two groups have an interactive relationship that has implications for the environment. While this may be the most obvious of the cases, the same mutuality exists between the other cross-sectional groups. School-age boys in most societies partake in the tasks their fathers perform, just as school-age girls partake in the tasks their mothers perform. Fathers and mothers, while each having clearly delineated tasks and niches in the environment, also, due to their interaction, have a joint role in which the differentiated tasks intersect. The most typical role of the mother is that of child-rearing and domestic service. That of the father is related to provision, and in rural agricultural economies typically consists of various aspects of farming. The mothers, however, also play a distinct role in agricultural life, in many societies actually partaking in farming activities. The main limiting factor in a woman's farming participation are her small children and the demands made upon her by them. Boys and girls, in most societies, at an age roughly approximating that of primary-school attendance, begin active participation in adult roles played by their parents in various capacities. Here, too, a mutuality of interests begins to emerge. The participation schema shown above can thus be superimposed on a similar schema of environmental roles undertaken by each of the peer groups indicated. The participation lines will be parallel to intersecting lines of roles and the resulting cross-sectional groups will be identical to those formed in actuality through analysis of subgroup participation in environmental tasks. This explains why the groups identified are constructed along the lines proposed.

This basic paradigm is subject to change according to different societal specifications. The key to its construction is the analysis of environmental roles and interactions. Changes should, therefore, be incorporated in cases in which the groupings do not approximate the societal function. Different groupings should be substituted for those listed according to a comparable analysis of roles and interactions in such a way that the educational frameworks arrived at should parallel the roles and interactions found. Examples of such deviations from the paradigm could, for instance, be manifest in the formation of an uncles–nephews group in societies such as the Arapesh, described by Margaret Mead.[1] Nonetheless, the basic construct remains the same, with a substitution of father and mother surrogates in place of the biological parents. Since the groups formed include groups of parents and groups of children, not just a mother and child or father and child, the actual difference is theoretical. By including many mothers with many fathers and children, it stands to reason that the surrogate parents will be present in the grouping in which their surrogate children participate. In societies in which the onus of child-rearing falls upon grandparents these should be included in the appropriate groupings as either mothers or fathers.

It is clear, thus far, that the system proposed encompasses most social strata in a community. The problem that immediately arises is that of time.

Indeed, it might seem from this paradigm that an onerous and unreal system of education is being suggested for a population already busy with its regular daily occupation. This is particularly so in the case of mothers, who, besides their taxing occupational roles, are being asked to participate in no fewer than four educational frameworks. Quite obviously, an educational system engaging the active participation of working adults is unrealistic if it entails the imposition of excessive time demands. This would not only make the proposed system of fundamental education dysfunctional, but would also be counterproductive to its basic intent of providing a coherent course of fundamental educational experience.

The formation of instructional groups, it has been shown, is both role- and environment-bound. So, too, are the contentual and organizational aspects of the model. Herein lies its functionality as a working system of education.

In order to arrive at a framework for the determination of the contentual and organizational inputs into the model, an analysis of tasks performed by the different individuals in a society and the place where these tasks are performed is required. The following table attempts such a delineation as it might occur in a prototypical developing rural community:

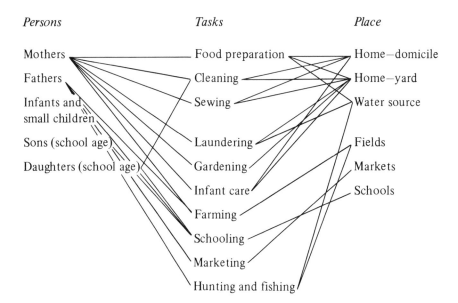

Persons	Tasks	Place
Mothers	Food preparation	Home—domicile
Fathers	Cleaning	Home—yard
Infants and small children	Sewing	Water source
Sons (school age)	Laundering	Fields
Daughters (school age)	Gardening	Markets
	Infant care	Schools
	Farming	
	Schooling	
	Marketing	
	Hunting and fishing	

The categories presented in this listing are broad ones. Farming, for instance, is a complex activity consisting of many different tasks performed by different people at different times. Indeed, not all of the tasks associated with farming are performed in the fields. Seed selection, threshing, and various aspects of processing are often performed elsewhere, depending on the particular crop. Nevertheless, this listing indicates the broad categories of tasks that are undertaken. The lines connecting the people with tasks and tasks with places indicate, in general terms, the person responsible for each set of tasks and the place in which these are undertaken. The listing is merely suggestive, consisting of those tasks and places that appear to have a fair degree of constancy in various cultural groups and societies. In the main, the tasks selected are those with which this model is most concerned. The connecting lines clearly indicate that certain tasks are performed by more than one participating group and that more than one group may be present at the same place at the same time, even if only one individual is performing the particular task specified. However, it is possible to further separate the tasks into broad categories and associate them with their major participants, as follows:

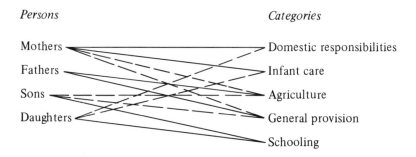

Clearly, the connecting lines indicate that mothers are primarily concerned with domestic responsibilities and infant care, fathers with agriculture and general provision (marketing, trading, hunting, etc.), and school-age children with schooling. The broken lines represent possible secondary areas of participation. Mothers might thus have a secondary interest and participatory role in agriculture and general provision, and children with any of the broad categories other than schooling as helpers or apprentices to their parents. Infants and small children are excluded from this listing, since they have no specific function to perform, and most typically accompany their mothers or remain in the home compound under the care of surrogates or caretakers.

Finally, it is possible to differentiate the tasks by the time of day at which they are performed. While this may differ widely in different societies, the following table indicates the way in which time factors can be superimposed upon the tasks. A mother's daily schedule might be as follows:

Time \ Task	Cooking	Sewing	Cleaning	Laundering	Child care	Gardening
Early morning	X				X	
Morning	X	X	X	X	X	X
Noon					X	
Afternoon		X		X	X	X
Late afternoon	X				X	
Evening		X			X	

It might be difficult, in most rural communities, to differentiate time elements as clearly as this. Certainly certain activities are performed at different times of the day, and the pattern emerging of relatively less activity during the late afternoon and evenings might not in fact be the case. Clearly, however, certain times of the day will be more occupied than others. Earlier it was noted that many women find participation in adult classes difficult at any time during the day due to the burden of activities they need to perform. One might conclude from the foregoing table, for example, that mornings are so full of activity that it would be difficult to assemble mothers in a formalized classroom situation. However, this would be equally as difficult in the evenings, when the mother must remain at home in order to care for her children. There is, indeed, a distinct difference between some of the activities delineated as they relate to time factors. Early-morning cooking for instance, is closely bound with schedules of fathers and school-going children. Since they must be fed by a certain time so that they can arrive at their respective occupational sites by a certain time, it would be difficult to occupy mothers with other activities at the same time. The same constraint would hold true during the late afternoon, and perhaps at noontime. Other tasks are not as stringently associated with a time factor. It is fairly immaterial at what hour of the day they are performed as long as they are completed. Cooking is a possible exception, as basic preparations must be made at certain times in order to adhere to a meal schedule. Thus, it becomes feasible to weigh activities and time factors accordingly. Similar schedule tables can be constructed for the other groups in order to determine which tasks are performed when, and which tasks must be performed at given times, and which leave a place for flexibility. This time-scheduling becomes an important factor in the design of the model, as it indicates some basic organizational procedures. It should be remembered that the schedule implicitly indicates not only the time during which tasks are being performed but also the place at which the different participants are found at given times. Contrary to what one might conclude from this exercise, namely that periods of minimal activity are those stipulated for the formation of instructional situations, it is the periods of maximum activity as well as minimum activity that are utilized. This will become further apparent as the model continues to unfold.

Thus far a set of ten interactive groups has been formed, tasks, places, and times indicated. Each of these will have a bearing upon the contentual and organizational aspects of the model. Prior to proceeding to a discussion of these, however, a discussion of the specific objectives the model seeks to attain is warranted.

Essentially this model of fundamental education is concerned with the provision of attitudes, knowledge, and specific skills aimed at introducing certain changes in various aspects of individual and community existence. In the first part of this study the possible role of education in the areas of health, nutrition, family planning, agriculture, and literacy attainment was indicated. In each of these areas education is seen as a vehicle for introducing change into existing behaviors. In the theory of fundamental education forwarded at the outset of the second part of the study it was argued that fundamental education consists of several distinct functions. First, it is necessary to inculcate an awareness of the need for change that would result in the formation of attitudes conducive to the adoption of innovations. Second, it becomes necessary to provide participants with the knowledge and skills required for the introduction of specific innovations. The cycle cannot be ended at this point. For the educative process to be successful these two stages must result in the actual adoption of the changes stipulated. Consequently, there is both an active and a passive aspect to the educational experience.

The specific objective of the model is to provide a blueprint for an educational system whereby each of these areas can be incorporated so that change will ensue in all. The exact nature of the changes desired cannot be determined globally, as these are contingent upon the specific conditions prevailing in each society and community. A generalized model is able to indicate little more than broad categories and show how these might be manifest.

To the extent that the introduction of innovations in each of the areas stipulated is contingent upon specific attitudinal and behavioral changes of individuals within a community, the educational system proposed is designed to facilitate such change. However, education alone cannot achieve the ultimate change objectives envisioned. These rely also upon various public health measures, introduction of new farming implements, availability of contraceptive devices, and other noneducational efforts. The model is primarily geared toward enabling people to better use the resources at their command, but not resources that are nonexistent. At best, increased awareness of needs and the inculcation of the notion that existing conditions can be changed through human actions can combine to create a demand for other measures. Indeed, these outcomes are also envisioned as objectives of the model.

The role of the model as it relates to the instruction of literacy skills can be stated more explicitly in terms that have more general validity. In the first part of the study it was noted that literacy skills are often considered essential tools for change to occur in other areas. It was also pointed out that existing research has not been able to indicate a definite correlation between literacy attainment and either attitude formation conducive to change or actual introduction of innovations. In the second part of the study the record of primary schooling and adult literacy programs as these pertain to literacy skill dissemination was examined, and it was concluded that this record was most bleak. Skills actually attained rapidly fell into disuse, because of a combination of lack of supporting systems and lack of appropriate reading materials. Earlier in this part of the study factors related to reading in both children and adults wre analyzed. The role of adequate preparation for reading was discussed, as was the particular role served by memory in the adult illiterate. Combining all of these factors, it is possible to articulate a series of objectives regarding reading and writing skills or, in broader but more accurate terms, communication skills. While the optimum objective remains that of inculcating literacy skills to both children and adults, the realities of existing situations necessitate the formulation of a more plausible objective. This objective for adults is to enable them to "read" and retain the materials presented to them in the program. Since for most participants these materials will most likely be the extent of materials ultimately used, they are planned and programmed to convey the essential information and skills required. They are also designed so that additional material can be added to them at later stages. The precise nature and method of the material will be further elaborated upon below. At this point it will be sufficient to note that adult reading is intended to be closely geared toward the ability to cope with the presented materials. For infants and children the objective of the model is to stress activities that enhance reading preparedness and to help create a supporting system, so that when literacy skills are eventually taught the hurdles currently extant will have been overcome. This does not rule out the possibility that in certain situations, in addition to these objectives, literacy skills will actually be taught to the participating youngsters. The literacy objectives of the model can, therefore, be seen as having a minimum and maximum. The minimal objectives would be the inculcation of "reading" skills to adults according to a prespecified set of materials and the creation of an apporpirate supporting system for reading, as well as the incorporation of activities aimed at reading preparation for infants and children. Maximal objectives would substitute actual literacy attainment for adults in place of the specialized mode of "reading" and literacy attainment for children, in addition to the preparation activities. In a sense the literacy objectives can also be stated in terms of an attempt to break the "vicious circle" of illiteracy, by means of a three-pronged approach entailing the attainment of a given modicum of literacy by adults, the creation and establishment of a supporting system, and the undertaking of reading preparation activities for infants and children.

In the area of health some broad objectives may be stated, although specifics are, of necessity, situation-bound. These broad objectives might include matters pertaining to personal and home hygiene, formation of positive attitudes toward cleanliness, medicine, and medical treatment, as well as specific measures that can be taken to prevent or treat certain illnesses. Some basic diagnosis and first aid could also be included.

Nutrition has been isolated, due to the severity of its incidence, from other aspects of health. Here, too, some broad objectives can be stipulated. These would consist of the impression of an awareness of the importance of proper nutritional habits, instruction pertaining to meal and diet construction emphasizing the use of readily available food-stuff and actual preparation of different foods. In many situations the attainment of the foregoing objectives may well require an attempt to change eating habits and even taste for different foods.

Family-planning objectives in the model, broadly stated, also include all three areas of attitude formation, knowledge, and skills. The exact nature of the manifestation of these three areas is, of course, determinable only by the variables extant in each specific situation. However, a maximum set of objectives could consist of motivation toward family planning, instruction relating to the functions of the body, procreation, and contraception, as well as the actual introduction of contraceptives and instruction in their use. The motivational aspects of this objective could include concepts of family size, spacing of children, and the broader notion of the family and its functions.

Similarly, objectives in agricultural change could contain the induction of attitudes conducive to the introduction of innovation, the transfer of specific knowledge and farming techniques that would lead to increased agricultural productivity and the actual implementation of these methods. As in each of the previously noted areas, emphasis should be placed on the utilization of existing and available materials. In some situations the formation of farm cooperatives might also be desired, and could subsequently be included in the objectives.

Implicit in many of these objectives is yet a further area of concern—that of child-rearing habits. While, if these are even partially successful, such change will occur by definition, an objective of introduction of change into child-rearing practices need not be only covert. Indeed, an overt objective to achieve changes in this area is also stipulated. However, since each of the other portents of change affects child-rearing habits, specific objectives need not be delineated.

The foregoing listing of objectives is quite broad. The model is so designed that one or all can be included in a particular program. Hence, the listing is merely of suggestions and does not imply that the model is only operative if the entire spectrum is included. Conversely, this listing need not be accepted as exhaustive. Indeed, the model lends itself to additions and deletions in these objectives according to the dictates of specific situations. A close relationship to the tasks performed within the community emerges from the objectives. In order to attain the objectives some measure of change must be introduced into each of the tasks outlined earlier. Thus, for example, nutrition is related to food preparation and health to infant care, cleaning, and laundering. Furthermore, the objectives also indicate the contentual aspects of the program entailed in the model. From the list of objectives an overall syllabus, or listing of topics, can be derived. Alongside these topics an overall indication of the attitudinal elements of the program can also be derived. The way in which some of the areas targeted for change intersect with performed tasks can be depicted as follows:

Tasks Objectives	Food Preparation	Cleaning	Sewing	Laundry	Infant care	Farming	Gardening
Health	X	X		X	X		
Nutrition	X				X	X	X
Agriculture						X	X

While these are the most obvious, a similar cross-tabulation can also be constructed for literacy, family-planning, and child-rearing objectives. By superimposing this table on that of the tasks and their performers, an indication of the target group to be reached, so that specific objectives are obtained. Finally, through the superimposition of the tables indicating the time and place in which the tasks are performed some important organizational specifications can be discerned.

Crucial to the model is an organizational framework that would facilitate the operation of this rather complex system. Underlying the organizational paradigm is a fundamental assumption that organizationally, learning situations should approximate, as far as possible, the natural settings in which tasks are performed and subgroup interaction occurs. The rather sacrosanct notion that instruction should be conducted in a formalized classroom situation is negated. Indeed, the contribution of the frontal classroom situation and the generally poor conditions prevailing in classrooms in rural developing areas, to the failure of both primary schooling and adult-literacy programs, has been discussed. Consequently, the organogram of the model consists of the utilization of existing structures and frameworks as well as the design of specialized ones. Obviously, the scope of the system and the heterogeneity of its participants necessitate several different organizational frameworks.

The core of the organizational structure is a specialized fundamental education center. This center can either be situated in an actual structure or in a combination of several existing ones. Theoretically such a structure should contain facilities for several of the subsystems indicated as participants in the model. Ideally the center should contain several different units and areas and can best be described in terms of a unified structure. The units and areas are, however, the significant aspects of the model and not the structure itself.

The areas within the center correspond to the objective areas. These include, therefore, a nursery for infants and small children, a cooking area, a domestic sciences area, a workshop area, a small room for gatherings, and a larger area to facilitate larger gatherings. The way in which each of these areas of the center combine to form a coherent educational system will be discussed below. Physical proximity is of essence for at least four of the areas: the nursery, cooking area, domestic sciences area, and small gathering area. Others can be situated in different sites. Basically, the four areas stipulated are similar to those found in most rural homes. Most rural homes have particular areas for cooking, small gatherings, performance of various domestic science activities, and for children. Thus, while a special structure would constitute optimal conditions for the model an alternative could be the utilization of one or more homes of participants. The structure with its various areas might look as in the following diagram:

1. nursery	2. cooking area
3. small gatherings	4. domestic sciences
5. large gatherings	6. workshop

As indicated above, only the first four need be geographically close together.

The shape and character of the structure should approximate as closely as possible the shape and character of a prototypical dwelling. In situations in which dwellings are extremely small the scale may have to be enlarged. Similarly the determination of whether some areas should be indoors or outdoors is a function of whether these typically are either indoors or outdoors. If, for instance, in a given community all cooking is performed outdoors, the cooking area in the center should also be outdoors. In both the cooking and the workshop areas the utensils present should be the same as those that participants normally have access to. The cooking area or model kitchen should be model in that a participating mother should feel as if she were in her own home, not that the utensils available are "magic" or beyond her reach. The workshop, primarily intended for men, should consist of the tools and materials the men normally use in their daily occupations. The specific activities undertaken in the workshop and the specific furnishings are determined by the nature of the occupations men engage in and the objectives of the program relating to men.

It is mainly in the nursery that changes are introduced. These changes are not aimed at changing the external environment or introducing into the nursery major furnishings that are unfamiliar. Rather, the changes are subtle and consist of introducing various objects and toys with which the children can play. Although many of these may be foreign to the environment and culture, the children will certainly not resist having them. Resistance is also not anticipated from the mothers, as it is intended that they both participate in the "manufacture" of these objects and learn their use through observation. In the majority of cultures small children are provided with various objects and toys with which to play. By having the traditional toys alongside the newly introduced ones whatever resistance may be incurred can be averted. Indeed, the traditional play objects may provide for the toddlers most of the learning objectives ascribed to the toys.

Besides the core center the system calls for other organizational frameworks. Any place in which the subgroups specified associate and at which any of the identified tasks are performed is a potential site for a learning experience. Thus, sessions pertaining to agriculture can best be conducted in those areas in which farming tasks are performed, sessions pertaining to gardening in gardens and so forth. For all practical purposes any area of the community is a potential site as long as it conforms to the basic criteria of being both a site where subgroups congregate and a site where tasks are performed.

It remains to outline the fashion in which the model operates. This will include an analysis of the mode of operation, the nature of the peer group and cross-sectional group associations, and some methodological suggestions. This analysis will begin with an examination of the three learning groups formed by mothers, infants and their combination into a cross-sectional group.

Operation of the Model

The key to the coherence of the model lies in its mode of operation. Indeed, without a clear notion of operation the system would be dysfunctional. In the following pages operational patterns will be discussed regarding each of the groups and phases stipulated.

Obviously the nursery, model kitchen, and domestic sciences areas in the center are primarily designed for use by groups of mothers and small children, and equally obviously both mothers and infants will be present at the center concurrently, as the former are charged with the care of the latter and cannot leave them untended elsewhere. While these compelling factors necessitate joint participation, this is also intended by design. Two of the peer-group and one of the cross-sectional group meetings can be conducted at the center through this arrangement. Attending mothers and their accompanying infants form two separate groups and the presence of both facilitates formation of the cross-sectional grouping to which both belong. While the mothers are engaged in a peer-group activity in either the model kitchen, domestic science, or small gathering areas the infants, together in the nursery, engage in their peer-group activity. Thus, clearly, one function of the nursery is to serve as a day-care facility. The objective of the nursery, however, is not merely to serve a baby-sitting function. The nature of the activities engaged in by the infants should be such that they receive a carefully designed fare replete with specified learning objectives. Interaction between the mothers and infants need not occur at one given time span but, rather, during a series of intervals interspersed throughout the period of attendance. As in the case of the nursery's function, here too, mothers and infants have a clearly specified series of learning objectives and the interaction is not merely one of "visiting."

From the foregoing it is clear that the sessions involving mothers, children, and their combination are conducted during daytime hours. Daytime sessions are desirable for several reasons. As was seen earlier, one cause of poor participation of women in adult-literacy programs is that these are typically conducted during the evening hours when mothers with babies and small children must remain at home to care for them. By convening daytime meetings to which mothers bring their babies and toddlers this constraint is eliminated. Moreover, a program involving active participation of children, like the one being proposed, cannot be conducted in the evenings. The compelling factor, however, is instructional and not administrative. The organization of daytime programs during hours normally considered working hours enables the association of the content and activities of the program with actual tasks being performed. In this the facilities of the center play a decisive role.

It is a basic contention of this model that a learning experience should be as practical and functional as possible. This is achieved by relating learning situations and experiences to actual task performance. Thus, the model kitchen and domestic sciences areas serve a distinct instructional purpose. They are used in lieu of classrooms as locations for instruction, supplemented when needed by short sessions in the small gathering area. It stands to reason that nonparticipating women are involved, at the same time that the sessions are being conducted, in similar working situations, performing like tasks. Indeed, one likely constraint to participation is the fact that the tasks must be performed and cannot be delayed. Here, too, the facilities of the center serve a distinct function. Since the instructional precept of "learning by doing" is manifest in having participants actually cook, sew, or launder, the products of these activities can be utilized by the women in partial fulfillment of their daily task requirements. Thus, for instance, if a learning unit consists of learning how to prepare a certain food and actually preparing it, participating women can take home part of their family's midday or evening meal. They might also feed the preparation to their infant children in the adjacent area and by so doing complete another necessary task. Similarly, if sewing or laundering constitute a learning activity, the chores that the women need, in any case, perform can be completed through the learning experience. Practically this means that participants bring the "raw" materials to the center with them and learn by "operating" on them. The framework and facilities are thus designed to enable participants, through a learning experience and in addition to that experience, to also perform some of their regular tasks. This greatly diminishes the occupational constraint to attendance. This combination of factors—the nursery facility, the task-centered curriculum, and the fact that sessions result in the performance of tangible products that form a part of regular task requirements—also serves to arouse motivation to attend.

In practice mothers arrive at the center or the alternative to the center bringing their small children and "materials" (food ingredients, laundry, clothes, cloth, etc.) required for the particular session. While the children undergo a peer-group activity in the nursery area, the mothers engage in their peer-group activities. From time to time, at appropriate intervals, mothers and children join together for a cross-sectional group experience. After the session mothers and children return home, taking with them the "finished product" from the particular session. Optimally, these meetings should occur several times each week, so that a continuous and fairly structured program can be presented. Two weekly meetings would seem to be the minimum.

The center facility also serves as a meeting ground for the two groups comprising school-age girls as a peer group and the combination of school-age girls and their mothers in a cross-sectional grouping. In areas where girls attend schools during the morning hours these meetings can be convened only in the afternoon. Indeed, where primary schools exist the peer group of girls can be conducted in the schools. Since mothers are accompanied by their small children, all three of the groups will be assembled at the center at one time allowing for the formation of yet another cross-sectional association—that of infants with their older sisters.

In their peer-group session, the young girls engage in a course of experiences that can, to a large extent, parallel that of their mothers. In this they can be served by the same facilities. In addition, certain games and other specialized experiences can be designed. The reasoning behind this similarity of learning experience is that the girls, at approximately school age, begin to partake in the same task activities as their mothers. Indeed, where this is not the case a different set of learning tasks should be designated. In the cross-sectional grouping of girls and mothers the latter can serve as instructors to their daughters in the same set of activities. In such a manner the mothers have a dual role, as both instructed and instructor.

Each of the other five subgroups of the system can also make use of the center. Along the same principles as those employed for the sessions of mothers, fathers can congregate around the workshop area and engage in an activity of interest and significance to them. Such activities could include the mending of farm implements, construction of home furnishings, seed selection and preparation, and others. Like the mothers they would bring basic materials for these activities, as stipulated, with them and return from the sessions with finished products. Due to the fact that during the day the men are usually involved in the performance of tasks in distant fields, evenings may be the optimum time for such meetings. If this is not the case, any time during the day when these activities are normally performed would be a suitable time for sessions at the center.

School-age boys can also utilize the center at the same time period as their fathers, engaging in peer-group activities and cross-sectional activities with their elders. As in the case of the mother–girl relationships, the nature of the activities might well be similar, with the fathers serving as instructors in the cross-sectional grouping. However, if only evenings can be utilized for meetings of groups of fathers at the center, it would be difficult to involve the young boys in either peer-group or cross-sectional groups at the center.

The center, as it relates to activities of fathers and boys, need not be physically the same facility as that utilized by the mothers, children, and girls. One alternative is to situate the learning experience for fathers and boys in the fields, where the bulk of agricultural tasks are performed. Indeed, some form of field experience would be requisite if sessions pertaining to farming are to maintain the principle of associating instruction with actual task performance. There is, hence, a possibility of forming a second "center" intended for boys and fathers in the general area where the majority of adult male tasks are carried out which would include that part of the workshop area designed for these groups. Proximity of this center to the farming areas would facilitate the use of these for the conduct of sessions. Many of the learning experiences designed for adult males may well involve performance of actual field farming activities so that such proximity would also be desirable. In such a manner portions of farming tasks that must in any case be undertaken can be completed in conjunction with the learning experience. Boys, insofar as they normally participate in farming tasks, can also convene for sessions, both in peer groups and cross-sectional groupings, in this center. If they are attending primary schools in the mornings, they may, of course, form these groupings in the afternoons. The nature of their cross-sectional contacts with their fathers can be conceived of as a form of apprenticeship where, under the tutelage of the fathers, they assist in the performance of appropriate tasks.

Two cross-sectional peer groupings remain to be discussed—those involving both fathers and mothers and boys and girls. For the former the large gathering area and possibly the small gathering area, depending on the size of the group and nature of the activity, serve as meeting grounds. Activities might be conducted during the evenings and include a variety of discussion groups, presentations, socialization, or even activities of a religious nature. Normally such a grouping would be extremely difficult to convene and, indeed, is quite similar to the groupings that most adult literacy programs attempt to form. However, in a situation where these meetings form only one part of a much larger experience chances for success are enhanced. Even so, in some situations it might be necessary to convene the father–mother grouping at irregular intervals around specific topics.

Boys and girls, in situations where both attend primary school, may well have occasion to interact there. Both in place of and in addition to whatever interaction might take place in school, they may further take advantage of the center or centers, as the case may be, for additional meetings. Since their time is often less task-bound than that of the adults, meetings can be conducted more frequently and with greater flexibility. The nature of their joint activities may include various games, tasks, and joint learning projects.

Each of the groups plays an important role in achieving the objectives of the model, and what occurs in each reinforces that which is taking place in each other. The system is a total one, involving all segments of a community. The operation of the system is not intended to be limited only to those families who conform to the father-mother-infant-school-age-boy-school-age-girl notion. Indeed older children, beyond the primary-school years but not yet married, can easily join in the fathers' group if their functions in a society are similar. Similarly, older adults whose children are no longer infants may also join groups of fathers and mothers if their performed tasks are similar. None of the cross-sectional groupings are predicated upon a sine qua non notion that only biological parents and children can participate in the system. The terms are utilized in this rendition of the model merely to denote a series of relationships that can more easily be understood by so labeling them. Obviously, in societies in which people other than those stipulated fill these role slots, they will be the persons to be included in the various groupings and resultant frameworks.

The center, too, is not intended as a rigid and requisite tool in the program. Rather, it is the various areas comprising the center that are of significance, and if it behooves a particular situation to situate those areas in places other than a special building or structural facility then that is where they should be. The foregoing pages merely outlined the operation of the model in one set of terms that seem to be the most generalizable. The operational model should provide an indication of the mode in which the model works, but it is also intended that it be flexible and adaptable to different situations.

Some Methodological Observations

It is difficult to prescribe precise methodological procedures for all aspects of the model, as specific content in different areas may vary widely and instructional methodologies should, to a degree, be bound to the subject matter.

Nevertheless, a basic methodological strategy must be determined if the program is to maintain an educational cohesiveness.

Earlier it was stated that a fundamental precept underlying the suggested instructional methodology is that, to the extent possible, task performance should be an integral part of the learning and instructional activities. This precept derives from the contention that actual innovations and changes have little chance of being introduced as a result of an educational strategy that is manifest in frontally delivered lectures and the distribution of written materials describing the desired change. There is somewhat more of a chance that innovations will be ultimately accepted and introduced through a strategy that includes performance of the desired change. The method proposed goes a step further and attempts to actually influence and bring about acceptance and introduction of change. Thus, the method is conceived as a total strategy encompassing the learning of a particular unit, actual performance of the content of the unit, and its incorporation into common practice.

In chapter 4 it was noted that awareness of the need for change and the nature of the specific change are important aspects of the educative process. Indeed, such awareness and understanding are crucial if change is to be sustained. Strategically the requirements of this facet of the educational experience are met in two distinct ways. On the one hand the actual instruction of material, through a process of problematizing a situation and discussion of possible solutions to that situation, is designed to arouse some degree of awareness. On the other hand the onus of creating the needed attitudes is placed on the specific units included in the program so that the perception of the benefits of change will result in formation of the attitudes. In practice, due to the complete circle of events envisioned in the method, the specific benefits should become apparent to participants without necessitating recourse to abstract lectures relating to the benefits. The best way of bringing about positive attitudes toward change and creating both awareness and understanding of the concepts of change is through enabling participants to have a positive experience with actual change. The suggested methodologies are geared toward the creation of such positive experiences.

For example, assuming that a unit of the program aimed at improving nutrition consists of the introduction of a certain food-stuff into the diet, that food-stuff would be incorporated into a recipe or series of recipes. The participating mothers would learn the recipe and then cook it, in the model kitchen. One of two things would then occur, or a combination of both. The prepared food could be fed by the mothers to their small children or school-age daughters in the appropriate cross-sectional grouping, or the food could be carried home by the mothers and served to the entire family at the appropriate meal. This final phase serves to introduce the food into the diet. It does not, however, guarantee that the new food will gain acceptance.

Acceptance of new foods might be facilitated by having the food fed to infants and younger children whose palates are not yet sufficiently formed to reject a food that differs in taste and possibly texture from the norm.[2] It is likely that the infants, after having been fed a certain food over a period of time, would develop a liking for it and continue to demand that it be served to them in the home. In this manner, the infant can become an agent of change. Even if the food is not served to adult members of a family, the nutritional status of children might be perceptibly improved so that, over time, the new food might gain wider acceptance.

Great care must be taken in the preparation of recipes for instruction. The closer the new foods are in taste and texture to the normative foods the more chance of acceptance they have. Careful preparation can reduce the factor of lack of palatability of new foods to a minimum. Over a period of time, after such foods have been introduced and accepted, the benefits of the improved diet will become apparent and positive attitudes will have been engendered. The innovation then stands a good chance of becoming permanent.

In this example each of the four phases of the suggested methodology is discernible. The first two phases, occurring in the peer group of mothers, are instruction of a topic and performance of the subject of instruction. The third phase takes place during the cross-sectional meetings of mothers and infants or school-age girls and entails the introduction of the products of the second. The fourth phase needs no instructors or instruction, and occurs after the accrued benefits of several rounds of the first three phases become apparent and perceptible.

Units in nutrition and some areas of health instruction can be approached in the described manner. Home hygiene, for example, might be taught by having participant mothers meticulously clean a kitchen after use and perceive, over time, that it is free of the bugs that might be common in home kitchens. Similarly, treatment of various common diseases might be taught by having participants learn about the treatment, prepare whatever is necessary, and then actually treat a member of their family afflicted by the disease. Again, the improvement in that person's condition over time should serve to form positive attitudes toward the treatment and facilitate its introduction. Although the specific content of instructional units will vary from situation to situation as it is dependent upon prevailing local needs and conditions, this general methodological strategy seems appropriate to most situations.

Units pertaining to sewing and laundering are included in the general design as much for motivational purposes as for instructional ones. If a garment is made or mended or dirty laundry is cleaned and a participating woman can carry home these clearly desirable objects, chances of her maintaining an interest and, hence, attendance, is enhanced. In addition, many aspects of personal hygiene can be taught through laundering clothes and mending or making new clothes. Both these units also lend themselves to the instruction of concepts of upkeep of personal possessions, maximum utilization of available materials, and the importance of clothing to general health.

Each of the activities of the program involving the various domestic activities is also aimed at building up confidence of the participants in the program. At a point at which such confidence exists it becomes relatively easier to broach such topics as family planning and contraception. Optimally, discussions on these topics, introduced casually over a period of time, might lead to participant demand to delve into them at greater length and detail. These certainly should not be topics for instruction early in a program before some degree of mutual confidence between participants and instructors exists. Depending on the conditions of a specific situation, sessions relating to family planning and contraception might be coordinated with a local health center. Basically, the method implied for instruction is one of problematization of the issue and the discussion of ways of approaching the problems. Discussion, indeed, emerges as a crucial element of the methodology.

The role of discussion in the methodology is essentially that of self-analysis. The objective is to enable participants to view their own situation and problematize it. This can be achieved through utilization of photographs or pictures. If these are taken in the area in which a particular program is being conducted, participants will be able to identify the depicted situations and discuss them, as the objects will be concrete ones with which they can readily identify. Creation of such a dialogical framework is considered essential for the problematization of issues.

The strategies outlined for instruction to mothers of topics in nutrition, health, and domestic sciences can be applied equally to groups of school-age girls, but at a different level. Indeed, as has been mentioned, the participating mothers might serve as instructors of these topics in a cross-sectional meeting. In addition, through a similar methodology, girls might participate in sessions on various crafts, dramatic performances, and others, all according to the specific situation.

The general strategy proposed for instruction of farming and workshop activities to the adult male groups is similar. Here too, a cycle consisting of instruction, performance, and observation of results is stipulated. If units pertaining to farming innovations are introduced on too large a scale, some resistance may arise. In the typical subsistence economy farm holdings are small and the tried and known methods of cultivation carry a certain warranty that known amounts of produce will result.[3] It may therefore be propitious to set aside a small plot of land where participants would experiment with the innovations. Over a period of time, once they have perceived the benefits of the changes proposed by the program, introduction of the innovations on a broader scale will become simpler to achieve. In a sense the methodology is geared to a form of demonstration wherein the participants themselves are the demonstrators.

In the various workshop activities an approach similar to that utilized in the instruction of nutrition to the mothers might be utilized. Different items can actually be produced by the participants at the workshop sessions and be taken home by them for use. The exact natue of the items would, of course, depend upon situational needs. Farm implements, house furnishings, various utensils could be produced through a similar fashion of first describing the uses of the product and manner in which it can be produced and then actually producing it. Since in many such undertakings it is unlikely that a product will be made and completed in one session, a project approach may be taken, so that each item produced becomes a project involving a number of meetings.

As in the case of the women participants, such topics as contraception and family planning should be delayed until confidence of the participants in the program is built up, although the topics could be raised casually. At the stage when more specifically explicit sessions are held on these topics it might, in some situations, be possible to conduct discussions on them in joint meetings of fathers and mothers. This could, for instance, be done in conjunction with a visit to a local health center and a lecture or presentation by a physician.

The peer group of school-age boys undertakes, in the model, a course of activities and experiences similar to those of their fathers. Also, as in the case of the girls, the fathers might be employed as the instructors of their sons. A project approach, whereby groups of boys undertake to cultivate a tract of land or build a given object as a group, is seen as the optimal approach. Sports, crafts, and dramatic presentations could also be undertaken, either in a separate group or in a cross-sectional activity with peer-group girls.

Infants and small children cannot, of course, undergo a similar program, nor indeed is that the intention of the model. Most of the activities designed for infants are intended to provide the type of stimulation required for reading preparation. Thus the program consists of providing "learning" toys for the children and of engaging them in "conversation" so that their verbal acuity will be developed. The nature of the infant activities should be nonformal but monitored. The basis for their program is the provision of a variety of toys, play objects, and materials that they can use at will, learning while playing.[4] Provision should also be made at the nursery to accommodate babies. Either a series of cribs or a large crib [5] in which babies can freely interact could be provided. Various mobiles and cause–effect toys could be placed within easy reach of the babies. Older children between the ages of four and six might be formally taught how to read if the situation permits.

Objects for the nursery need not be expensive or sophisticated. Indeed, objects easily obtainable in the environment should be used to the extent possible, so that mothers can introduce them into the home environments. Some of the workshop projects could undertake to produce various toys and objects for the nursery. Simply constructed blackboards, chalk, pencils, paper, and crayons can all be provided for the nursery at small cost. In some situations children might be given milk and various foods at the nursery, so that actual nutritional rehabilitation could result from attendance.

The methods for the cross-sectional groupings have been clearly implied in the foregoing discussion. Some additions, however, can be made. Mothers and young girls in their cross-sectional grouping with infants can play with them so that the playing activities, from time to time, cast mother and infant or infant and older sister in a mutual learning experience. Merely getting down on the floor and playing with the infants, drawing with them, talking to them, and similar activities will have the effect of creating interaction beneficial to both infants and mothers and sisters. Both mothers and older girls can aid in teaching older children basic reading skills, such as letter identification. (This, of course, can occur only in situations in which some elementary reading instruction has been given the mothers and girls.)

Since in most societies young boys and girls are typically initiated into various adult tasks at about school age they can, in interactive groupings with adults, serve as helpers or apprentices on jointly undertaken projects. Thus, for example, in a joint cooking session they may be given preparatory tasks, such as kneading dough or stirring food in a pot. Similarly, in a joint agricultural undertaking children might perform tasks such as weeding under the direction of their fathers. Such joint activity can be most beneficial to both children and adults in forming cohesiveness and stressing mutual interests. Traditional authority patterns should not, however, as a rule, be broken. If absolute authority is vested in adult males the cross-sectional experience should be structured to preserve that pattern.

The observations made on methodologies in this section are not intended to be exhaustive or prescriptive. Rather, they attempt to present a methodological strategy that is aimed at putting the model into an educational perspective. It is clear from this methodological recitation that careful preparation of materials and content is vital to the strategy. Indeed, due to the general lack of qualified instructional personnel in rural developing areas, much of the onus of such a program falls upon the design of the curriculum and the production of adequate materials.

Literacy and Materials in the Model

The precepts underlying the role of literacy and reading instruction in the model have been discussed above. Here these precepts will be translated into a methodological paradigm for the blueprint.

As stated, literacy instruction per se is not an overt objective of the system; it is introduced covertly through its use in the instructional materials as an instructional tool. Thus, a discussion of literacy instruction cannot be divorced from a consideration of the materials intended for use. A reciprocal relationship exists between the nature of the materials and the method of literacy skill instruction. Indeed, each is contingent upon the other. Both together are considered inseparable from the content they purvey and the actual performance of tasks as outlined above. The materials, their literacy component, their content, and the approach toward implementing them are intended to project a methodological unity.

Basic features of the materials are a form of looseleaf binder and a series of separate sheets or cards designed to be inserted into the binder. At the first session of the program participants are given the empty binder and the sheet or card that is the subject of that particular session. Thereafter, at each session a sheet or card relating to the session is distributed and inserted into the binder. Over a period of time, in this manner, participants build up their own books. This in itself becomes a motivating factor for attendance. Essentially, this is a reverse strategy to that employed in the typical primer approach to adult-literacy programs, where adult learners are given a book or booklet which they laboriously work through, page by page. The contention underlying the binder-card approach is that the primer, by the very nature of its format, discourages learners and abets attrition. Progress in the primer is usually quite slow and difficult, and the beginning learner can easily become discouraged just by looking at the more advanced pages that are, initially, far beyond his reach. When this is coupled with undue emphasis on the reading aspect of the primer rather than upon its content and with the fact that attendance in programs is rarely regular, making a sequentially structured program difficult to maintain, the need for an alternative to the primer becomes apparent.[6] Several other factors are contributory to the binder-card design. Since stress is laid in the model upon the content of the experience rather than reading instruction, and since that content is derivative from specific local conditions, the production of a set of materials to be used on national or even regional scales may well be counterproductive. Situational differences prevailing between various locales could easily create a situation whereby materials suitable for one area are unusable in another. The production of several different specialized primers may be quite costly, but the card format is designed so that situational differences can be more economically accommodated through the addition of some cards and the deletion of others. In addition, the sequence of presentation of the materials to participants can be altered to suit different situational contexts. In this manner a program becomes more readily adaptable to different sectors of a country. A final consideration is based on an attempt to functionalize the materials themselves. It has been seen that the likelihood that adult illiterates undergoing literacy programs will actually read materials other than those presented to them in the programs is indeed slim. Furthermore, it has been seen that primers are usually more concerned with teaching the mechanics of reading than any specific content. This being the case, the cards are designed so that participants can constantly refer to them if they wish to recall the specific content. Thus, for example, if a particular card contains a recipe that a participating mother wishes to reproduce in her home all she need do is extract the card with that recipe from her binder and refer to it. In a sense, the cards join to form a type of reference library. In addition, once the card format becomes clear to participants and they are proficient in its use, cards can be added to the collection with new material. The binder-card materials strategy, although specifically designed for the adult groups in the system, can also be used for the groups of young boys and girls.

These could, indeed, make use of the same sets of cards utilized by their parents.

Clearly, the format of the sheets or cards is crucial in this strategy. Based on the discussion of communication with illiterates and the role of literacy in reading in the model above, these have two separate but complementary parts. On one side of the sheet or card a photograph or drawing of the object of the card is depicted. On the other side a text explains the picture. In this fashion either the picture or the text, or a combination of both, can be utilized to aid recall of the content of the card. For example, if the content of a particular card is devoted to the preparation of a certain food, one side of the card would depict a drawing or photograph of the finished food, while the other would present the recipe in a written text. The women would be taught how to prepare the food through a discussion of the picture and a reading of the text. Then they would go to the model kitchen where the preparation would actually be made, referring to both the picture and the text for directives. A woman wishing to reproduce the food at a later date in her home would be able to recall the particulars of the recipe by looking at both components of the card and associating them with the practical experience she had in preparing the food. Thus, while she may not be able to "read" the text in a traditional manner of reading, the text will become meaningful as it serves to strengthen recall. In fact, memorization skills are such that the text might be memorized verbatim through association with the pictorial representation.

Over a period of time the same words can reappear several times so that the participant will begin to identify them. In addition, it is possible to isolate a key word or series of key words in each card and teach these phonetically, so that over a period of time participants will be able to identify all letter symbols and be able to actually read the texts.

Similarly, a unit in agriculture may be aimed at showing farmers that rice planted at twenty-five-centimeter intervals yields a greater quantity of crop. One side of the card would depict a rice field stressing such intervals (possibly alongside a picture of a rice paddy in which spaces are not discernible for comparison purposes), while the opposite side would describe the spacing procedure in a written text. After learning the content of the card through a discussion of the pictures and a reading of the text, the participating farmers would actually plant a portion of a field in the manner stipulated. If, after the crop has grown, the participating farmers can perceive an increase in yield, they may decide to plant all of their land holdings in like manner. Then they will be able to extract the appropriate card from the binder and recall the planting procedure through associating the picture with the text and with their actual experience. A further aid would be to design the card with one edge actually the length of the desired spacing (25 cm.). In areas in which the climate is moist it might be desirable to coat the cards in a preservative plastic coating, so that they can be used repeatedly with minimal deterioration.

As the system of fundamental education proposed in this model is not conceived of as an educational experience with a definite termination point, but rather as an ongoing enterprise, literacy abilities will result over a period of time. Obviously, the time needed to inculcate literacy skills in this model is much greater than that usually stipulated in literacy programs. This is justified, however, on the grounds that the content and accruing changes are the primary objective, literacy attainment being a by-product. Moreover, literacy skills taught in the fashion described may well prove better engrained, and retained longer than those taught in traditional literacy programs. Once participants prove to be functionally literate more traditional types of materials can be offered them, such as pamphlets, books, etc.

There are two other roles the model has pertaining to literacy. The first, not programmed or taught in any way, is that of creating a supporting system among the adult participants so that the teaching of reading to their children will be more effective. The cards, to a large extent, contribute to this. While they may not succeed in making adults "properly" literate, they may well have the effect of introducing a literacy consciousness. Indeed, the written texts on the cards may be used more by the young children learning how to read than by the adults, who may rely more on the pictorial representations. The mere introduction of written texts that have functional value and use into the home environment should serve to underscore the importance of literacy as a means of communication, and create an atmosphere conducive to its spread.

A further role of the model regarding literacy is also aimed at facilitating its spread and usage among the younger generation. The various games and toys employed in the program for small children are largely aimed at laying a solid foundation for reading, through emphasizing the development of skills associated with reading. Similarly, stress is laid upon increasing verbal interaction between children and adults. As suggested, actual reading instruction may be offered to older children. It might even be feasible to have the mothers teach their children the letters of the alphabet as they themselves learn them. This would result in a dual benefit—the children would learn the alphabet while the meager reading capabilities of the parents would be reinforced. Similarly, school-age girls could be the reading instructors of their younger siblings, teaching them to identify letters and their sounds.

In consequence of these roles and the way in which they are manifest, the literacy strategy of the model is a three-pronged one. On the first level materials designed for the adult groups and primarily aimed at communicating specific content also have an inadvertent objective of "literalization." Part of this "literalization" (and the second prong of the strategy) is intended to create a system supportive of literacy as a means of communication. The third prong is designed to lay the foundation for bringing up a new generation of literates. In this sense the program and the model are, in addition to other objectives literacy efforts. Through this strategy it is hoped that the vicious cycle of illiteracy might be broken.

Sequencing and Organization of Materials

Two additional points regarding the sequencing of materials and general organization of the curriculum are of significance to the model. Most formal educational endeavors are conceived of in systematic terms and the material to be presented is sequenced accordingly. This is certainly the case in traditional literacy programs, where the alphabet is systematically and sequentially instructed until all letters, sounds, and possible combinations are known. As this is the case, a systematic notion of a program ensues in which each lesson is contingent upon the previous one having been learned.

Sequencing in this fashion has been observed to encourage attrition from programs. A participant who has for one reason or another missed several sessions discovers upon returning that an important link has been taught in his absence. The new texts cannot be read because several new letters with which the learner may not be familiar are prominently included in most of the words. Several such absences—and they are most common—will create wide gaps which will not enable the participant to continue attending the program.

In the current model the curriculum and material are not intended to be sequenced. Units may be instructed as the instructor sees fit to insert them into the learning situation. If participant interests at a particular time lean toward a particular topic, then that topic should become the focus of attention. If an instructor feels that some of the prepared materials are not relevant to the particular group of people with whom he is working, then these should be omitted. The method suggested for the teaching of reading does not in any way contradict this approach; indeed, it permits it. As reading instruction within the model is a function of association of texts with concrete situations depicted in the illustrations, and participants are taught the accompanying texts whether they can or cannot read, it makes no difference which texts or units are taught when. Actual reading abilities, as has been stated, will develop over time as a function of continued experience with numerous texts.

Closely related to this idea is that relating to the organization of material. In addition to being nonsequenced, the entire curriculum is conceived of as being a composite of several self-contained units. This means that each and every session in the program is understood to be a singular instructional unit, so that learners can perceive that they are departing the meeting having gained something of value to them. This format provides a solution to the problem of in-program attrition in that participants can miss several sessions without having missed a crucial link in the material. They also receive a substantive reward with each session in that an entire concept, skill, or unit has been taught. A recipe, for instance, will be taught in its entirety and not on an "installment" basis. Each session attended provides the participant with a complete learning experience. Self-contained, nonsequenced instructional units become, then, the organizational format of the model from a materials point of view.

A Note on Staffing

Lack of adequately trained personnel is the nemesis of both primary schooling and adult-literacy programs. It could be equally as injurious to the proposed system. However, several of the features of the model mitigate the staffing problem.

The center and its program require a staff composed of three different types of instructors and an administrator. The role of the administrator is crucial, as he is the person who must regulate all of the elements so that the system can function smoothly. The administrator might find it both useful and desirable to work with local counterparts drawn from among the acknowledged leadership of a community. Over a period of time the administrative function could be entirely transferred to local hands. Indeed, even initially administration of the program could be undertaken by a local person or group of persons. Local involvement in the administration of the center and its programs would serve to bring the community closer to the undertaking, making of it a community center or project.

A number of full-time instructors for the adult groups are needed, their exact numbers a function of the number of participants. Employing a full-time core staff of instructors for adults would lessen the need for part-time teachers such as those staffing most current literacy programs. A specialized staff would be more readily available for training and supervision and could specialize in the instruction of adults. The instructors need not be expert in each of the topics included in the curriculum. The cards, in fact, are designed to contain all the information an instructor needs to introduce a particular unit. Literacy would thus be the basic skill required of the instructors. Other than literacy skills, training in the methodology and approaches contained in the model would be requisite. These, however, are not complex or difficult and do not necessitate a high level of prior training. Female instructors for the mothers and male instructors for the fathers seem to be desirable, particularly in view of the specialized vocational nature of the curriculum. Indeed, some basic training in cooking and domestic sciences for the female instructors, and in agriculture and various aspects of workshop work for the male instructors, would seem desirable. This training need not be intensive or aimed at making experts of the instructors in each of the areas covered by the program. Common sense, a basic aptitude for the mechanical aspects of these areas and an ability to follow written instructions are the main skills necessary.

In areas in which agricultural extension and public health workers are present, coordination of efforts would prove most profitable. The center might, indeed, provide these workers with an appropriate framework through which they can perform part of their functions. Similarly, community development agents might find the center to be a useful base of operations. Each of these functionaries could, in turn, supplement the core instructional staff of the center.

A second type of instructor required for the system is one who would work with the school-age children. In areas in which primary schools function activities for these groups would be limited, of necessity, to after-school hours. These would also tend to be periods of unemployment for primary-school teachers. Primary school-teachers, aptly suited to work with the younger groups, with a minimal amount of additional training could undertake instructional responsibilities for them.

The third person needed for the instructional staff is a nursery-school teacher to work with the infants. Local girls would perhaps offer the best source. The amount of training necessary is not extensive, and locally recruited personnel would have the advantage of knowing the children and their parents and be familiar with the local environment. Mothers may be wary of handing their children over to a stranger for care, and feel more comfortable about someone they know and trust.

It has been suggested that mothers and fathers might serve as partial instructors to their children. Although this is primarily intended to be a methodological input to the functioning of some of the cross-sectional groupings, it also has the effect of providing staffing for these groups. Similarly, the use of young girls as aides in the infant groups, while having methodological benefits, also contributes to the staffing of the groups. In such manner the model is not only a consumer of staff time but also a generator and producer of staff inputs to the system. It is not inconceivable that over a period of time, after the system has been in operation and gained community acceptance, the majority of staff needs might be met locally, requiring only minimal training and a modicum of supervision.

One distinct problem arises regarding program instructors. Most teachers in rural areas in developing countries have been observed to give frontal instruction—to base their activities on lecturing. This is surely not conducive to an approach based on initiating dialogue. It is hardly likely that conventional forms of teacher training will correct this in a meaningful way.

A system consisting of close supervision and consistent in-service training sessions during the course of a program might alleviate this problem. Another possibility is to create a training format for prospective instructors that, from the point of view of method, would parallel the approach taken in the model. An old adage holds that teachers tend to teach in the way in which they themselves were taught, not necessarily in the way in which they were told to teach. Capitalizing on this untested theory, it might be possible to create a training manual for teachers that would have the same format—cards—the same organizational precepts—nonsequenced and self-contained units of instruction—and be based on dialogue rather than the canonical lectures. Prospective teachers will only be asked to repeat this technique with their future program participants. Over time, of course, local residents in target areas might well be able to serve as instructors. They, too, will have been in contact with the methodology as participants.

Concluding Observations

The system of fundamental education proposed in the preceding pages is primarily intended to promote change. Any system so geared need be aware of the fact that the old and tried patterns of life that in traditional societies have been ingrained in generation after generation are not likely to give way to new practices without some resistance. The intensity of this resistance will no doubt reflect the characteristics peculiar to each society. To some extent, however, local characteristics might also reflect the program of fundamental education that is being presented.

This model of fundamental education has been developed in such a way as to attempt to diminish the extent of the potential resistance. Several of the model's features play a role in this. By relating the contents of the program to the functional world of participants, the likelihood of resistance decreases. It stands to reason that the familiarity of much of the content, as well as the settings provided in the model, will reduce the anxieties that often result from being subjected to unknown and foreign situations. Group stratification as it is manifest in the model is also intended to replicate existing structures, in order not to upset existing patterns of communication. Through the participation of all segments of a community, the situation wherein one group attempts to introduce an innovation and is met by resistance from others is also averted.

It has not been sufficiently emphasized that this system of fundamental education is not intended as a short-lived educational experience. A program of short duration would, indeed, undermine the notion of fundamental education as posited in this study. The system proposed is aimed at becoming a permanent institution in those areas for which it is intended. The complexity and never-ending roster of tasks and objectives that fundamental education is required to come to grips with makes this a foregone conclusion. The system, as laid forth in this blueprint, is designed to be as flexible as possible so that it can be constantly redefining its role and methodologies. This flexibility also relates to the pace of the program. The pace should reflect the receptivity of the participants rather than the urgency of the problems. While this can mean slow progress, the possibility of having the various innovations and changes introduced and accepted will be enhanced.

The multiple roles that participants play in the program is also partially intended to reduce resistance. Participants, being both learners and instructors, become totally involved on both the receiving and giving ends of the program. They join in the determination of the nature of the program, its content and methodologies. The model is thereby incorporated into the traditional system, becoming a part of it, rather than being imposed entirely from without and posing a threat to the existing order.

As one set of objectives is met and, it is hoped, attained, new ones will arise that may well necessitate the design of new modes of operation and methodologies. It is the basic framework of the blueprint, aimed at facilitating communication between various groups and building on the existing interactive network, that lies at the core of the system. Through this network and the institutions and methodologies that are superimposed upon it, fundamental education can become a dynamic force in the introduction and sustenance of change.

Notes

Part I: On the Role of Education in Development

Chapter 1: Introduction

1. Clifton R. Wharton, Jr., "Education and Agricultural Growth: The Role of Education in Early Stage Agriculture," in C. Arnold Anderson and Mary Jean Bowman (Eds.), *Education and Economic Development,* Chicago, Aldine, 1965, p. 202.
2. John Dewey, *Lectures in the Philosophy of Education,* Lecture XII: "A Formal Definition of Education. Discussion of its Formal Elements" (January 26, 1899), New York, Random House, 1966.
3. Malcolm S. Adiseshiah, *Let My Country Awake,* UNESCO, Paris, 1970, p. 49.
4. See, for example, Frederick Harbison and Charles A. Myers, *Education, Manpower and Economic Growth: Strategies of Human Resource Development,* New York, McGraw-Hill, 1964.
5. Peter F. Duker, "The Education Revolution," in A.H. Halsey, Jean Floud, and C. Arnold Anderson, *Education, Economy and Society,* New York, Free Press, 1961, pp. 15–19.
6. Carlo M. Cipolla, *Literacy and Development in the West,* London, Penguin, 1969.
7. Adam Curle, *Educational Problems of Developing Societies,* New York, Praeger, 1969, p. 3.
8. C.E. Black, *The Dynamics of Modernization,* New York, Harper, 1967, p. 19.
9. Mary Jean Bowman, "The Human Investment Revolution in Economic Thought," in Mark Blaug (Ed.), *Economics of Education, I,* London, Penguin, 1968, pp. 101–2.
10. T.W. Schultz, "Investment in Human Capital," in Blaug, op. cit., pp. 13–31, is an example of this approach. More recently (1970) Malcolm S. Adiseshiah, op. cit., has argued along similar lines, chapter 3.
11. The economic emphasis as it relates to human resource development is certainly a major consideration of educational planning. See, for example, George Skorov, "Manpower Approach to Educational Planning," in *Economic and Social Aspects of Educational Planning,* UNESCO, 1964.
12. United Nations, *The Universal Declaration of Human Rights,* Art. 26, para. 1.
13. Jan Tinbergen and H.C. Bos, "The Global Demand for Higher and Secondary Education in the Under-Developed Countries in the Next Decade," OECD *Conference on Economic Growth and Investment in Education,* 1962, p. 5.

14. C.E. Beeby, *The Quality of Education in Developing Countries,* Harvard University Press, 1966, Chapter II; and Adam Curle, op. cit., p. 4.

Chapter 2: Literacy and Development

1. Gunnar Myrdal, *Asian Drama,* Vol. III, New York, Pantheon, 1968, p. 1667.
2. Ibid.
3. *Literacy as a Factor Development,* UNESCO, Minedlit/3, Paris, 1965, p. 7.
4. J.F. Abel and N.J. Bond, *Illiteracy in Several Countries of the World,* Washington, D.C., Government Printing Office, 1929 (U.S. Bureau of Education Bulletin, No. 4, 1929), cite this as being in practice in England, Wales, Scotland, Northern Ireland, Irish Free State, the Netherlands, Switzerland, and Uruguay. Hilda Herz Golden, "Literacy and Social Change in Underdeveloped Countries," in *Rural Sociology* XX, No. 1, (1955), mentions that the ability to read and write one's name is the dividing line used by most governments for purposes of census enumeration (p. 1).
5. Edward Sapir, *Language,* Vol. I, New York, Harcourt, Brace, 1921, p. 132.
6. UNESCO, *World Illiteracy at Mid-Century:* A Statistical Study, Paris, 1957, p. 18.
7. United Nations Population Commission, *Report of the Third Session,* 10–15, May 1948, Lake Success (mimeo), pp. 17–18.
8. Expert Committee on Standardization of Educational Statistics, *Report,* UNESCO, Paris, 1952, p. 3.
9. William S. Gray, *The Teaching of Reading and Writing,* Monographs on Fundamental Education, No. 10, UNESCO, 1956, p. 24.
10. International Committee of Experts on Literacy, *Report,* UNESCO, Paris, 1962.
11. Ibid.
12. Ibid.
13. World Conference of Ministers of Education on the Eradication of Illiteracy, *Final Report,* Teheran, 1965, p. 7.
14. Paulo Freire: "The Adult Literacy Process as Cultural Action for Freedom," Harvard Educational Review, 40, No. 2, May 1970, p. 212.
15. See David, Harman, "Illiteracy: An Overview," ibid., p. 228.
16. For the United States, for example, the author developed a formula for determination of an Adult Proficiency Level (APL) in lieu of the basic fundamental literacy level which includes a base standard of reading, writing, numeracy, and knowledge variables. This formulation is in the Report of the Task Force on Planning a Nationwide Adult Right-to-Read Effort, Washington, D.C., U.S. Office of Education, June 1970 (mimeo).
17. *Literacy as a Factor in Development,* p. 10.
18. C. Arnold Anderson, "Literacy and Schooling on the Development Threshold: Some Historical Cases," in C. Arnold Anderson and Mary Jean Bow-

man, *Educational and Economic Development,* Chicago, Aldine, 1965, p. 347.

19. This figure was arrived at independently by both W.L. Sargant, "On the Progress of Elementary Education," in *Journal of the Royal Statistical Society,* 30, 1867, pp. 127–8, and W.P. Baker, *Parish Registers and Illiteracy in East Yorkshire,* New York, Oxford, 1961, p. 12.

20. Anderson, op. cit., pp. 352–54;

21. Cipolla, *Literacy and Development in the West,* London, Penguin, 1969, p. 115.

22. Ibid., pp. 114 and 89.

23. Herbert Passin, "Portents of Modernity and the Meiji Emergence," in Anderson and Bowman, op. cit., pp. 399–400.

24. Cipolla, op. cit., pp. 74–75 and 115.

25. Ibid.; Anderson, op. cit. pp. 350–51.

26. Cipolla, op. cit., Table 4.

27. Anderson, op. cit., p. 349.

28. C. Arnold Anderson and Mary Jean Bowman, "Concerning the Role of Education in Development," in C. Geertz (Ed.), *Old Societies and New States: The Quest for Modernity,* Glencoe, Illinois, Free Press, 1963, pp. 247–79.

29. Mark Blaug, "Literacy and Economic Development," in *School Review,* 74, Winter 1966, p. 400.

30. Ibid.

31. Peter C. Wright, *Literacy and Custom in a Ladino Peasant Community,* Ed.D. Dissertation, Michigan University, 1967.

32. Rose K. Goldsen and Max Ralis, *Factors Related to Acceptance of Innovations in Bang Chan, Thailand,* Ithaca, Cornell University Department of Far Eastern Studies, Data Paper 25, 1957.

33. D. Alfredo Mendez and F.B. Waisanen, "Some Correlates of Functional Literacy," paper presented at the Ninth Congress of the Inter-American Society of Psychologists, Miami, 1964.

34. Blaug, op. cit., p. 405.

35. Everett M. Rogers and William Herzog, "Functional Literacy Among Columbian Peasants," in *Economic Development and Cultural Change,* XIV, No. 2, January 1966.

36. Howard Schuman, Alex Inkeles, and David H. Smith, "Some Social Psychological Effects and Non-Effects of Literacy in a New Nation," in *Economic Development and Cultural Change,* XVI, No. 1, October 1967.

37. Peter C. Wright, Thomas A. Rich, and Edmund E. Allen, *The Impact of a Literacy Program in a Guatemalan Ladino Peasant Community,* University of South Florida, 1967.

38. William A. Herzog, Jr., *The Effect of Literacy Training on Modernization Variables,* Unpublished Ph.D. Thesis, Michigan State University, 1967.

39. Frederick C. Fliegel, "Literacy and Exposure to Instrumental Information Among Farmers in Southern Brazil," in *Rural Sociology,* XXI, No. 1, March 1966.

40. Daniel Lerner, *The Passing of Traditional Society,* New York, Free Press, 1958, pp. 52–65.

41. Lerner based his calculations on United Nations and UNESCO data. Their reliability will be discussed below. See also Wilbur Schramm and W. Lee Ruggles, "How Media Systems Grow," in Daniel Lerner and Wilbur Schramm (Eds.), *Communication and Change in Developing Countries,* Honolulu, East–West Center Press, 1967, pp. 63–67, for an examination of Lerner's hypothesis with newer data.

42. Lerner, op. cit., pp. 49–50.

43. Lerner, op. cit., Schuman, Inkeles, and Smith, op. cit.; Rogers and Herzog, op. cit.; Herzog, op. cit.; Wright, op. cit.; and others have all studied this relationship.

44. Besides the studies quoted above, the following have also dealt with these questions: Seymour Martin Lipset, "Some Social Requisites of Democracy: Economic Development and Political Legitimacy," in *American Political Science Review,* 53, March 1959, pp. 69–105 (political participation). Samuel P. Huntington, *Political Order in Changing Societies,* New Haven, Yale University Press, 1968 (political participation—Huntington formulates an argument that literacy actually increases instability based on a series of comparative international statistics). Prodipto Roy and Joseph Kivlin, *Health Innovation and Family Planning: A Study in Eight Indian Villages,* National Institute of Community Development, Hyderabad, India, 1968 (health innovations stressing family planning). R.S. Smith, "Population and Economic Growth in Central America," in *Economic Development and Cultural Change,* II, No. 1, January 1962, pp. 134–50 (birth control).

45. Lerner, op. cit., pp. 54–61.

46. Ibid., p. 61.

47. W.W. Rostow, *The Stages of Economic Growth,* Cambridge University Press, 1967, Chapter 3.

48. *World Illiteracy at Mid-Century,* op. cit. *Statistics of Illiteracy,* UNESCO, Minedlit 5, Paris, 1965. The most recent figures appear in *Literacy 1967–1969,* UNESCO, Paris, 1970.

49. *Literacy 1967–1969,* pp. 9–11. Assuming an increase in the rate of decrease in the 1960s, of 1.5 times the rate during the 1950s, the figures would be 760 million and 32.6 percent.

50. *Statistics of Illiteracy.*

51. See *Progress of Literacy in Various Countries,* UNESCO, Paris, 1953, Chapter 1 for examples of such questions in 26 countries.

52. *World Illiteracy at Mid-Century,* Chapter 2.

53. Nevertheless, some have hazarded such guesses. Gray, op. cit., estimated a 60–70 percent functionally illiterate population in the world.

Chapter 3: Some Aspects of Underdevelopment

1. Malnutrition relates to undernourishment, which denotes actual hunger and quantitative deficiency of calories and malnourishment related to

qualitative deficiency of such essential nutrients as proteins, minerals, and vitamins.

2. Food and Agriculture Organization, *Third World Food Survey,* Rome, 1963. More recent calculations give approximately the same result. See K.C. Abercrombie, "Food and Agriculture," in Richard Symonds (Ed.), *International Targets for Development,* New York, Harper, 1970, pp. 113–14.

3. Moisés Béhar, M.D., "Prevalence of Malnutrition Among Pre-School Children of Developing Countries," in Nevin Scrimshaw (Ed.), *Malnutrition, Learning and Behavior,* Cambridge, M.I.T. Press, 1968, p. 40.

4. Jean A.S. Ritchie, *Learning Better Nutrition,* FAO, Rome, 1967, pp. 18–20.

5. P. Gyorgi, "Report of the Symposium 'How to Reach the Pre-School Child,' Villa Serbelloni, Lake Como, Italy, August, 1963, in *American Journal of Clinical Nutrition* 14:65, 1964.

6. See, for example, Angus M. Thomson, "Historical Perspectives of Nutrition, Reproduction and Growth," in Scrimshaw, op. cit., pp. 17–27.

7. *Malnutrition and Disease,* World Health Organization, Geneva, Freedom from Hunger Campaign Basic Study No. 12, 1963.

8. Oscar Gish, "Health Planning in Developing Countries," in *Journal of Development Studies* VI, No. 4, p. 68.

9. Ritchie, op. cit., pp. 7–18.

10. Derrick B. Jelliffe, *Child Nutrition in Developing Countries,* Washington, D.C., AID (revised edition), 1969, pp. 75–86.

11. See Mavis B. Stoch and P.M. Smythe, "Undernutrition During Infancy and Subsequent Brain Growth and Intellectual Development," in Scrimshaw, op. cit., pp. 278–88.

12. Ritchie, op. cit., pp. 24–26.

13. Jelliffe, op. cit., pp. 75–86.

14. Margaret Mead (Ed.), *Cultural Patterns and Technical Change,* Mentor Book, 1955, pp. 194–96.

15. "New Directions in Family Planning," *Studies in Family Planning,* no. 32, The Population Council, June 1968, p. 1.

16. Bert F. Hoselitz and H.W. Hargreaves, "Population Growth and Economic Development," in Art Gallaher, Jr. (Ed.), *Perspectives in Development Change,* Lexington, University of Kentucky Press, 1968, pp. 100–27, contains a discussion of some of these implications. A general discussion can be found in Halvor Gille, "Population," in Symonds, op. cit., pp. 59–91.

17. Gille, op. cit., pp. 54–55.

18. Ibid., pp. 55–56.

19. Dorothy Nortman, *Population and Family Planning Programs: A Factbook,* Population Council and the International Institute for the Study of Human Reproduction, Columbia University, Reports on Population/Family Planning No. 2 (1970 Edition), July 1970.

20. Max F. Millikan and David Hapgood, *No Easy Harvest; the Dilemma of Agriculture in Underdeveloped Countries,* Boston, Little, Brown & Co., 1967, pp. 3–4.

21. Theodore W. Schultz, *Transforming Traditional Agriculture,* New Haven, Yale University Press, 1964, pp. 11–15.

22. *The Growth of World Industry 1938-1961; International Analysis and Tables,* UN, New York, 1965, pp. 320-27.
23. The State of Food and Agriculture, 1966, FAO, Rome, 1966.
24. Abercrombie, op. cit., pp. 117-18, and Lester R. Brown "New Directions in World Agriculture," *Studies in Family Planning,* No. 32, The Population Council, June 1968, pp. 1-6.
25. *The Food Problem of Developing Countries,* OECD, 1967, p. 25.
26. Millikan and Hapgood, op. cit., p. 91.
27. Schultz, op. cit., pp. 175-206.
28. *United Nations Demographic Yearbook, 1969,* New York, 1970, Table.
29. Gish, op. cit., pp. 68, 73-74, and Dr. V. Zammit-Tabona, "The Health Aspects of Development," in Symonds, op. cit., pp. 98-99.
30. Zammit-Tabona, op. cit., pp. 100-3.

Part II: Fundamental Education:
Theory and Practice

Chapter 4: A Theory of Fundamental Education

1. *Fundamental Education—Common Ground for all Peoples,* UNESCO, New York, Macmillan, 1947.
2. *Fundamental Education—A Description and Program,* Monographs in Fundamental Education No. I, UNESCO, Paris, 1949, pp. 9-11.
3. *Fifteenth Report of the Administrative Committee on Coordination to the Economic and Social Council,* New York, 1953, pp. 8-10.
4. Ibid., p. 9.
5. A Bulletin published by UNESCO and entitled *Fundamental Education* began appearing in June 1952 as *Fundamental and Adult Education.*
6. *Guide for the Preparation of Pilot Experimental Work Oriented Literacy Projects,* UNESCO, Paris, April 1967 (mimeo), p. 1.
7. See Margaret Mead, "Our Educational Emphasis in Primitive Perspective," in John Middleton (Ed.), *From Child to Adult: Studies in the Anthropology of Education,* New York, American Museum of Natural History, 1970, pp. 8-10.
8. Daniel Lerner, *The Passing of Traditional Society: Modernizing the Middle East,* Glencoe, Illinois, Free Press, 1958, p. 64.
9. Hortense Powdermaker, *Copper Town: Changing Africa,* New York, Harper, 1962, p. 228.
10. Lerner, op. cit., p. 64.
11. David Riesman, *The Oral Tradition, the Written Word and the Screen Image,* Antioch College Founders Day Lecture No. 1, Yellow Springs, Antioch Press, 1956, pp. 27-34.
12. William S. Gray, "Reading and Factors Influencing Reading Efficiency," in William S. Gray (Ed.), *Reading in General Education,* Washington, D.C., 1940, pp. 30-31.

13. Charles C. Fries, *Linguistics and Reading,* New York, Holt, Rinehart and Winston, 1962, p. 120.

14. Ibid., p. 208.

15. Jeanne Chall, *Learning to Read: The Great Debate,* New York, McGraw-Hill, 1967, p. 34.

16. William A. Herzog, Jr., op. cit., p. 20.

Chapter 5: Primary Schooling as Fundamental Education

1. For a brief discussion of the lack of clarity in the goals of primary education see C.E. Beeby, *The Quality of Education in Developing Countries,* Cambridge, Harvard University Press, 1966, pp. 35–36 and 41–42.

2. *The United Nations Development Decade: Proposals for Action,* UN, New York, 1962, p. 30.

3. Nicholas Bennett, "Primary Education in Rural Communities: An Investment in Ignorance?" in *The Journal of Development Studies,* Vol. 6, No. 4, July 1970, p. 92.

4. Statistics on primary education expansion are reported annually in the *International Yearbook of Education,* International Bureau of Education, Geneva and UNESCO, Paris.

5. See, for example, *Report of Meeting of Ministers of Education of Asian Member States Participating in the Karachi Plan,* UNESCO, Tokyo, 1962, for individual country reports on the attainment of the quantitative goals for primary-school expansion contained in the Karachi Plan.

6. For a discussion of what is meant by "quality of education" see Beeby, op. cit., Chapter 1.

7. Philip H. Coombs, *The World Educational Crisis,* London, Oxford University Press, 1968, p. 106.

8. R.S. Peters, "The Meaning of Quality in Education," in *Qualitative Aspects of Educational Planning,* UNESCO, IIEP, 1969, pp. 150–59.

9. Torsten Husén, "Some Views on Cross-National Assessment of the Quality of Education," ibid., p. 275.

10. See Beeby, op. cit., pp. 10–11, and Bennett, op. cit., p. 92.

11. Coombs, op. cit., p. 106.

12. *Facilities for Education in Rural Areas,* UNESCO, International Bureau of Education, Geneva, Publication No. 192, 1958.

13. See Bennett, op. cit., pp. 93–94.

14. See *Report of Meeting of Ministers of Education of Asian Member States Participating in the Karachi Plan,* pp. 4–12.

15. Ibid., p. 5.

16. Coombs, op. cit., pp. 34–35.

17. See discussion in ibid., pp. 34–35, and, for an example relating to the situation in Africa, *Survey of the Status of Teaching Professions in Africa,* Washington, D.C., World Confederation of Organizations of the Teaching Profession, 1964, pp. 1–13.

18. Beeby, op. cit., p. 31.

19. Christopher Cox, "Presidential Address to the Education Section of the British Association for the Advancement of Science," 1956, quoted in ibid., p. 30.

20. Much has been written on the popular demand for education in developing countries. See, for example, Beeby, op. cit., Chapter III; Coombs, op. cit., Chapter II.

21. Paul Mort, *Principles of School Administration,* New York, McGraw-Hill, 1946, pp. 199–200.

22. C.E. Beeby, "Educational Quality in Practice," in *Qualitative Aspects of Educational Planning,* p. 41.

23. Bennett, op. cit., p. 94.

24. *Wastage and Stagnation in Primary and Middle Schools in India,* NIE–HEW Project 005, Department of Educational Administration, New Delhi, 1967 (mimeo), p. 14.

25. The countries included are Cameroon, Chad, Togo, Central African Republic, Dahomey, Congo (Brazzaville), Gabon, Ivory Coast, Madagascar, Upper Volta, Niger, Mauritania, Senegal. See Coombs, op. cit., Appendix 9, p. 192.

26. Conference on Education and Economic and Social Development in Latin America, *Final Report,* United Nations Economic and Social Council, UNESCO/ED/CEDES/37, Paris, March 1962, pp. 35–36.

27. Gunnar Myrdal, *Asian Drama,* New York, Pantheon, 1968, Table 33–34, pp. 1718–20.

28. See Beeby, *The Quality of Education in Developing Countries,* pp. 15–17, for a discussion of the accuracy of drop-out and wastage statistics.

29. G. Flores, "A Study of Functional Literacy for Citizenship in the Philippines," in *Quarterly Bulletin of Fundamental Education,* Vol. II, No. 3, July 1950.

30. Ithiel de Sola Pool, "The Mass Media and Politics in the Modernization Process," in Lucien Pye (Ed.), *Communications and Political Development,* Princeton, Princeton University Press, p. 247.

31. J.C. Carothers, "Culture, Psychiatry and the Written Word," in *Psychiatry,* Vol. XXII, November 1959, p. 308.

32. W.D. Wall, "Unconscious Resistance to Education," in John W. Hanson and Cole S. Brembeck (Eds.), *Education and the Development of Nations,* New York, Holt, 1966, p. 277.

33. Francis E. Dart, "The Rub of Cultures," in Hanson and Brembeck, op. cit., p. 97.

34. See Marion J. Levy, Jr., *Modernization and the Structure of Societies,* Vol. I, Princeton, Princeton University Press, 1966, Part I, Chapter 2.

35. Carothers, op. cit., p. 308.

36. UN, *Pulp and Paper Prospects in Asia and the Far East,* Vol. I, Bangkok, 1962, p. 8.

37. UNESCO, *Statistics of Illiteracy,* Minedlit 5, Paris, 1965, gives these statistics for 96 countries.

38. See Charles Granston Richards, *The Provision of Popular Reading Materials,*

UNESCO, Monographs on Fundamental Education No. XII, 1959, for an in-depth discussion of this problem and some case studies.

39. William S. Gray, *The Teaching of Reading and Writing*, UNESCO, Monographs on Fundamental Education No. X, Second Edition, 1969, pp. 136–44.

40. See Bennett, op. cit., p. 94, and Beeby, *The Quality of Education in Developing Countries*, pp. 31–32.

41. Clifton R. Wharton, Jr., "The Role of Education in Early Stage Agriculture," in C. Arnold Anderson and Mary Jean Bowman, (Eds.), *Education and Economic Development*, Chicago, Aldine, 1965, p. 207.

42. Cited in ibid.

43. Ibid., pp. 208–11.

44. Prodipto Roy and Joseph Kivlin, *Health Innovations and Family Planning*, National Institute of Community Development, Hyderabad, India, 1968, pp. 12–13.

45. C. Woodruff, "Nutritional Aspects of Metabolism Growth and Development," in the *Journal of the American Medical Association*, Vol. 196, p. 214, 1966.

46. See, for example, J. Craviato and B. Robles, "Evolution of Adaptive and Motor Behavior During Rehabilitation from Kwashiorkor," in the *American Journal of Orthopsychiatry*, Vol. 35, p. 449, 1965.

47. Joaquin Cravioto and Elsa R. De Licardie, "Intersensory Development of School-Age Children," in Nevin S. Scrimshaw (Ed.), *Malnutrition, Learning and Behavior*, Cambridge, M.I.T. Press, 1968, pp. 252–67.

48. Mavis B. Stoch and P.M. Smythe, "Undernutrition During Infancy and Subsequent Brain Growth and Intellectual Development," in Scrimshaw, op. cit., p. 287.

49. Alex Inkeles, "Making Men Modern: On the Causes and Consequences of Individual Change in Six Developing Countries," in the *American Journal of Sociology*, Vol. 75 No. 2, September 1969, p. 213. The six countries are Argentina, Chile, India, Israel, Nigeria, and Pakistan.

50. Ibid., p. 212. The "modernity scale" is based on a set of "personal qualities which reliably cohere as a syndrome and which identify a type of man who may validly be described as fitting a reasonable theoretical conception of modern man" (p. 210).

51. Ibid., p. 212.

52. Alex Inkeles, "The Modernization of Man," in Myron Weiner (Ed.), *Modernization*, New York, Basic Books, 1966, p. 146. Since the six-country data were all collected by 1964, it can be assumed that this reservation is derived from the same empirical evidence.

Chapter 6: Community Development as Fundamental Education

1. United Nations Economic and Social Council, *Official Records of the 24th Session, Annexes, Agenda Item 4: 20th Report of the Administrative*

Committee on Coordination to the Council, Annex III, Geneva, 1957, p. 14.

2. Peter du Sautoy, *The Organization of a Community Development Program,* London, Oxford University Press, 1962, p. 126.
3. UN Economic and Social Council, op. cit., p. 14.
4. Ibid., pp. 14–15.
5. Ibid., p. 15.
6. Louis Miniclier, "Community Development Defined," in International Cooperation Administration, *The Community Development Review,* No. 3, 1956, p. 1.
7. See, for example, William W. Biddle and Loureide J. Biddle, *The Community Development Process: The Rediscovery of Local Initiative,* New York, Holt, 1965, Chapters 2 and 3.
8. Great Britain, Colonial Office, *Social Development in the British Colonial Territories,* Report of the Ashbridge Conference on Social Development, Miscellaneous Papers No. 523, London, HMSO, 1965, p. 14.
9. T.R. Batten, *Communities and Their Development,* London, Oxford University Press, 1957, pp. 46–47.
10. du Sautoy, op. cit., p. 2.
11. Batten, op. cit., p. 2.
12. Alexis de Tocqueville, *Democracy in America,* Vol. I (Henry Reeve text revised by Phillip Bradley), New York, Knopf, 1948, p. 191.
13. Charles Erasmus, *Man Takes Control: Cultural Development and American Aid,* Minneapolis, University of Minnesota Press, 1961, p. 95.
14. Adam Curle, *Educational Strategy for Developing Countries,* London, Tavistock Publications, 1963, p. 114.
15. See Batten, op. cit., Chapter IX.
16. Harold Houghton and Peter Tregear (Eds.), *Community Schools in Developing Countries,* UNESCO, Institute for Education, Hamburg, 1969, pp. 15–16.
17. Ibid., pp. 27–37.
18. Ibid., Chapter IV, and Batten, op. cit., pp. 103–6.
19. Jack D. Mezirow, *Dynamics of Community Development,* New York, Scarecrow Press, 1963, p. 193.
20. B.B. Schaffer, "Deadlock in Development Administration," in Colin Leys (Ed.), *Politics and Change in Developing Countries,* Cambridge, Cambridge University Press, 1969, p. 209.
21. Ibid., p. 209.
22. Ibid., p. 204.
23. Mezirow, op. cit., p. 193.
24. One such example is that of the Comilla experiment in East Pakistan. See Howard Schuman, *Economic Development and Individual Change,* Center for International Affairs, Harvard University, Cambridge, 1967.
25. T.R. Batten, *The Human Factor in Community Work,* London, Oxford University Press, 1965, p. 1.
26. V.L. Griffiths, "The Field Worker," in Phillips Roupp (Ed.), *Approaches to Community Development,* The Hague, 1953, pp. 218–26.
27. Batten, *The Human Factor in Community Work,* is a casebook in which

many failures due to the field worker are documented and analyzed. See also the cases reported in Edward H. Spicer, *Human Problems in Technological Change*, New York, Russell Sage Foundation, 1952.

28. Griffiths, op. cit., p. 221. This would explain, perhaps, part of the success reported in such efforts as the Comilla experiment.

29. Schaffer, op. cit., p. 203.

30. Leonard Doob, *Becoming More Civilized: A Psychological Exploration*, New Haven, Yale University Press, 1960, pp. 104–5.

31. Quoted in Herbert H. Hyman, Gene N. Levine, and Charles R. Wright, *Inducing Social Change in Developing Communities*, United Nations Institute for Social Development, n.d., p. 81.

32. Margaret Mead (Ed.), *Cultural Patterns and Technical Change*, UNESCO, 1955 (Mentor Book), p. 258.

33. See United Nations Seminar, *Administrative Aspects of Community Development*, The Hague, 1959.

Chapter 7: Adult Literacy Programs:
The Record

1. Adults are generally considered to be people from the age of fifteen upwards. See United Nations Population Commission, *Report of the Third Session*, 10–25 May 1948, Lake Success, p. 17.

2. See, for example, profiles of participants in Adult Basic Education classes in the United States in Curtis Ulmer, *Teaching the Disadvantaged Adult*, University of Georgia and Georgia State Department of Education, December 1968, Chapter III. See also discussion of history of adult education in Denmark, England, Germany, and the United States, Mary Ewen Ulich, *Patterns of Adult Education*, New York, Pageant Press, 1965.

3. James E. Allen, Jr., "The Right-to-Read—Target for the 70's," Address before the 1969 Annual Convention of the National Association of State Boards of Education, Los Angeles, California, September 23, 1969.

4. James E. Allen, Jr., "The Educational Third Dimension," Address before the Galaxy Conference on Adult and Continuing Education, Washington, D.C., December 9, 1969.

5. Julius Nyerere, quoted in *Literacy—A Social Experience*, International Council of Women, Teheran, 1965, p. 3. (In address to Parliament at the inauguration of the first Five Year Development Plan, May 1964.)

6. See *International Yearbook of Education*, UNESCO and International Bureau of Education, Geneva, 1967, 1968, 1970, and the *United Nations Demographic Yearbook*, where comparative statistics are given for budgetary outlays and number of teachers and participants in the various levels of education. This is also true, incidentally, of Nyerere's Tanzania.

7. See descriptions of literacy programs in 110 countries in *Literacy and Education for Adults*, UNESCO and International Bureau of Education, Geneva, 1964, Publication No. 226, and *Supplement 1965*, Publication No. 278.

8. Ibid., and UNESCO, *Literacy 1967–1969*, UNESCO, Paris, 1970, pp. 5–6.

9. Benson Snyder, *The Hidden Curriculum,* New York, Knopf, 1970. (The "hidden curriculum" referred to is the dichotomy between the explicit and implicit aspects of university curricula).

10. Sir Charles Jeffries, *Illiteracy: A World Problem,* London, Pall Mall Press, 1967, pp. 31–33.

11. Ulich, op. cit., pp. 50–55, for instance, describes such activities in eighteenth-century England.

12. Jeffries, op. cit., pp. 37–40, and Frank C. Laubach, *Literacy as Evangelism,* Committee on World Literacy and Christian Literature, New York, 1950.

13. Frank C. Laubach and Robert S. Laubach, *Toward World Literacy the Each-One-Teach-One Way,* Syracuse, Syracuse University Press, 1960, pp. 3–30. Appendix D of this book lists 274 languages. The revised figure of 312 was received in personal communication with Robert Laubach.

14. Quoted in *Elimination of Illiteracy in U.S.S.R.,* Moscow, n.d., p. 6. The campaign began in 1919 and continued through 1940. It is described in the above-cited booklet as well as in *The Abolition of Adult Illiteracy in the U.S.S.R. (1917–1940),* UNESCO Journal of Fundamental and Adult Education, XI, 3, 1959.

15. Brother Joseph F. Keimeg, *The Use of Adult Education in the Emergence of a New Order in Puerto Rico,* unpublished Ph.D. Dissertation, University of Chicago, March 1964, chapters 3, 4,

16. Anna Lorenzetto and Karel Neijs, "The Cuban Literacy Campaign," in *Convergence,* Vol. 1, No. 3, September 1968, p. 46.

17. Paulo Freire, *Pedagogy of the Oppressed,* New York, Herder and Herder, 1970, p. 19.

18. Ibid., pp. 70–71.

19. UNESCO, *World Campaign for Universal Literacy: Request Addressed to Unesco by the General Assembly of the United Nations at its 16th Session,* Paris, 10 October 1962, p. 36.

20. Seymour Martin Lipset, "Some Social Requisites of Democracy: Economic Development and Political Legitimacy," in *American Political Science Review,* Vol. 53, March 1959, pp. 69–105. Samuel P. Huntington, *Political Order in Changing Societies,* New Haven, Yale University Press, 1968.

21. Advisory Committee on Education in the Colonies, *Mass Education in African Society,* Colonial No. 186, HMSO, London, 1943, p. 11.

22. Mahatma Gandhi, quoted in *Literacy 1967–1969,* UNESCO, Paris, 1970, p. 25.

23. UNESCO, Resolutions of the 12th General Conference (Provisional), Paris, 12 January 1963 (mimeo), p. 26.

24. UN Economic and Social Council, *World Campaign for Universal Literacy,* New York, 15 May 1963 (E/3771), p. 39.

25. Ibid., p. 35.

26. UNESCO, 13th General Conference, *Addendum and Corrigendum to Proposed Program and Budget for 1965–1966* (13C/5), Paris, 4 September 1964, p. 5.

27. UNESCO, *Literacy as a Factor in Development,* Minedlit/3, Paris, 1965, pp. 7–8.

28. Ibid., p. 15.
29. Jeffries, op. cit., p. 63.
30. William S. Gray, *The Teaching of Reading and Writing*, UNESCO, Monographs on Fundamental Education No. X, Paris, 1956, p. 18.
31. UN, *The United Nations Development Decade: Proposals for Action*, UN, New York, 1962, p. 33.
32. UNESCO, *The Concept of Functional Literacy and its Application*, Round Table, 22–24 April, 1970 (mimeo), p. 5.
33. UNESCO, *Resolutions of the 12th General Conference*, p. 27.
34. Adam Curle, *World Campaign for Universal Literacy: Comment and Proposal*, Harvard University Graduate School of Education, Center for Studies in Education and Development, Occasional Papers in Education and Development No. 1, February 1964, p. 10.
35. UN Economic and Social Council, op. cit., p. 53.
36. Curle, op. cit., pp. 9–10
37. See Jeffries, op. cit., p. 37.
38. A.M. Ivanova, "Survey of the Literacy Campaign in the U.S.S.R.", in *Convergence*, Vol. 1, No. 3, September 1968, p. 21.
39. UNESCO, *World Illiteracy at Mid-Century:* A Statistical Study, Paris, 1957, p. 15.
40. Ivanova, op. cit., p. 22.
41. See *Elimination of Illiteracy in U.S.S.R.*, Moscow, n.d.
42. Arcadius Kahan, "Social Structure, Public Policy and the Development of Education and the Economy in Czarist Russia," in C. Arnold Anderson and Mary Jean Bowman (Eds.), *Education and Economic Development*, Chicago, Aldine, 1965, p. 367.
43. Arcadius Kahan, "Determinants of the Incidence of Literacy in Rural 19th Century Russia," in Anderson and Bowman, op. cit., p. 302.
44. *UNESCO Statistical Yearbook–1965*, Paris, p. 76.
45. UNESCO, *World Illiteracy at Mid-Century*, p. 187.
46. See Herbert Passin, "Portents of Modernity and the Meiji Emergence," in Anderson and Bowman, op. cit., pp. 394–421
47. Lorezetto and Neijs, op. cit., p. 49.
48. UNESCO, *World Campaign for Universal Literacy*, p. 20.
49. Lorenzetto and Neijs, op. cit., p. 46.
50. See, for example, D.R. Gadgil, "Report of Investigation into the Problem of Lapse into Illiteracy in the Satara District," in D.R. Gadgil and V.M. Dandekar, *Primary Education in Satara District*, Gokhale Institute of Politics and Economics, Publication No. 32, 1955, p. 67. Also, Ekavidya Nathalang and Kamol Sudaprasert, *The Effects of Primary Schooling in Rural Thailand* (in Thai), Department of Elementary and Adult Education, Ministry of Education, Bangkok, 1970. Also, G. Flores, "A Study of Functional Literacy for Citizenship in the Philippines," in *Quarterly Bulletin of Fundamental Education*, Vol. 2, No. 3, July 1950.
51. Lorenzetto and Neijs, op. cit., pp. 49–50.
52. Ramon Eduardo Ruiz, *Mexico; The Challenge of Poverty and Illiteracy*, The Huntington Library, San Marino, California, 1963, pp. 81–84.

53. Ibid., p. 84.
54. Descriptions of such campaigns can be found in *Literacy and Education for Adults* and *Supplement 1965.*
55. Curle, op. cit., p. 30.
56. UNESCO, *World Literacy Program* (13C/PRG/4), Paris, 4 September 1964, p. 4.
57. UNESCO, World Conference of Ministers of Education on the Eradication of Illiteracy, *Final Report,* Teheran, 1965, p. 13.
58. Ibid.
59. UNESCO, *World Literacy Program,* p. 8.
60. Ibid.
61. J.D.N. Versluys, "Functional Literacy in Rural Areas," in *Prospects in Education,* No. 2, 1969, p. 29.
62. UNESCO, *UNESCO and the Eradication of Illiteracy or the Metamorphosis of Fundamental Education,* Paris, 20 October 1967, p. 7.
63. UNESCO, *Addendum and Corrigendum . . .* p. 5. See also UNESCO, *Guide for the Preparation of Pilot Experimental Work-Oriented Literacy Projects,* Paris, April 1967.
64. The countries are Algeria, Ecuador, Ethiopia, Guinea, India, Iran, Madagascar, Mali, Sudan, Syria, Tanzania, Venezuela, Brazil, Chile, Jamaica, Nigeria, Tunisia, and Upper Volta. Only ten of the pilot projects actually became operational. See UNESCO, *Meeting on the Experimental Work Literacy Program, Working Paper, Experimental Functional Literacy Projects,* Paris, 13 November 1969, Annex I and II.
65. UNESCO, *Literacy: Three Pilot Projects,* Paris, 1966, pp. 8–9, 11–12.
66. UNESCO, *Working Paper, Experimental Functional Literacy Projects,* Annex I.
67. Ibid., p. 7.
68. UNESCO, Third Meeting of the Panel for the Evaluation of Experimental Literacy Projects, *Progress Made Since December 1969 and Present Situation,* Paris, 20 August 1970, p. 2.
69. Ibid., p. 7.
70. UNESCO, *Literacy: Three Pilot Projects,* pp. 15–16.
71. UNESCO, *Working Paper,* Annex I, and *Progress Made . . . ,* p. 2.
72. "Functional Literacy Materials for Cotton Growing," Supplement to *Literacy–A Newsletter,* UNESCO, 1970.
73. UNESCO, *Working Paper,* Annex I, and *Progress Made . . . ,* p. 2.
74. Dr. H.S. Bhola, *Literacy Teachers of Adults,* UNDP/Tanzania Work-Oriented Adult Literacy Pilot Projects, Lake Regions, Tanzania, 1970, pp. 11–12.
75. UNESCO, *Working Paper,* Annex I.
76. Merga Gobena and Kenneth Brooks, *The Ethiopian Work-Oriented Literacy Project,* Paper presented to UNESCO Workshop on Functional Literacy, Addis Ababa, May 4, 1970, pp. 1 and 6.
77. B.N. Singh, *Work-Oriented Adult Literacy Project–Ethiopia: Evaluation and Research Section: Problems and Difficulties Encountered in the Field,* Paper presented at UNESCO Workshop on Functional Literacy, Addis Ababa, April 13, 1970, p. 1.

78. UNESCO, *Progress Made* . . . , p. 2.

79. Gobena and Brooks, op. cit., p. 7.

80. Amir H. Nasution, *Work-Oriented Functional Literacy in Nigeria,* UNESCO Workshop on Functional Literacy, Addis Ababa, April 6, 1970, p. 3.

81. Ibid., pp. 5–7.

82. Ibid., p. 7. (Level of reading and writing attained are not specified.)

83. Ibid., p. 10.

84. *Literacy: Three Pilot Projects,* pp. 13–14. In the Isphahan area the program was aimed at both an industrially and agriculturally occupied population.

85. "Functional Literacy Experiments in Iran," Supplement to *Literacy—A Newsletter,* UNESCO, 1970, p. 2.

86. N. Soraya, *A Functional Literacy Approach in Iran,* Paper presented at the UNESCO Workshop on Functional Literacy, Addis Ababa, 4 May 1970.

87. *List of Functional Literacy Programmes—Iran,* Document 2-Misc. SN. 31, UNESCO Workshop on Functional Literacy, Addis Ababa, 7 May 1970.

88. M. Bazany, H.D. Kaufman, and A. Safavi, *Problems and Difficulties of the Work-Oriented Adult Literacy Pilot Project in Iran,* Paper presented at UNESCO Workshop on Functional Literacy, Addis Ababa, March 29, 1970, pp. 2–3.

89. UNESCO, *Working Paper,* Annex I, and *Progress Made* . . . , p. 2.

90. Bazany, Kaufman, and Safavi, op. cit., pp. 1–4.

91. S.N. Saraf, *Functional Literacy Component Under Farmers' Training and Functional Literacy Project,* UNESCO Workshop on Functional Literacy, Addis Ababa, May 4, 1970, pp. 9–11.

92. Ibid., pp. 12–15, and F.M. Ragheb, *Farmers' Training and Functional Literacy Project in India,* UNESCO Workshop on Functional Literacy, Addis Ababa, 30 April 1970.

93. UNESCO, *Progress Made* . . . , p. 2.

94. Saraf, op. cit., pp. 12–15.

95. See, for example, the following: "A Functional Literacy Experiment in an Industrial Environment; Brazil—Vale do Rio Doce," Supplement to *Literacy—A Newsletter,* UNESCO, 1970; A. Sammak, *Problems and Experience in Evaluation of Work-Oriented Adult Literacy Project: Sudan,* UNESCO Workshop on Functional Literacy, Addis Ababa, May 6, 1970; Maher F. Abdalla, *Integrated Ghab Development Project: Syrian Arab-Republic: Problems, Difficulties and Experience,* UNESCO Workshop on Functional Literacy, Addis Ababa, May 17, 1970.

96. Curle and UNESCO also broach the subject of costs of literacy programs. Despite the absence of cost-benefit analyses both agree that the tremendous costs envisioned by advocates of the world campaign approach create a situation whereby programs cannot be effectively instituted, whereas the reduced costs of a selective strategy permit the conduct of smaller but sounder efforts.

97. *Report on Gram Shikshan Mohim of Maharashtra,* Government of India Planning Commission, 1964, pp. 2, 11, 19–20, 30.

98. John L. Simmons, *Towards an Evaluation of Literacy and Adult Education in a Developing Country: A Pilot Study,* September 1970 (mimeo), Harvard University UNESCO Contract ED 6284.

99. Ibid., p. 10.

100. Ibid., Part II, pp. 70–110; and John Simmons and James Allman, *Literacy Retention and Adult Education in a Tunisian Village* (mimeo), 1969; and James Allman, *Preliminary Results of a Follow-up Study of an Adult Education Program in Tazerka, A Tunisian Village,* Term Paper submitted at Harvard University, January 1970.

101. Prodipto Roy and J.M. Kapoor, *Retention of Literacy,* Council for Social Development, New Delhi, 1970 (mimeo).

102. Ibid., p. 84.

103. T.R. Singh, *Functional Literates: Six Case Studies,* Literacy House, Lucknow, India, n.d. (mimeo), pp. 10–11; and T.R. Singh, "Literacy in Two Indian Villages," in *Literacy Discussion,* Vol. I, No. 3., September 1970, pp. 111–21.

104. David Harman, *Mimtsaim Al Matsav Haskalat Hamevugarim Bamoshavim* (Findings Pertaining to Adult Education in the Moshavim), Ministry of Education and Culture, Department of Adult Hebrew and Elementary Education, Israel, 1968.

105. Joanna Landy–Tolwinska, "Former Participants in Literacy Courses– Poland" in *Literacy Discussion,* Vol. I, No. 3, September 1970, pp. 107– 10.

106. Peter du Sautoy, *The Planning and Organization of Adult Literacy Programmes in Africa,* UNESCO, Manuals on Adult and Youth Education No. 4, Paris, 1966, p. 21.

107. Cyril O. Houle, *The Inquiring Mind,* Madison, University of Wisconsin, 1961.

108. David C. McClelland, *The Achieving Society,* New York, Free Press, 1961, p. 104.

109. M. Bazany and H.D. Kaufman, *Motives of Participation in Functional Literacy Courses,* Evaluation Studies No. 5, Work-Oriented Adult Literacy Pilot Project in Iran, Esphahan, July 1970, pp. 9–20.

110. Ora Grabelsky, *From Illiteracy to Literacy,* Adult Education Center, Hebrew University of Jerusalem, 1970, pp. 60–61.

111. See, for example, Bazany and Kaufman, op. cit., pp. 21–22.

112. Karel Neijs, *Literacy Primers, Construction, Evaluation and Use,* UNESCO, Manuals on Adult and Youth Education No. 2, Paris, 1961, pp. 19–22.

113. Frank C. Laubach, *Teaching the World to Read,* London, 1947; and Laubach and Laubach, *Toward World Literacy,* Chapter 2.

114. Gray, op. cit., pp. 163–64.

115. Jeffries, op. cit., p. 112.

116. Gray, op. cit., pp. 87–88.

117. Neijs, op. cit., pp. 23–24.

118. Gray, op. cit., p. 259.

119. During 1967 supervisors in the Israel literacy program were asked to collect data on the drop-out phenomenon. These data are derived from a number of internal reports and memoranda in which seven supervisors reported early attrition in programs.

120. Robert F. Barnes and Andrew Hendrickson, *A Review and Appraisal of*

Adult Literacy Materials and Programs, Columbus, Ohio State University Research Foundation, 1965.

121. A.J. Carpenter, "Adult Literacy—A Survey," in *Community Development Bulletin,* Vol. II, No. 4, September 1951, London, University of London Institute of Education.

122. UNESCO Conference of African States on the Development of Education in Africa, Addis Ababa, 15–25 May 1964, *Final Report,* Paris, 1961, Chapter VII, para. 23.

123. Samples of materials can be seen in Charles Richards (Ed.), *Simple Reading Materials for Adults: Its Preparation and Use,* UNESCO Manuals on Adult and Youth Education No. 3, Paris, 1963.

124. UNESCO, *Literacy as a Factor in Development,* p. 13.

125. Iran, for example, imposes stiff fines on literate adults refusing "literacy duty." See "Iran Proposes Fines to Fight Illiteracy," in *New York Times,* September 4, 1969.

126. See UNESCO, *Literacy and Education for Adults,* pp. xxvii–xxxii. In 51 countries primary-school teachers are reported to be employed in literacy programs, making up from 6 to 70 percent of the entire teaching force.

127. A.S.M. Hely, *School Teachers and the Education of Adults,* UNESCO Manuals on Adult and Youth Education No. 5, Paris, 1966, pp. 12–13.

128. See, for example, Bazany and Kaufman, op. cit., pp. 15–17.

129. See UNESCO, *Literacy and Education for Adults,* pp. xlii–xliii.

130. *The Use of Vernacular Languages in Education,* UNESCO, Monographs on Fundamental Education No. 8, Paris, 1953, Chapter I.

131. Ibid., pp. 17–18.

132. UNESCO, Meeting of Experts on the Use of Vernacular Languages, *Regional Paper on Vernacular Languages No. 4,* Paris, 1951.

133. Ralph C. Staiger, "Developments in Reading and Literacy Education 1956–1967," Chapter XIII in Gray, op. cit. (second ed. 1969), p. 290, and John Bowers, "Language Problems in Literacy," in Joshua A. Fishman, Charles A. Ferguson, and Jyotirindra Das Gupta (Eds.), *Language Problems of Developing Nations,* New York, Wiley, 1968, p. 385.

134. Jyotirindra Das Gupta, "Language Diversity and National Development," in Fishman, Ferguson, and Das Gupta, op. cit., p. 19.

135. See, for example, Bazany and Kaufman, op. cit., pp. 15–17.

136. Richards, op. cit., pp. 71–72, and Gray, op. cit., pp. 260–61.

137. UNESCO, *Equality of Access of Women to Literacy,* Paris, August 31, 1970, p. 14.

138. World Conference of Ministers of Education, op. cit., p. 12.

139. UNESCO, *Literacy as a Factor in Development,* p. 11.

140. UNESCO, *Literacy—A Social Experience,* op. cit., p. 4.

141. UNESCO, *Equality of Access of Women to Literacy,* op. cit., summarizes replies received to a questionnaire from 99 Member States, 2 Associate Members, 19 Self-Governing Territories and one Member State of the World Health Organization.

142. UNESCO, Meeting of Experts on the Access of Girls and Women to Education in *Rural Areas in Asia,* Final Report, Paris, 8 July, 1962, p. 6.

143. M. Bazany, H.D. Kaufman, and A. Safavi, *Demographic Characteristics and Interest in Participation in Functional Literacy Courses,* Evaluation Studies No. 4, Work-Oriented Adult Literacy Pilot Project in Iran, Esphahan, April 1970.

Part III: A System of Community-Based Fundamental Education—A Model

Chapter 8: An Alternative Approach to Fundamental Education: Precepts of a Model

1. Jerome S. Bruner, *Toward a Theory of Instruction,* Cambridge, Harvard University Press, 1967, p. 1.
2. Jerome S. Bruner, *The Process of Education,* New York, Vintage Books, 1960, pp. 17–18.
3. Orville G. Brim, Jr., "Socialization Through the Life Cycle," in Orville G. Brim and Stanton Wheeler, *Socialization After Childhood: Two Essays,* New York, Wiley, 1966, p. 9.
4. Ibid., p. 8.
5. Raymond G. Hunt, "Role and Role Conflict," in Edwin P. Hollander and Raymond G. Hunt (Eds.), *Current Perspectives in Social Psychology,* (second ed.), New York, Oxford University Press, 1967, p. 259.
6. Robert J. Havinghurst and Bernice L. Neugarten, *Society and Education,* Boston, Allyn and Bacon, 1957, p. 83.
7. Norman W. Bell and Ezra F. Vogel, "Toward a Framework for Functional Analysis of Family Behavior," in Norman W. Bell and Exra F. Vogel (Eds.), *A Modern Introduction to the Family* (revised ed.), New York, Free Press, 1968, pp. 7–8.
8. George Peter Murdock, *Social Structure,* New York, Macmillan, 1949, Chapter 1.
9. Robert H. Lowie, *Primitive Society,* New York, Boni and Liveright, 1920, pp. 66–67.
10. Morris Zelditch, Jr., "Role Differentiation in the Nuclear Family: A Comparative Study," in Talcott Parsons and Robert F. Bales, *Family, Socialization and Interaction Process,* New York, Free Press, 1955, pp. 307–42.
11. Ibid., p. 309.
12. Murdock, op. cit., p. 4.
13. Talcott Parsons, "Family Structure and the Socialization of the Child," in Parsons and Bales, op. cit., p. 37.
14. Ibid., p. 49.
15. Jerome Kagan, "The Concept of Identification," in *Psychological Review,* Vol. 65, No. 5, September 1958, p. 299.
16. Roger Brown, "Language: The System and its Acquisition." Part I: Phonology and Grammar. Part II: The Semantic System: Language, Thought and Society" in *Social Psychology,* New York, Free Press, 1965,

pp. 246–349; Courtney B. Cazden, *Environmental Assistance in the Child's Acquisition of Grammar,* unpublished Ph.D. Thesis, Harvard University, 1965.

17. See Mary B. Meader, *Position Paper: Language Development,* Pre-School Project, Harvard University, December 1967 (mimeo), pp. 2–9.

18. See, for example, Howard A. Moss and Jerome Kagan, "Maternal Influences on Early I.Q. Scores," in *Psychological Reports,* Vol. 14, 1959, pp. 655–61.

19. See, for example: Paul Mussen and Eldred Rutherford, "Parent–Child Relations and Parental Personality in Relation to Young Children's Sex-Role Preferences," in *Child Development,* Vol. 34, 1963, pp. 589–607; J. McV. Hunt, "Experience and the Development of Motivation: Some Reinterpretations," in *Child Development,* Vol. 31, 1960, pp. 489–504; Jerome S. Bruner, "On Cognitive Growth, I," in Jerome S. Bruner, Rose R. Oliver, and Patricia M. Greenfield (Eds.), *Studies in Cognitive Growth,* New York, Wiley, 1966, pp. 1–29.

20. See, for example, Jerome Kagan and Howard A. Moss, "The Stability of Passive and Dependent Behavior From Childhood Through Adulthood," in *Child Development,* Vol. 31, 1960, pp. 577–91.

21. Brim, op. cit., p. 18.

22. Orville G. Brim, Jr., *Education For Child Rearing,* New York, Russell Sage Foundation, 1959, p. 61.

23. Yonina Talmon, "Comparative Analysis of Adult Socialization," Paper prepared for the Social Science Research Council Conference, 1964.

24. Brim, "Socialization . . . ," p. 35.

25. See Lois Meek Stolz, *Influences on Parent Behavior,* London, Tavistock Publications, 1967, pp. 164–65, 289.

26. Ibid., pp. 290–91.

27. See J. Nash, "The Father in Contemporary Culture and Current Psychological Literature," in *Child Development,* Vol. 36, No. 1, 1965, pp. 261–97.

28. Zelditch, op. cit., pp. 329–33.

29. Parsons, op. cit., p. 35.

30. Tamotsu Shibutani, "Reference Groups as Perspectives," in *American Journal of Sociology,* Vol. 60, 1955, pp. 565–66.

31. N.W. Ackerman, *The Psychodynamics of Family Life: Diagnosis and Treatment of Family Relationships,* New York, Basic Books, 1958, Chapter 21.

32. Stolz, op. cit., p. 29.

33. Bernard Barber, *Social Stratification,* New York, Harcourt, 1957, p. 280.

34. Jesse Pitts, "The Family and Peer Groups," in Bell and Vogel, op. cit., p. 292.

35. Herbert Kelman, "Three Processes of Social Influence," in Hollander and Hunt, op. cit., pp. 439–42.

36. Pitts, op. cit., p. 294.

37. See, for example: Howard S. Becker, "Schools and Systems of Stratification," in A.H. Halsey, Jean Floud, and C. Arnold Anderson, *Education, Economy and Society,* New York, Free Press, 1961, pp. 93–104; Talcott

Parsons, "The School Class as a Social System: Some of its Functions in American Society," in *Harvard Educational Review,* Vol. 29, Fall 1959, pp. 297–318.

38. Talcott Parsons and Neil J. Smelser, *Economy and Society,* Glencoe, Illinois, Free Press, 1956, p. 16.

39. See Zelditch, op. cit., p. 320.

40. Many anthropological descriptions of nonliterate cultures and societies point out this rigidity in role differentiation as a fundamental societal precept. See, for example, James L. Gibbs, Jr. (Ed.), *Peoples of Africa,* New York, Holt, 1965. Fifteen such cultures are described in different papers, and in each roles are clearly differentiated according to the pattern described.

41. See UNESCO: International Bureau of Education, *Facilities for Education in Rural Areas,* Geneva, Publication No. 192, 1958, pp. 14–18.

42. Andreas Fuglesang, *Communication With Illiterates: A Pilot Study of the Problem of Social Communication in Developing Countries,* The National Food and Nutrition Commission, Lusaka, Zambia, 1969, p. 9.

43. S.C. Dube, *India's Changing Villages: Human Factors in Community Development,* London, Routledge and Kegan Paul, 1958, p. 128.

44. See Wilbur Schramm, "Communication and Change." in Daniel Lerner and Wilbur Schramm, *Communication and Change in the Developing Countries,* Honolulu, East–West Center Press, 1967, pp. 11–16.

45. Jerome S. Bruner, J.J. Goodnow and G.A. Austin, *A Study of Thinking,* New York, Wiley, 1956, p. vii.

46. Patricia M. Greenfield, "Oral or Written Language: The Consequences for Cognitive Development in Africa and the United States," Paper presented at Symposium on Cross-Cultural Cognitive Studies, American Educational Research Association, Chicago, February 9, 1968 (mimeo), pp. 3–4.

47. Jack Goody and Ian Watt, "The Consequences of Literacy," in Jack Goody (Ed.), *Literacy in Traditional Societies,* Cambridge, Cambridge University Press, 1968, p. 29.

48. William S. Gray, *The Teaching of Reading and Writing,* UNESCO Monographs on Fundamental Education, No. 10, Paris, 1956, p. 73.

49. Goody and Watt, op. cit.

50. Bronislaw Malinowski, "The Problem of Meaning in Primitive Languages," in C.K. Ogden and I.A. Richards (Eds.), *The Meaning of Meaning,* New York, 1930, passim.

51. Julian Hochberg, "The Psychophysics of Pictorial Perception," in *Audio-Visual Communication Review,* Supplement, September–October 1962, p. 32.

52. Luiz Fonseca and Bryant Kearl, *Comprehension of Pictorial Symbols: An Experiment in Rural Brazil,* Bulletin 30, Department of Agricultural Journalism, University of Wisconsin, 1960, p. 17.

53. W. Hudson, "Cultural Problems in Pictorial Perception," in *South African Journal of Science,* Vol. 58, No. 7, July 1962, pp. 189–95.

54. Luiz Fonseca and William R. Lassey, *Comprehension and Meaning in Visual Communication Among Illiterate, Low-Literate and Higher Literate*

Individuals, Programa Interamericano de Informacion Popolár, Costa Rica, February 10, 1964 (Preliminary Report), p. 74.

55. Fuglesang, op. cit., pp. 48–53.
56. Goody and Watt, op. cit., p. 30.
57. A.B. Lord, *The Singer of Tales,* Cambridge, Harvard University Press, 1960, p. 20.
58. Based on the author's observations in literacy programs in Israel and Thailand.
59. Gray, op. cit., p. 112.
60. See Jeanne Chall, *Learning to Read: The Great Debate,* New York, Mc-Graw-Hill, 1967, passim, particularly pp. 57–60 and 90–92.
61. Ibid., p. 59.
62. Gertrude Hildreth, "Interrelationships Among the Language Arts," in *Elementary School Journal,* Vol. 48, No. 10, June 1948, pp. 538–49.
63. Walter D. Loban, *The Language of Elementary School Children,* Illinois, National Council of Teachers of English, 1963, p. 93.
64. See Ralph Staiger, "Developments in Reading and Literacy Education; 1956–1967," in Gray, op. cit. (second ed.), Paris, 1969, pp. 290–92.
65. L.S. Vygotsky, *Thought and Language,* edited and translated by E. Hanfmann and C. Vakov, Cambridge, M.I.T. Press, 1962, p. 51.
66. See Eleanor and George Kaplan, "The Prelinguistic Child," in John Eliot (Ed.), *Human Development and Cognitive Processes,* New York, Holt, 1971, p. 377.
67. See N.H. Mackworth and J.S. Bruner, "How Adults and Children Search and Recognize Pictures," in *Human Development,* Vol. 13, 1970, pp. 149–77.
68. See P. Lieberman, *Intonation, Perception and Language,* Cambridge, M.I.T. Press, 1971.
69. Samuel Y. Gibbon, Jr., and Edward L. Palmer, *Pre-Reading on Sesame Street,* Paper submitted to the Committee on Reading of the National Academy of Education, June 1, 1970, particularly pp. 13–21.

Chapter 9: The Model: A Blueprint

1. See Margaret Mead, *Growing Up in New Guinea,* New York, Morrow, 1930.
2. For an example of rejection of an innovation due to its effect on taste of food, see Anacleto Apodaca, "Corn and Custom: The Introduction of Hybrid Corn to Spanish American Farmers in New Mexico," in Edward H. Spicer (Ed.), *Human Problems in Technological Change,* New York, Russell Sage Foundation, 1952, pp. 35–40.
3. See Jack D. Mezirow, *Dynamics of Community Development,* New York, Scarecrow Press, 1963, pp. 203–5.
4. Jerome S. Bruner, "Competence in Infants," Paper presented at the meeting of the Society for Research in Child Development, Minnesota, March 30, 1971.

5. See Urie Bronfenbrenner, *Two Worlds of Childhood,* New York, Russell Sage Foundation, 1970, pp. 16–17 on use of large cribs.

6. While I have been unable to locate empirical evidence relative to this point in the available literature, my own observations of literacy programs in Israel, India, and Thailand have led to this conclusion. Attempts to introduce a binder-card approach into a pilot literacy program in Thailand have thus far proven successful.

Bibliography

Abdalla, Maher F.: *Integrated Ghab Development Project: Syrian Arab Republic: Problems, Difficulties and Experience.* Paper presented at UNESCO Workshop on Functional Literacy, Addis Ababa, May 17, 1970.

Abel, James Frederick, and Norman J. Bond.: *Illiteracy in the Several Countries of the World,* Washington, U.S. Govt. Print. (offset), 1929.

Abercrombie, K.C.: "Food and Agriculture," in Richard Symonds (Ed.), *International Targets for Development,* New York, Harper & Row, 1970.

Ackerman, N.W.: *The Psychodynamics of Family Life: Diagnosis and Treatment of Family Relationships,* New York, Basic Books, 1958.

Adiseshiah, Malcolm S.: *Let My Country Awake,* UNESCO, Paris, 1970.

Adult Schools: A Letter from a Priest on Adult Schools in Agricultural Areas, London, Longman, Brown, Longman & Green, 1850.

Advisory Committee on Education in the Colonies: *Mass Education in African Society,* Colonial No. 186, HMSO, 1943.

Aguilar, J.V.: *This is Our Community School,* Manila, Bookman, Inc., 1951.

Al-Bassam, Hassan Kadhum: *An Evaluation of the Rural Development Program of Iraq,* unpublished Ph.D. Thesis, Ithaca, Cornell University, September 1959.

Allen, James E., Jr.: "Liberal Education for Adults in a Changing Society," in *School and Society,* Vol. 94, 1966, pp. 454–58.

——: "The Educational Third Dimension," Address Before the Galaxy Conference on Adult and Continuing Education, Washington, D.C., December 9, 1969.

——: "The Right-to-Read-Target for the 70's," Address Before the 1969 Annual Convention of the National Association of State Boards of Education, Los Angeles, California, September 23, 1969.

Allman, James: "Preliminary Results of a Follow-Up Study of an Adult Education Program in Tazerka—A Tunisian Village," Harvard University (typewritten), January 1970.

Almond, Gabriel A., and James S. Coleman (Eds.): *The Politics of the Developing Areas,* Princeton, Princeton University Press, 1960.

Anderson, C. Arnold: "Literacy and Schooling on the Development Threshold: Some Historical Cases" in C. Arnold Anderson and Mary Jean Bowman (Eds.): *Education and Economic Development,* Chicago, Aldine Publishing Co., 1965, pp. 347–62.

Arensberg, Conrad M., and Solon T. Kimball, *Culture and Community,* New York, Harcourt, Brace, and World, 1965.

Axford, Roger W.: *Adult Education: The Open Door,* Scranton, Pennsylvania, International Textbook Co., 1969.

Baker, W.P.: *Parish Registers and Illiteracy in East Yorkshire,* New York, Oxford University Press, 1961.

Barber, Bernard: *Social Stratification,* New York, Harcourt, Brace and World, 1957.

Barnes, Robert F., and Andrew Hendrickson: *A Review and Appraisal of Adult*

Literacy Materials and Programs, Columbus, Ohio State University Research Foundation, 1965.

Barnett, Homer G.: *Innovation*, New York, McGraw-Hill, 1953.

Bartlett, Frederick: *Remembering*, Cambridge, Cambridge University Press, 1954.

Batten, T.R.: *The Human Factor in Community Work*, London, Oxford University Press, 1965.

——: *Communities and Their Development*, London, Oxford University Press, 1957.

Bazany, M., and H.D. Kaufman: *Motives of Participation in Functional Literacy Courses*, Evaluation Studies No. 5, Work-Oriented Adult Literacy Pilot Project, Iran, Isphahan, July 1970.

—— and A. Safavi: *Demographic Characteristics and Interest in Participation in Functional Literacy Courses*, Evaluation Studies, No. 4, Work-Oriented Adult Literacy Pilot Project in Iran, Isphahan, April 1970.

——: *Problems and Difficulties of the Work-Oriented Adult Literacy Pilot Project in Iran*, Paper presented at UNESCO Workshop on Functional Literacy, Addis Ababa, March 29, 1970.

Becker, Howard S.: "Schools and Systems of Stratification," in A.H. Halsey, Jean Floud, and C. Arnold Anderson, *Education, Economy and Society*, New York, The Free Press, 1961.

Beeby, C.E.: "Educational Quality in Practice," in *Qualitative Aspects of Educational Planning*, UNESCO, IIEP, 1969.

——: *The Quality of Education in Developing Countries*, Cambridge, Harvard University Press, 1966.

——: "Stages in the Growth of a Primary Education System," in *Comparative Education Review*, Vol. 6, No. 1, 1962, pp. 2–11.

Behar, Moises, M.D.: "Prevalence of Malnutrition Among Pre-School Children of Developing Countries," in Nevin S. Scrimshaw (Ed.), *Malnutrition, Learning and Behavior*, Cambridge, M.I.T. Press, 1968.

Beirn, Russell: "A Review of Quantitative Research on Literacy and Development," Harvard University Internal Report 34: Research Project—North Africa, March 1969 (mimeo).

Bell, Norman W., and Ezra F. Vogel: "Toward a Framework for Functional Analysis of Family Behavior," in Norman W. Bell and Ezra F. Vogel (Eds.), *A Modern Introduction to the Family* (revised ed.), New York, The Free Press, 1968.

Bennett, Nicholas: "Primary Education in Rural Communities—Investment in Ignorance?" in *The Journal of Development Studies*, Vol. 6, No. 4, July 1970, pp. 92–103.

Berredday, George Z.F., and Joseph A. Lanwerys (Eds.): *Educational Planning: The World Year Book of Education*, New York, Harcourt, Brace and World, and London, Evans Bros., 1967.

Bergevin, Paul Emile: *Adult Education in Sweden: an Introduction*, Bloomington, Bureau of Studies in Adult Education, Indiana University, 1961.

Bertelson, P.: "Problems of Priorities in Adult Education," in C.G. Widstrand (Ed.), *Development and Adult Education in Africa*, Upsala, Sweden: Scandinavian Institute of African Studies, 1965, pp. 22–39.

Bhola, H.S.: *Literacy Teachers for Adults,* UNESCO/UNDP/Tanzania Work-Oriented Adult Literacy Pilot Project, Lake Regions, Tanzania, 1970.

——: "The Methods and the Materials of Functional Literacy," UNESCO, Workshop on Functional Literacy, Addis Ababa (29 April–12 May 1970), F/W Addis/ 2–3, 4/ SN. 2 26:3:70.

Biddle, William W., and Loureide J. Biddle: *The Community Development Process,* The Rediscovery of Local Initiative, New York, Holt, Rinehart and Winston, Inc., 1965.

Bindra, Dalbir, and Jane Steward (Eds.): *Motivation: Selected Readings,* London, Penguin Books, 1966.

Black, C.E.: *The Dynamics of Modernization,* A Study in Comparative History, New York, Harper & Row (Harper Torchbooks), 1967.

Blakely, R.J.: *Notes and Essays on Education for Adults,* "Toward a Homeo-dynamic Society," Boston University, Center for the Study of Liberal Education for Adults.

Blaug, Mark: "Approaches to Educational Planning," in *Economic Journal,* Vol. 77, June 1967, pp. 262–87.

——: *The Role of Education in Enlarging the Exchange Economy in Middle Africa: The English-Speaking Countries,* Paris, UNESCO Document SSAD/ 103, 18 September 1964, pp. 75–81.

——: "Literacy and Economic Development," in *The School Review,* Vol. 74, No. 4, Winter 1966, pp. 393–415.

——: "The Evaluation of Functional Literacy: An Economist's View," in Freddie Wood: *The Evaluation of Functional Literacy Projects: UNESCO Workshop,* London, 3–22 August 1969, London, University of London Institute of Education, 1969.

Bose, Santi Priya: "Characteristics of Farmers Who Adopt Agricultural Practices in Indian Villages," in *Rural Sociology,* Vol. 26, No. 1, June 1961, pp. 138–45.

Bostian, Lloyd R., and Fernando C. Oliveira: *Relationships of Literacy and Education to Communication and to Social and Economic Conditions on Small Farms in Two Municipios in Southern Brazil,* Paper read at the annual meetings of the Rural Sociological Society, Chicago, Illinois, August 1965.

Bowers, John: "Language Problems and Literacy," in Joshua A. Fishman, Charles A. Ferguson, and Jyotirindra Das Gupta (Eds.), *Language Problems of Developing Nations,* New York, John Wiley and Sons, 1968.

Bowers, John: "Functional Literacy: Definition and Evaluation," working paper in Freddie Wood (Ed.): *The Evaluation of Functional Literacy Projects: UNESCO Workshop,* London, August 1969, pp. 15–24.

Bowman, Mary Jean: "The Human Investment Revolution in Economic Thought," in Mark Blaug (Ed.), *Economics of Education, I,* London, Penguin Books, 1968.

Bowman, Mary Jean, and C. Arnold Anderson: "Concerning the Role of Education in Development," in C. Geertz (Ed.), *Old Societies and New States: The Quest for Modernity,* Glencoe, Illinois, Free Press, 1963, pp. 247–79.

Brim, Orville G., Jr.: *Education for Child Rearing,* New York, Russell Sage Foundation, 1959.

——: "Socialization Through the Life Cycle," in Orville G. Brim, Jr., and

Stanton Wheeler: *Socialization After Childhood: Two Essays,* New York, John Wiley and Sons, 1966.

Bronfenbrenner, Urie: *Two Worlds of Childhood,* New York, Russell Sage Foundation, 1970.

Brown, J.S.: *The Motivation of Behavior,* New York, McGraw-Hill, 1961.

Brown, Lester R.: "New Directions in World Agriculture," Studies in Family Planning, No. 32, The Population Council, June 1968.

Brown, Thomas Kite: *Adult Education for Social Change,* Philadelphia, Little, Brown and Company, 1936.

Bruner, Jerome S.: *The Process of Education,* New York, Vintage Books, 1960.

——: *Toward a Theory of Instruction,* Cambridge, Harvard University Press, 1967.

——: "On Cognitive Growth: I," in Jerome S. Bruner, Rose R. Oliver, and Patricia M. Greenfield (Eds.), *Studies in Cognitive Growth,* New York, John Wiley and Sons, 1966.

——, J.J. Goodnow, and G.A. Austin: *A Study of Thinking,* New York, John Wiley and Sons, 1956.

Brunner, Edmund deS., David S. Wilder, Corinne Kirchner, and John S. Newberry, Jr.: *An Overview of Adult Education Research,* Chicago, Adult Education Association of the U.S.A., 1959.

Buasri, Saroj: *A Study of Methods of Teaching Adults to Read as Developed for Literacy Campaigns by Some Member States of UNESCO,* unpublished Ph.D. Thesis, Ohio State University, 1951.

Butt, Helen: *Integrated Literacy Method,* Manual for Teachers, Kurukshetra (Haryana), Kurukshetra University Press, 1967.

Calvin, Allen D.: "Teaching Adults to Read," in *Adult Learning:* Adult Basic Education Pre-Institute Seminar, Detroit, Wayne State University, May 1967.

——, Edgar L. Harden, Thomas L. Clifford, Betsy Clifford, and Russell Schulz: "Studies in Adult Learning Since 1930," *Journal of Educational Research,* Vol. 50, December 1956.

Campagnac, E.T.: *Converging Paths,* Cambridge, Cambridge University Press, 1916.

Cantril, Hadley: *The Pattern of Human Concerns,* New Brunswick, Rutgers University Press, 1965.

Carothers, J.C.: "Culture, Society and the Written Word," in *Psychiatry,* Vol. 22, No. 4, November 1959, pp. 307–20.

Carpenter, A.J.: "Adult Literacy—A Survey" in *Community Development Bulletin,* Vol. 2, No. 4, September 1951.

Cartwright, Morse Adams: *Adult Adjustment,* New York, Teachers College Press, Columbia University, 1945.

Chall, Jeanne: *Learning to Read: The Great Debate,* New York, McGraw-Hill, 1967.

Chen, Sih Kong: *A Plan for Adult Education in China Based on the Experiences of Major Experiments of Adult Education, the Resources of the Social Conditions in China, and the History of Chinese Education in the Last Fifty Years,* unpublished Ph.D. Thesis, Columbia University, 1942.

Cipolla, Carlo M.: *Literacy and Development in the West,* London, Penguin Books, 1969.

Clark, J.W.: "The Aging Dimension: A Factorial Analysis of Individual Differences With Age on Psychological and Physiological Measurements," in *Journal of Gerontology, XV,* 1960, pp. 183–87.

Clausen, John A.: "Family Structure, Socialization and Personality," in Martin L. Hoffman and Lois Wladis Hoffman (Eds.), *Review of Child Development Research,* Vol. I, New York, Russell Sage Foundation, 1964, pp. 1–53.

Clay, Horace F.: *Some Effects of Cultural Factors on Adult Educational Processes: A Comparison of Cooperative Extension Techniques as They Apply to Small Farm Operators in Costa-Rica, Guatemala and Hawaii,* unpublished Ph.D. Thesis, University of Chicago, 1950.

Clower, Robert W., George Dalton, Mitchell Harwitz, and A.A. Walters: *Growth Without Development, An Economic Survey of Liberia,* Evanston, Northwestern University Press, 1966.

Cofer, C.N., and M.H. Appley: *Motivation: Theory and Research,* New York, John Wiley and Sons, 1964.

Cognitive Development in Children, with a foreword by Roger Brown, Chicago, University of Chicago Press, 1962 (last printing–1970).

Cohen, Arthur Robert: *Attitude Change and Social Influence,* New York, Basic Books, 1964.

Collomb, H., and S. Valantin: "Patterns of Mothering, Organization of the Personality and Rapid Social Changes," in *International Social Science Journal,* Vol. XX, No. 3, 1968.

Colombain, Maurice: *Co-operatives and Fundamental Education,* UNESCO Monographs on Fundamental Education, No. 2, Paris, 1950.

Cook, Huldah Florence, and Edith May Walker: *Adult Elementary Education,* New York, Charles Scribner's Sons, 1927.

Coombs, Philip H.: *The World Educational Crisis,* New York, Oxford University Press, 1968.

Cotton, Webster: *On Behalf of Adult Education: A Historical Examination of the Supporting Literature,* Notes and Essays on Education for Adults #56; Boston, Center for Study of Liberal Education for Adults, Boston University, 1968.

Cox, Christopher: "Presidential Address to the Education Section of the British Association for the Advancement of Science," 1956.

Cratty, Bryant J.: *Perceptual and Motor Developments in Infants and Children,* New York, Macmillan Company, 1970.

Cravioto, Joaquin, and Elsa R. De Licardie: "Intersensory Development of School Age Children," in N.S. Scrimshaw, *Malnutrition, Learning and Behavior,* Cambridge, M.I.T. Press, 1968.

—— and B. Robles: "Evolution of Adaptive and Motor Behavior During Rehabilitation from Kwashiorkor," in *American Journal of Orthopsychiatry,* Vol. 35, 1965.

Cripwell, Kenneth K.: "Teaching Adults by Television, A Report on an Experiment in the Teaching of Elementary English and Arithmetic to Adult Africans," Zambia, Salisbury University College of Rhodesia, 1966.

Curle, Adam: *Educational Strategy for Developing Countries,* London, Tavistock Publications, 1963.

———: *World Campaign for Universal Literacy: Comment and Proposal,* Cambridge, Harvard University Graduate School of Education, Center for Studies in Education and Development, Occasional Papers in Education and Development, No. 1, February 1964.

———: *Educational Problems of Developing Societies,* New York, Praeger Publishers, 1969.

Dabasi–Schweng, Lorand: "The Problem of Transforming Traditional Agriculture," in *World Politics,* Vol. XVII, No. 3, April 1965.

Dart, Francis E.: "The Rub of Cultures," in John W. Hanson and Cole S. Brembeck, *Education and the Development of Nations,* New York, Holt, Rinehart and Winston, 1966.

Das Gupta, Jyotirindra: "Language Diversity and National Development, in Joshua A. Fishman, Charles A. Ferguson and Jyotirindra Das Gupta (Eds.), *Language Problems of Developing Nations,* New York, John Wiley and Sons, 1968.

David, Marcel: *Adult Education in Yugoslavia,* Paris, 1962.

De Beauvais, Michel: "Education in Former French Africa," in J.S. Coleman (Ed.): *Education and Political Development,* Princeton, Princeton University Press, 1965.

———, Le Thanh Choi, et al.: *Les rélations de l'alphabetization et du développement économique, Etudes Tiers Monde,* Paris, Presses Universitaires de France, 1964.

De Clerck, M.: "Education for Community Development," in Quoc Thuc Vu (Ed.), *Social Research and Problems of Rural Development in South-East Asia,* Brussels, UNESCO, 1963.

de Sola Pool, Ithiel: "The Mass Media and Politics in the Modernization Process," in Lucien Pye (Ed.): *Communications and Political Development,* Princeton, Princeton University Press, 1963.

Dees, Norman: *Approaches to Adult Teaching,* Oxford, Pergamon Press, 1965.

Deutschmann, Paul J., Alfredo Mendez, and W. Herzog: *Adoption of Drugs and Foods in Five Guatemalan Villages,* San José, Costa Rica: Program Interamericano de Information Popular, 1967.

Deutschmann, Paul J.: "The Mass Media in an Underdeveloped Village," *Journalism Quarterly XL:* 1, Winter 1963, pp. 27–35.

Dewey, John: *Lectures in the Philosophy of Education,* Lecture XII, "A Formal Definition of Education. Discussion of its Formal Elements," January 26, 1899, New York, Random House, 1966.

De Young, John E., and Chester L. Hunt: "Communication Channels and Functional Literacy in the Philippine Barrio," in *Journal of Asian Studies,* Vol. 22, no. 1, November 1962, pp. 67–77.

Doob, Leonard W.: *Communication in Africa,* New Haven, Yale University Press, 1961.

———: "The Use of Different Test Items in Non-literate Societies," in *Public Opinion Quarterly,* Vol. 30, Winter 1966–67, pp. 551–68.

——: *Communication in Africa: A Search for Boundaries,* New Haven, Yale University Press, 1961.

——: *Becoming More Civilized: A Psychological Exploration,* New Haven, Yale University Press, 1960.

Dore, Ronald: "Social Planning for the Family," in *The Journal of Development Studies,* Vol. 6, No. 4, July 1970, pp. 57–66.

Dube, S.C.: *India's Changing Villages: Human Factors in Community Development,* London, Routledge and Kegan Paul, 1958.

Duker, Peter F.: "The Education Revolution," in A.H. Halsey, Jean Floud, and C. Arnold Anderson (Eds.), *Education, Economy and Society,* New York, The Free Press, 1961.

du Sautoy, Peter: *The Organization of a Community Development Program,* London, Oxford University Press, 1962.

——: *The Planning and Organization of Adult Literacy Programs in Africa,* UNESCO Manuals on Adult and Youth Education, No. 4, Paris, 1966.

Dye, Marjorie, Davida Finney, Adib Galdas, and Samuel Habib: *Literacy – The Essential Workers,* A Handbook for Literacy Workers, The Committee on World Literacy and Christian Literature, n.d.

Educational Materials Center, *Adult Basic Education,* U.S. Department of Health, Education and Welfare, 1968.

Elkind, D., and J. Weiss: "Studies in Perceptual Development: III. Perceptual Organization," in *Child Development,* Vol. 38, 1967, pp. 553–61.

—— and J.A. Deblinger: "Perceptual Training and Reading Achievement in Disadvantaged Children," in *Child Development,* Vol. 40, 1969, pp. 11–19.

——: "Piaget's Theory of Perceptual Development: Its Application to Reading and Special Education," in *Journal of Special Education,* No. 1, 1967, pp. 357–61.

Ely, Mary L.: *Adult Education in Action,* New York, American Association for Adult Education, 1936.

Emery, F.E., and D.A. Oeser: *Information, Decision and Action,* Melbourne, Melbourne University Press, 1958.

Erasmus, Charles: *Man Takes Control: Cultural Development and American Aid,* Minneapolis, University of Minnesota Press, 1961.

ERIC Clearinghouse on Adult Education: *A Register of Research and Evaluation in Adult Education – 1968 Edition,* Syracuse, New York.

——: *Occupational Training For Disadvantaged Adults,* 1970.

Essert, Paul L., M.B. Lourenco–Filho, and Angelica W. Cass: "Developments in Fundamental Education for Adults," in *Review of Educational Research,* Vol. 23, No. 3, June 1953.

Fagen, Richard R.: *Cuba: The Political Content of Adult Education,* Stanford, Hoover Institution on War, Revolution and Peace, Stanford University Press, 1964.

Festinger, Leon: *Changing Attitude Through Social Contact,* Lansing, University of Michigan, Research Center for Group Dynamics, Institute for Social Research, 1951.

Fliegel, Frederick C.: "Literacy and Exposure to Instrumental Information

Among Farmers in Southern Brazil," in *Rural Sociology*, Vol. 31, No. 1, March 1966, pp. 15–28.

Flores, G.: "A Study on Functional Literacy for Citizenship in the Philippines," in *Quarterly Bulletin of Fundamental Education*, Vol. 2, No. 3, July 1950, pp. 24–28.

Fonseca, Luis, and Bryant Kearl: *Comprehension of Pictorial Symbols: An Experiment in Rural Brazil*, Bulletin 30, Department of Agriculture Journalism, Madison, University of Wisconsin, 1960.

—— and William R. Lassey: *Comprehension and Meaning in Visual Communication Among Illiterate, Low, Literate, and Higher Literate Individuals*, San José, Costa Rica, Institute of Interamerican Social Sciences of the O.A.S., 1964 (mimeo).

Food and Agriculture Organization: *The State of Food and Agriculture, 1966*, Rome, FAO, 1966.

——: *Third World Food Survey*, Rome, FAO, 1963.

Fourre, Pierre: *Adult Education Techniques in Developing Countries: A Greek Case Study*, Paris: Organization for Economic Cooperation and Development, 1963.

Forde, Cyril Daryll: *African Worlds: Studies in the Cosmological Ideas and Social Values of African Peoples*, London, Oxford University Press, 1955.

Freire, Paulo: *Pedagogy of the Oppressed*, New York, Herder and Herder, 1970.

——: "The Adult Literacy Process as Cultural action for Freedom," in *Harvard Educational Review*, Vol. 40, No. 2, May 1970.

Frey, Frederick W.: "The Politicization of the Peasant," Cambridge, Center for International Studies, M.I.T., 1961 (unpublished paper).

Fries, Charles C.: *Linguistics and Reading*, New York, Holt, Rinehart and Winston, 1962.

Fuglesang, Andreas: *Communication With Illiterates:* A Pilot Study of the Problem of Social Communication in Developing Countries, The National Food and Nutrition Commission, Lusaka, Zambia, 1969.

Gadgil, D.R.: "Report of Investigation into the Problem of Lapse Into Illiteracy in Satara District" in D.R. Gadgil and V.M. Dandikar: *Primary Education in Satara District,* Gokhale Institute of Politics and Economics, Publication No. 32, 1955.

Geiger, H. Kent: *National Development: Cultural, Political and Social Aspects of Modernization,* Metuchen, New York, Scarecrow Press, 1969.

Getzels, J.W.: *Learning Theory and Classroom Practice in Adult Education,* Syracuse, Syracuse University, University College, 1956.

Gibbon, Samuel Y., Jr., and Edward L. Palmer: *Pre-Reading on Sesame Street,* Paper submitted to the Committee on Reading of the National Academy of Education, June 1, 1970.

Gibbs, James L. (Ed.): *Peoples of Africa,* New York, Holt, Rinehart and Winston, 1965.

Gibson, Eleanor J.: "A Working Paper Summarizing Theory-Based Research on Reading and its Implications for Instruction," Ithaca, Cornell University, n.d. (mimeo).

Gille, Halvor: "Population," in Richard Symonds (Ed.), *International Targets for Development*, New York, Harper & Row, 1970, pp. 59–91.

Gish, Oscar: "Health Planning in Developing Countries," in *The Journal of Development Studies*, Vol. 6, No. 4, July 1970, pp. 67–76.

Gobena, Merga, and Kenneth Brooks: *The Ethiopian Work-Oriented Literacy Project*, Paper presented to UNESCO Workshop on Functional Literacy, Addis Ababa, May 4, 1970.

Golden, Hilda Hertz: "Literacy and Social Change in Underdeveloped Countries," in *Rural Sociology*, Vol. 20, No. 1, March 1955, pp. 1–7.

Goldsen, Rose K., and Max Ralis: *Factors Related to Acceptance of Innovations in Bang Chan, Thailand*, Ithaca, Cornell University Department of Far Eastern Studies Data Paper 25, 1957.

Goody, Jack and Ian Watt: "The Consequences of Literacy," in Jack Goody (Ed.), *Literacy in Traditional Societies*, Cambridge, Cambridge University Press, 1968.

Gordon, Morton: "Daytime School for Adults: A New Program Dimension at University of California at Berkeley," Brookline, Massachusetts, Center for the Study of Liberal Education for Adults at Boston University, 1962.

Grabelsky, Ora: *From Illiteracy to Literacy*, Adult Education Center, Hebrew University of Jerusalem, 1970.

Gray, William S.: *The Teaching of Reading and Writing*, UNESCO Monographs on Fundamental Education No. X, Paris, 1956.

——: *Manual for Teachers of Adult Illiterates*, Washington, D.C., Sub-Committee on Techniques, October 1930.

——: "Reading and Factors Influencing Reading Efficiency" in William S. Gray, (Ed.), *Reading in General Education*, Washington, D.C., 1940.

Great Britain, Colonial Office: *Social Development in the British Colonial Territories*, Report of the Ashbridge Conference on Social Development, Miscellaneous Papers No. 523, London, HMSO, 1965.

Greenfield, Patricia M.: "Oral or Written Language: The Consequences for Cognitive Development in Africa and the United States," Paper presented at Symposium on Cross-Cultural Cognitive Studies, American Educational Research Association, Chicago, February 9, 1968.

Greenwald, Anthony (Ed.): *Psychological Foundations of Attitudes*, New York, Academic Press, 1968.

Griffiths, V.L.: "The Field Worker," in Phillip Roupp (Ed.), *Approaches to Community Development*, The Hague, 1953.

Groombridge, Brian: *Adult Education and Television, A Comparative Study in Canada, Czechoslovakia and Japan*, London, National Institute of Adult Education, 1966.

Gyorgi, P.: "Report of the Symposium 'How to Reach the Pre-School Child,' Villa Serbelloni, Lake Como, Italy, August, 1963," in *American Journal of Clinical Nutrition*, 14:65, 1964.

Hagen, Everett E.: *On the Theory of Social Change: How Economic Growth Begins*, Illinois, Dorsey Press, 1962.

Hanks, Lucian M., Jr.: "Indifference to Modern Education in a Thai Farming

Community," in *Practical Anthropology*, Tarrytown, New York, Vol. 7, 1960, pp. 18–29.

Harbison, Frederick: "High Level Manpower for Nigeria's Future," in Report of the Commission on Post-School Certificate and Higher Education in Nigeria, *Investment in Education:* Federal Ministry of Education, 1960 (Ashby Report).

—— and Charles A. Myers: *Education, Manpower and Economic Growth: Strategies of Human Resource Development*, New York, McGraw-Hill, 1964.

Harman, David: "Illiteracy: An Overview," in *Harvard Educational Review*, Vol. 40, No. 2, May 1970.

——: *Mimtsaim Al Matsav Haskalat Hamevugarim Bamoshavim* (Findings Pertaining to Adult Education in the Moshavim), Jerusalem, Ministry of Education and Culture, Department of Adult Hebrew and Elementary Education, 1968.

——: *Functional Education for Family Life Planning: Program Design*, New York, World Education Monographs, 1973.

Hart, Joseph K.: *Adult Education*, New York, Thomas Y. Crowell Co., 1927.

Havinghurst, Robert J., and Bernice L. Neugarten: *Society and Education*, Boston, Allyn and Bacon, 1957.

Hawkins, T.: *Adult Education: The Record of the British Army*, London, Macmillan and Company, 1947.

Hedley, Howard W.: *A Study of the Education of Illiterates in the Canadian Army*, unpublished Ph.D. Thesis, Ontario Institute for Studies in Education, 1949.

Hely, A.S.M.: *New Trends in Adult Education*, UNESCO Monographs on Education–IV, 1962.

——: *School Teachers and the Education of Adults*, UNESCO Manuals on Adult and Youth Education No. 5, Paris, 1966.

Hertert, Patricia C.: *Elementary Education for Adults*, unpublished Ph.D. Thesis, University of California, Berkeley, 1958.

Herzog, William Adam, Jr.: *The Effect of Literacy Training on Modernization Variables*, Michigan State University, Ph.D. Thesis, 1967.

Hewitt, Dorothy, and Kirtley F. Mather: *Adult Education: A Dynamic for Democracy*, New York, D. Appleton-Century Co., Inc., 1937.

Hildreth, Gertrude: "Interrelationships Among the Language Arts," in *Elementary School Journal*, Vol. 48, No. 10, June 1948.

Hochberg, Julian: "The Psychophysics of Pictorial Perception," in *Audio-Visual Communication Review*, Supplement, September–October 1962.

Hoffman, Martin L., and Lois Wladis Hoffman (Eds.): *Review of Child Development Research*, New York, Russell Sage Foundation, Vol. 1–1964, Vol. II–1966.

Hoggart, Richard: *The Uses of Literacy*, London, Penguin Books, 1957.

Holmes, Alan C.: *Health Education in Developing Countries*, Edinburgh, Thomas Nelson and Sons, Ltd., 1964.

Hoselitz, Bert: "Investment in Education and Its Political Impact," in J.S. Coleman (Ed.): *Education and Political Development*, Princeton, Princeton University Press, 1965.

—— and H.W. Hargreaves: "Population Growth and Economic Development," in Art Gallaher, Jr. (Ed.): *Perspectives in Development Change*, Lexington, University of Kentucky Press, 1968.

Houghton, Harold, and Peter Tregear (Eds.): *Community Schools in Developing Countries*, UNESCO, Institute for Education, Hamburg, 1969.

Houle, Cyril O.: *The Inquiring Mind*, Madison, University of Wisconsin Press, 1961.

Howard, K.L.: *Diet and Achievement Among School Children in a Depressed Community*, unpublished M.Sc. Thesis, University of Hawaii, 1966.

Howes, H.W.: *Fundamental Adult Literacy and Community Education in the West Indies*, No. XV: "Educational Studies and Documents" series, UNESCO, Paris, 1955.

Hudson, W.: "Cultural Problems in Pictorial Perception," in *South African Journal of Science*, Vol. 58, No. 7, July 1962.

Hughes, Lloyd H.: *The Mexican Cultural Mission Program*, UNESCO Monographs on Fundamental Education No. 3, UNESCO, Paris, 1950.

Hunt, J. Mc V.: "Experience and the Development of Motivation: Some Re-interpretations," in *Child Development*, Vol. 31, 1960.

Hunt, Raymond G.: "Role and Role Conflict," in Edwin P. Hollander and Raymond G. Hunt (Eds.), *Current Perspectives in Social Psychology* (second ed.), New York, Oxford University Press, 1967.

Hunter, Guy: *The Best of Both Worlds*, New York, Oxford University Press, 1965.

Huntington, Samuel P.: *Political Order in Changing Societies*, New Haven, Yale University Press, 1968.

Husen, Torsten: "Some Views on Cross-National Assessment of the Quality of Education," in *Qualitative Aspects of Educational Planning*, UNESCO, IIEP, 1969,

Hyman, Herbert H., Gene N. Levine, and Charles R. Wright: *Inducing Social Change in Developing Communities:* An International Survey of Expert Advice, United Nations Research Institute for Social Development, n.d.

India: *Report on Gram Shikshan Mohim of Maharashtra*, Government of India Planning Commission, New Delhi, 1964.

——: *Wastage and Stagnation in Primary and Middle Schools in India*, NIE-HEW Project 005, Department of Educational Administration, New Delhi, 1967 (mimeo).

Inkeles, Alex: "The Modernization of Man," in Myron Weiner (Ed.), *Modernization*, New York, Basic Books, 1966.

——: "Making Men Modern: On the Causes and Consequences of Individual Change in Six Developing Countries," in the *American Journal of Sociology*, Vol. 75, No. 2, September 1969.

Insko, Chester A.: *Theories of Attitude Change*, Appleton-Century-Crofts, 1967.

International Council of Women: *Literacy—A Social Experience*, Teheran, 1965.

International People's College in Elsinore: *Adult Education in the Struggle for Peace*, Copenhagen, 1949.

Ivanova, A.M.: "Survey of the Literacy Campaign in the U.S.S.R.," in *Convergence*, Vol. 1, No. 3, September 1968.

Jacks, L.P.: *The Education of the Whole Man,* London, University of London Press, 1931.

Jeffries, Sir Charles: *Illiteracy: A World Problem,* London, Pall Mall Press, 1967.

Jelliffe, Derrick B.: *Child Nutrition in Developing Countries,* Washington, D.C., A.I.D. (revised ed.), 1969.

Jones, M.R. (Ed.): *Symposium on Motivation,* Lincoln, University of Nebraska Press, 1954.

Joshi, P.C., and M.R. Rao: "Social and Economic Factors in Literacy and Education in Rural India," in *Economic Weekly,* January 4, 1964, pp. 21–27.

Kagan, Jerome: "The Concept of Identification," in *Psychological Review,* Vol. 65, No. 5, September 1958.

—— and Howard A. Moss: "The Stability of Passive and Dependent Behavior From Childhood Through Adulthood," in *Child Development,* Vol. 31, 1960.

Kahan, Arcadius: "Social Structure, Public Policy and the Development of Education and the Economy in Czarist Russia," in C.A. Anderson and M.J. Bowman (Eds.), *Education and Economic Development,* Chicago, Aldine Publishing Co., 1965.

——: "Determinants of the Incidence of Literacy in Rural Nineteenth-Century Russia" in C.A. Anderson and M.J. Bowman (Eds.), *Education and Economic Development,* Chicago, Aldine Publishing Co., 1965.

Kahl, Joseph: *The Measurement of Modernism,* Austin, University of Texas Press, 1969.

Kallen, Horace: *Notes and Essays on Education for Adults,* "The Liberation of the Adult," Chicago, Center for the Study of Liberal Education for Adults 1954.

Katz, Elihu: "The Diffusion of New Ideas and Practices," in Wilbur Schramm (Ed.): *The Science of Human Communication,* New York, Basic Books, 1963.

Keimig, Joseph F.: *The Use of Adult Education in the Emergence of a New Order in Puerto Rico,* Ph.D. Thesis, University of Chicago, 1964.

Kelman, Herbert: "Three Processes of Social Influence," in Edwin P. Hollander, and Raymond G. Hunt (Eds.), *Current Perspectives in Social Psychology* (second ed.), New York, Oxford University Press, 1967.

Kidd, J. Roby: *How Adults Learn,* New York, Association Press, 1959 (5th Edition—1965).

King, Clarence: *Working With People in Small Communities,* New York, Harper & Row, 1958.

King, Jane: *Planning Non-Formal Education in Tanzania,* Paris, UNESCO, 1967.

Knox, Alan B.: *The Audience for Liberal Adult Education,* Chicago, Center for Study of Liberal Education for Adults, 1962.

Kuhler, R.G. (Ed.): *Psychological Backgrounds of Adult Education,* Chicago, The Center for the Study of Liberal Education for Adults, 1963.

Kushner, Gilbert, et al.: *What Accounts for Sociocultural Change? A Propositional Inventory,* Chapel Hill, North Carolina, Institute for Research in Social Science, 1962.

Landy–Tolwinska, Joanna: "Former Participants in Literacy Courses—Poland," in *Literacy Discussion,* Vol. 1, No. 3, September 1970.

Lassey, William R., et al.: *The Consequences and Meaning of Literacy for Attitudes and Social Behavior,* San José, Costa Rica: Program Interamericano de Información Popular, 1965 (mimeo).

Lasswell, Howard: "The Structure and Function of Communication in Society," in Lyman Bryson (Ed.): *The Communication of Ideas,* New York, Institute for Religious and Social Studies, 1948.

Laubach, Frank C.: *Literacy as Evangelism,* Committee on World Literacy and Christian Literature, New York, 1950.

——: *Teaching the World to Read,* London, 1947.

—— and Robert S. Laubach: *Toward World Literacy the Each-One-Teach-One Way,* Syracuse, Syracuse University Press, 1960.

——: *How to Make the World Literate the Each-One-Teach-One Way,* n.p., n.d.

Leasure, Nettie Norris: *Education for the Bakongo Village Based on a Sociological Study of Bakongo Life,* unpublished Ph.D. Thesis, Columbia University, 1939.

Lehrman, D.S.: "The Organization of Maternal Behavior and the Problem of Instinct," in *L'instinct dans les comportement des animaux et de l'homme,* Masson, Paris, 1956, pp. 475–520.

Lerner, Daniel: "Toward a Communication Theory of Modernization," in Lucien W. Pye (Ed.), *Communications and Political Development,* Princeton, Princeton University Press, 1963, pp. 327–50.

——: *The Passing of Traditional Society: Modernizing the Middle East,* Glencoe, Illinois, The Free Press, 1958.

Levin, H., and Joanna F. Williams (Eds.): *Basic Studies on Reading,* New York, Harper & Row, 1969.

Levy, Marion J., Jr.: *Modernization and the Structure of Societies,* Vol. I, Princeton, Princeton University Press, 1966.

Lewis, J.L.: *Education and Political Independence in Africa,* Edinburgh, Thomas Nelson and Sons, Ltd., 1962.

Linton, Ralph: "Cultural and Personality Factors Affecting Economic Growth," in B. Hozelitz (Ed.), *The Progress of Underdeveloped Areas,* Chicago, University of Chicago Press, 1952.

Lionberger, Herbert F.: *Adoption of New Ideas and Practices,* Ames, Iowa State University Press, 1960.

Lipsitt, Lewis P., and Charles C. Spiker (Eds.): *Advances in Child Development and Behavior,* Vol. I–1963, Vol. II–1965, Vol. III–1967, Vol. IV–1969 (Lipsitt, Lewis P. and Reese, Hayne W. Eds.), New York, Academic Press.

Lipset, Seymour Martin: "Some Social Requisites of Democracy: Economic Development and Political Legitimacy," in *American Political Science Review,* Vol. 53, March 1959, pp. 69–105.

Litchfield, Ann: *The Nature and Pattern of Participation in Adult Education Activities,* unpublished manuscript, Department of Education, University of Chicago, September 1965.

Literacy House: *A Guide to Literacy and Adult Education,* Lucknow, India, 1969.

Liveright, Alexander Albert: *A Study of Adult Education in the United States,* Brookline, Massachusetts, Center for the Study of Liberal Education for Adults, 1968.

Loban, Walter D.: *The Language of Elementary School Children,* Illinois,
    National Council of Teachers of English, 1963.
Lord, A.B.: *The Singer of Tales,* Cambridge, Harvard University Press, 1960.
Lorenzetto, Ann, and Karel Neijs: "The Cuban Literacy Campaign," in *Conver-
    gence,* Vol. 1, No. 3, September 1968.
Lowie, Robert H.: *Primitive Society,* New York, Boni and Liveright, 1920.
Lund, Ragnar: *Scandinavian Adult Education: Denmark, Finland, Norway,
    Sweden,* Copenhagen, Danske Falag, 1952.
McClelland, David: *The Achieving Society,* New York, The Free Press, 1961.
——: *Studies in Motivation,* New York, Appleton-Century-Crofts, 1955.
——: "Does Education Accelerate Economic Growth?" in *Economic Develop-
    ment and Cultural Change,* Vol. 14, No. 3, April 1966, pp. 257–78.
McClusky, Howard Y.: *The Psychology of Adults,* Ann Arbor, University of
    Michigan, n.d.
McLeish, John: "Adult Motives: Education and Propaganda," in *UNESCO
    Journal of Adult and Youth Education,* 3/1960.
MacLean, Malcolm S., Jr.: "Mass Media Audiences: City, Small City, Village and
    Farm," in *Journalism Quarterly,* Vol. 29, 1952, pp. 271–82.
Maguerez, C.: *La Promotion Technique du Travailleur Analphabete,* Paris,
    Eyrolles, 1966.
Malinowski, Bronislaw: "The Problem of Meaning in Primitive Languages," in
    C.K. Ogden and I.A. Richards (Eds.), *The Meaning of Meaning,* New York,
    Harcourt, Brace, 1930.
Martin, Everett Dean: *The Meaning of a Liberal Education,* New York, W.W.
    Norton & Co., 1926.
Mathur, J.C., and H.P. Saksena: *T.V. for Better Citizenship. Report of an AIR-
    UNESCO Project in Adult Education Through T.V.,* New Delhi, UNESCO,
    1962 (2 vols.), Indian State of Maharashtra.
Mayer, Albert, et al.: *Pilot Project, India: The Story of Rural Development at
    Etawah, Uttar Pradesh,* Berkeley, University of California Press, 1958.
Mead, Margaret: *Growing Up in New Guinea,* New York, William Morrow, 1930.
——: "Our Educational Emphasis in Primitive Perspective," in John Middleton
    (Ed.): *From Child to Adult: Studies in the Anthropology of Education,*
    New York, The American Museum of Natural History, 1970.
——: "The Contemporary Challenge of Adult Education," in *Fundamental and
    Adult Education,* Vol. 12, No. 3, Paris, UNESCO, 1960.
—— (Ed.): *Cultural Patterns and Technical Change,* UNESCO, 1955 (Mentor
    Book).
Meader, Mary B.: *Position Paper: Language Development,* Pre-School Project,
    Harvard University, December 1967.
Mearns, Hughes: *The Creative Adult,* New York, Doubleday, Doran & Company,
    Inc., 1940.
Mendez, D. Alfredo, and F.B. Weisanen: *Some Correlates of Functional Literacy,*
    Paper presented at Ninth Congress of the Inter-American Society of Psy-
    chologists, Miami, 1964.
Menlo, Allen: *Adult Self-Perception of Ability to Learn,* Ann Arbor, University
    of Michigan, 1960.
Mezirow, Jack D.: *Dynamics of Community Development,* New York, Scarecrow
    Press, 1963.

Michaels, Leila: *A Study of the UNESCO Latin American Fundamental Education Center (CREFAL)*, M.A. Thesis, University of California, Los Angeles, 1956.

Miles, Catherine C., and W.R. Miles: "The Correlation of Intelligence Scores and Chronological Age From Early to Late Maturity," in *American Journal of Psychology*, Vol. 44, 1932, pp. 44–78.

Miller, Harry L.: *Teaching and Learning in Adult Education*, New York, The Macmillan Company, 1964.

—— and Christine McGuire: *Evaluating Liberal Adult Education*, Chicago, Center for Study of Liberal Education for Adults, 1961.

—— and Marvin Sussman: *An Attempt to Develop a Typology of Community Development Programs*, Chicago, Center for the Study of Liberal Education for Adults, 1956.

Millikan, Max F., and David Hapgood: *No Easy Harvest: The Dilemma of Agriculture in Underdeveloped Countries*, Boston, Little, Brown and Co., 1967.

Miniclier, Louis: "Community Development Defined," in *The Community Development Review*, No. 3, 1956.

Morgaut, M.: *Etudes Tiers Monde: Cinq années de psychologies africaines*, Paris, Presses Universitaires de France, 1962.

Morrow, Evelyn: *Analysis of Family Needs and Problems as a Basis for Planning an Integrated Cooperative Extension Home Program*, unpublished Ph.D. Thesis, University of Minnesota, 1957.

Mort, Paul: *Principles of School Administration*, New York, McGraw-Hill, 1946.

Moss, Howard A., and Jerome Kagan: "Maternal Influences in Early I.Q. Scores," in *Psychological Reports*, Vol. 14, 1959.

Mossaheb, Shamsol Molouk: *After Literacy*, Teheran, Iran, July 1958.

Mowrer, O.H.: *Learning Theory and the Symbolic Process*, New York, John Wiley and Sons, 1960.

Mukherjee, Kartick C.: *Underdevelopment Educational Policy and Planning*, Asia Publishing House, 1969.

Murdock, George Peter: *Social Structure*, New York, The Macmillan Company, 1949.

Mussen, Paul, and Eldred Rutherford: "Parent-Child Relations and Parental Personality in Relation to Young Children's Sex-Role Preferences," in *Child Development*, Vol. 34, 1963.

Myrdal, Gunnar: *Asian Drama* (especially Vol. III), New York, Pantheon, 1968.

Nash, J.: "The Father in Contemporary Culture and Current Psychological Literature," in *Child Development*, Vol. 36, No. 1, 1965.

Nash, Manning: "Education in a New Nation: The Village School in Upper Burma," in John Middleton (Ed.), *From Child to Adult: Studies in the Anthropology of Education*, New York, The American Museum of Natural History, 1970.

Nasution, Amir H.: *Work-Oriented Functional Literacy in Nigeria*, Paper presented at UNESCO Workshop on Functional Literacy, Addis Ababa, April 6, 1970.

Nathalang, Ekavidya, and Kamol Sudarrasert: *The Effects of Primary Schooling in Rural Thailand* (in Thai), Department of Elementary and Adult Education, Ministry of Education, Bangkok, 1970.

Neijs, Karel: *Literacy Primers, Construction, Evaluation and Use,* UNESCO, Manuals on Adult and Youth Education, No. 2, Paris, 1961.

——: *Literacy in the South-Western Pacific: A General Survey,* Noumea (New Caledonia), South Pacific Commission, 1957.

Neisser, Charlotte S.: "Community Development and Mass Education in British Nigeria," in *Economic Development and Cultural Change,* Vol. 3, No. 4, July 1955, pp. 352–65.

Neugarten, Bernice L. (Ed.): *Middle-Age and Aging,* Chicago, University of Chicago Press, 1968.

Nikallranjan, Ray: *Adult Education in India and Abroad,* Delhi, S.S. Chaud, 1967.

Nortman, Dorothy: *Population and Family Planning Programs: A Factbook,* Population Council and the International Institute for the Study of Human Reproduction, Columbia University, Reports on Population/Family Planning No. 2 (1970 Edition), July 1970.

Nyerere, Julius: *Education for Self Reliance,* Ministry of Education and Tourism, Dar-es-Salaam, 1967.

OECD: *The Food Problem of Developing Countries,* OECD, 1967.

Ogburn, William Fielding: *Social Change,* New York, the Viking Press, 1950.

Oguz-Kan, Turhan: *Adult Education in Turkey,* UNESCO, 1955.

Ostheimer, John M.: "Modernization in Tropical Africa: Changing Perspectives and Future Prescriptions," in *Social Science Quarterly,* Vol. 51, No. 1, June 1970, pp. 97–107.

Otto, Wayne, and David Ford: *Teaching Adults to Read,* Boston, Houghton Mifflin Co., 1967.

Owens, W.A.: "Age and Mental Abilities: A Second Follow-Up," in *Journal of Educational Psychology,* Vol. 57, 1966, pp. 311–25.

Palermo, David: "Word Associations and Children's Verbal Behavior," in Lipsitt and Spiker: *Advances in Child Development and Behavior,* Vol. I, New York, Academic Press, 1963, pp. 31–68.

Pan American Union: *Programas para Adultos y su Integración con los Planes Nacionales de Desarrollo Economico y Social en el Ecuador, el Peru y Venezuela,* Washington, D.C., 1965.

Pareek, Udai: "Motivational Patterns and Planned Social Change," in *International Social Science Journal,* Vol. 20, No. 3, 1968 (UNESCO).

——: "A Motivational Paradigm of Development," in *Indian Educational Review,* Vol. 2, No. 2, 1967, pp. 105–11, and *Journal of Social Issues,* Vol. 24, No. 2, 1968, pp. 115–22.

Parker, Edwin B., et al.: *Patterns of Adult Information Seeking,* Stanford University Institute for Communication Research, California, 1966.

Parsons, Talcott: "The Organization of Personality as a System of Action," in Talcott Parsons and Robert F. Bales: *Family Socialization and Interaction Process,* New York, The Free Press, 1955.

——: "Family Structure and Socialization of the Child," in Talcott Parsons and Robert F. Bales: *Family, Socialization and Interaction Process,* New York, The Free Press, 1955.

——: "The School Class as a Social System: Some of Its Functions in American Society," in *Harvard Educational Review,* Vol. 29, Fall 1959.

—— and Neil J. Smelser: *Economy and Society*, Glencoe, Illinois, The Free Press, 1956.

Passin, Herbert: "Portents of Modernity and the Meiji Emergence," in C.A. Anderson and M.J. Bowman, *Education and Economic Development*, Chicago, Aldine Publishing Co., 1965.

Pearce, William Cliff: *The Adult Bible Class*, New York, Pilgrim Press, 1908.

Peers, Robert: *Adult Education: A Comparative Study*, London, Routledge and Kegan Paul, 1958.

Peters, R.S.: "The Meaning of Quality in Education," in *Qualitative Aspects of Educational Planning*, UNESCO, IIEP, 1969.

Phifer, B.M.: *Change of Interest Between Young Adulthood and Early Middle-Age Among Participants in Adult Education Programs*, University of Chicago, unpublished manuscript, 1964.

The Philippines: Human Relations Area Files Vol. II, pp. 877–82.

Pirot, H.: "Problèmes de psychologie appliqués au Maroc," in *La promotion humaine dans les pays sans-développés*, Paris, Presses Universitaires de France, 1960.

Pitts, Jesse: "The Family and Peer Groups" in Norman W. Bell and Ezra F. Vogel (Eds.): *A Modern Introduction to the Family* (revised ed.), New York, The Free Press, 1968.

Pons, V.G., N. Xydias, and P. Clement: *Social Implications of Industrialization and Urbanization in Africa South of the Sahara*, Paris, UNESCO, 1956.

Population Council: New Directions in Family Planning," in *Studies in Family Planning*, No. 32, New York, The Population Council, June 1968.

Powdermaker, Hortense: *Copper Town: Changing Africa*, New York, Harper & Row, 1962.

Primrose, Sister Vincent Marie: *A Study of the Effectiveness of the Educational Program of the Radio-Phonic Schools of Sutatenza on the Life of the Colombian Peasant Farmers*, St. Louis University, 1965.

Prosser, Roy: *Adult Education for Developing Countries*, East Africa Publication House, 1967.

Rabah, Taoufik: "La Motivation chez l'adulte Analphabete Tunisien" in *IBLA-Revue de l'Institut des Belles Lettres Arabes*, No. 1, 1970, pp. 7–39.

Ragheb, F.M.: *Farmers' Training and Functional Literacy Project in India*, Paper presented at UNESCO Workshop on Functional Literacy, Addis Ababa, 30 April, 1970,

Rao, Y.V. Lakshamana: *Communication and Development: A Study of Two Indian Villages*, Minneapolis, University of Minnesota Press, 1966.

Raybould, Sidney Griffith: *Adult Education at a Tropical University* (Nigeria), London, Longmans Green, 1957.

Redfield, Robert: *The Primitive World and Its Transformation*, Ithaca, Cornell University Press, 1953.

——: *A Village That Chose Progress*, Chicago, University of Chicago Press, 1950.

Review of Educational Research: *Growth, Development and Learning*, American Educational Research Association, Vol. 37, No. 5, December 1967.

Ribeiro, Lyra De Raugel: *Mass Adult Education for Rural India*, unpublished Ph.D. Thesis, Harvard University, 1946.

Richards, Charles Granston: *The Provision of Popular Reading Materials*,

UNESCO Monographs on Fundamental Education, No. XII, Paris, 1959.

—— (Ed.): *Simple Reading Material for Adults: Its Preparation and Use,* UNESCO, Manuals on Adult and Youth Education, No. 3, Paris, 1963.

Riesman, David: *The Oral Tradition, the Written Word and the Screen Image,* Antioch College Founders Day Lecture, No. 1, Yellow Springs, Antioch Press, 1956.

Ritchie, Jean A.S.: *Learning Better Nutrition,* Rome, FAO, 1967.

Rogers, Everett M.: *Modernization Among Peasants,* New York, Holt, Rinehart and Winston, 1969.

——: *Social Change in Rural Society,* New York, Appleton-Century-Crofts, Inc., 1960.

—— and Ralph Neill: *Achievement Motivation Among Colombian Peasants,* East Lansing, Department of Communication, Michigan State University, Diffusion of Innovations Research Report 5, n.d.

—— and William Herzog: "Functional Literacy Among Colombian Peasants," *Economic Development and Cultural Change,* Vol. 14, No. 2, January 1966, pp. 190–203.

Rosenberg, M.J.: *Attitude Organization and Change,* New Haven, Yale University Press, 1960.

Rossiter, Charles M., Jr.: "Chronological Age and Listening of Adult Students," in *Adult Education Journal,* Vol. 21, No. 1, Fall 1970, pp. 40–43.

Rostow, W.W.: *The Stages of Economic Growth,* Cambridge, Cambridge University Press, 1967.

Roy, Prodipto, and J.M. Kapoor: *Retention of Literacy,* Council for Social Development, New Delhi, 1970.

—— and Joseph Kivlin: *Health Innovation and Family Planning: A Study in Eight Indian Villages,* Hyderabad, India, National Institute of Community Development, 1968.

——, Frederick B. Waisanen, and Everett M. Rogers: *The Impact of Communication on Rural Development,* An Investigation in Costa Rica and India, UNESCO and National Institute of Community Development, Hyderabad, India, March 1969.

Rubin, Vera: "The Anthropology of Development," in Bernard J. Siegal (Ed.): *Biennial Review of Anthropology,* Stanford, 1961, pp. 120–72.

Ruiz, Ramon Eduardo: *Mexico: The Challenge of Poverty and Illiteracy,* San Marino, California, Huntington Library, 1963.

Russell, Bertrand: *Education and the Modern World,* New York, W.W. Norton & Co., 1932.

Rycroft, W. Stanley, and Myrtle M. Clemmer: *The Struggle Against Illiteracy,* United Presbyterian Church in the U.S.A., New York, 1964.

Sammak, A.: *Problems and Experience in Evaluation of Work-Oriented Adult Literacy Project: Sudan,* Paper presented at UNESCO Workshop on Fundamental Literacy, Addis Ababa, May 6, 1970.

Sapir, Edward: *Language,* Vol. 1, New York, Harcourt, Brace, 1921.

Saraf, S.N.: *Functional Literacy Component Under Farmers' Training and Functional Literacy Project,* Paper presented at UNESCO Workshop on Functional Literacy, Addis Ababa, May 4, 1970.

Sargant, W.L.: "On the Progress of Elementary Education," in *Journal of the Royal Statistical Society,* Vol. 30, 1867.

Schaffer, B.B.: "Deadlock in Development Administration," in Colin Leys (Ed.), *Politics and Change in Developing Countries,* Cambridge, Cambridge University Press, 1969.

Schramm, Wilbur: *Mass Media and National Development,* Stanford, Stanford University Press, 1964.

——: "Communication and Change," in Daniel Lerner and Wilbur Schramm: *Communication and Change in the Developing Countries,* Honolulu, East-West Center Press, 1967.

—— and W. Lee Ruggles: "How Media Systems Grow," in Daniel Lerner and Wilbur Schramm (Eds.): *Communication and Change in Developing Countries,* Honolulu, East-West Center Press, 1967.

Schultz, T.W.: "Investment in Human Capital," in Mark Blaug (Ed.), *Economics of Education, I,* London, Penguin Books, 1968.

Schuman, Howard: *Economic Development and Individual Change: A Social-Psychological Study of the Comilla Experiment in Pakistan,* Cambridge, Occasional Papers in International Affairs, No. 15, Harvard University, Center for International Affairs, February 1967.

——, Alex Inkeles, and David H. Smith: "Some Social Psychological Effects of Noneffects of Literacy in a New Nation," in *Economic Development and Cultural Change,* Vol. 16, No. 1, October 1967.

Scottish Council For Research in Education: *Studies in Reading,* Vol. II, London, University of London Press, 1949.

Scrimshaw, Nevin S.: "Food, World Problem," in David F. Sils (Ed.): *International Encyclopedia of the Social Sciences,* Vol. 5, New York, Macmillan Co., pp. 502–7.

——: *Pre-School Child Malnutrition: Primary Deterrent to Human Progress,* National Research Council Publication, Number 1282, National Academy of Science and National Research Council, Washington, D.C., 1964.

—— (Ed.): *Malnutrition, Learning and Behavior,* Cambridge, M.I.T. Press, 1968.

Seay, Maurice Farris: *Description of the Educational and Training Program of the Tennessee Valley Administration,* Lexington, University of Kentucky, 1938.

Serruys, Paul L.M.: *Survey of the Chinese Language Reform and the Anti-Illiteracy Movement in Communist China,* Studies in Chinese Communist Terminology, No. 8, Berkeley, Center for Chinese Studies, Institute of International Studies, University of California, 1962.

Shacklock, Floyd: *World Literacy Manual,* Committee on World Literacy and Christian Literature, New York, 1967.

Shapiro, Irving S.: *Changing Child-Rearing Attitudes Through Group Discussion,* unpublished Ph.D. Thesis, Columbia University, 1954.

Sharman, Anne: "Nutrition and Social Planning," in the *Journal of Development Studies,* Vol. 6, No. 4, July 1970, pp. 77–91.

Sherif, Carolyn W.: *Attitude and Attitude Change: The Social Judgement-Involvement Approach,* Philadelphia, W.B. Saunders Company, 1965.

Shibutani, Tamotsu: "Reference Groups as Perspectives," in *American Journal of Sociology,* Vol. 60, 1955.

Shrimali, Kalulal L.: *The Wandha Scheme: The Ghandian Plan of Education for Rural India,* unpublished Ph.D. Thesis, Columbia University, 1950.

Shultz, Theodore W.: *Transforming Traditional Agriculture,* New Haven, Yale University Press, 1964.

Sicault, George (Ed.): *The Needs of Children: A Survey of the Needs of Children in the Developing Countries,* UNICEF, New York, The Free Press, 1963.

Simmons, John L.: *Towards an Evaluation of Literacy and Adult Education in a Developing Country: A Pilot Study,* Harvard University, UNESCO Contract ED 6284, September 1970 (mimeo).

—— and James Allman: *Literacy Retention and Adult Education in a Tunisian Village,* Harvard Tunisia Project (mimeo), 1969.

Simpson, C.E.E.B.: "An African Village Undertakes Community Development on Its Own" in *Community Development Bulletin,* Vol. 2, No. 1, pp. 7–9.

Singh, B.N.: *Work-Oriented Adult Literacy Project—Ethiopia: Evaluation and Research Section: Problems and Difficulties Encountered in the Field,* Paper presented at UNESCO Workshop on Functional Literacy, Addis Ababa, April 13, 1970.

Singh, Rudra Datt: "The Village Level: An Introduction of Green Manuring in Rural India," in Edward H. Spicer (Ed.): *Human Problems in Technological Change: A Casebook,* New York, Russell Sage Foundation, 1952, pp. 55–67.

Singh, T.R.: *Functional Literates: Six Case Studies,* Lucknow, Literacy House, n.d.

——: "Literacy in Two Indian Villages," in *Literacy Discussion,* Vol. 1, No. 3, September 1970.

Skorov, George: "Manpower Approach to Educational Planning," in *Economic and Social Aspects of Educational Planning,* UNESCO, 1964.

Smith, Robert McCaughlan: *Adult Education in Liberia,* Bloomington, Indiana University Bureau of Studies in Adult Education, 1966.

Smith, R.S.: "Population and Economic Growth in Central America," in *Economic Development and Cultural Change,* Vol. 2, No. 1, January 1962, pp. 134–50.

Snyder, Benson: *The Hidden Curriculum,* New York, Alfred A. Knopf, Inc., 1970.

Soraya, N.: *A Functional Literacy Approach in Iran,* Paper presented at UNESCO Workshop on Functional Literacy, Addis Ababa, May 7, 1970.

Spaulding, Seth S.: *An Investigation of Factors Which Influence the Effectiveness of Fundamental Education Reading Materials for Latin-American Adults,* Ph.D. Thesis, Ohio State University, 1954.

Spector, Paul, et al.: *Communication and Motivation in Community Development,* Washington, D.C.: Institute for International Services, 1963.

Spence, K.W.: *Behavior Theory and Learning,* Englewood Cliffs, New Jersey, Prentice-Hall, 1960.

Spicer, Edward H. (Ed.): *Human Problems in Technological Change: A Casebook,* New York, Russell Sage Foundation, 1952.

Sprott, W.J.H.: *Social Psychology,* London, Methuen & Co., 1952.

Staiger, Ralph C.: "Developments in Reading and Literacy Education 1956–1967," Chapter XIII, in William S. Gray.: *The Teaching of Reading and*

Writing, UNESCO Monographs on Fundamental Education No. X, Paris, 1969 (second ed.).

Steward, Julian H.: "Perspectives on Modernization: Introduction to the Studies," in Julian H. Steward (Ed.): *Contemporary Change in Traditional Societies*, Vol. I, Chicago, University of Chicago Press, 1967.

Stoch, Mavis B., and P.M. Smythe: "Undernutrition During Infancy and Subsequent Brain Growth and Intellectual Development," in N.S. Scrimshaw: *Malnutrition, Learning and Behavior*, Cambridge, M.I.T. Press, 1968.

Stolz, Lois Meek: *Influences on Parent Behavior*, London, Tavistock Publications, 1967.

Stycos, J. Mayone: "Patterns of Communication in a Rural Greek Village," in *Public Opinion Quarterly*, Vol. 16, No. 1, Spring 1952, pp. 59–70.

Swift, Joan W.: "Effects of Early Group Experience," in Martin L. Hoffman and Lois Wladis Hoffman (Eds.): *Review of Child Development Research*, Vol. I, New York, Russell Sage Foundation, 1964, pp. 249–88.

Tadmor, Shlomo: *Adult Education in Israel—Problems and Principles for Future Development*, Ed.D. Thesis, Columbia University, June 1958.

Talmon, Yonina: "Comparative Analysis of Adult Socialization," Paper presented for the Social Science Research Council Conference, 1964.

Taylor, Katharine Whiteside: *Parents and Children Learn Together*, New York, Teachers College Press, Columbia University, 1967.

Thailand Ministry of Education: *Survey of Five Villages For a Literacy/Family Planning Project*, Department of Elementary and Adult Education, Bangkok, August 1970 (unpublished).

Thomson, Angus M.: "Historical Perspectives of Nutrition, Reproduction and Growth," in Nevin S. Scrimshaw (Ed.), *Malnutrition, Learning and Behavior*, Cambridge, M.I.T. Press, 1968.

Thomson, E.C.: *An Assessment of Activities in Zambia*, East African Conference on Nutrition and Child Feeding (stencil), N.F.N.C., 1969.

Thompson, James Westfall: *The Literacy of the Laity in the Middle Ages*, Berkeley, University of California Press, 1939.

Thorndike, Edward L.: *Psychology and the Science of Education*, Teachers College, Columbia, Bureau of Publications, 1962.

——: *Adult Interests*, New York, The Macmillan Company, 1935.

——, Elsie O. Bregman, Warren J. Tilton, and Ella Woodyard: *Adult Learning*, New York, The Macmillan Company, 1928.

Thorton, Alan Henry: *Adult Education and the Industrial Community*, London, National Institute of Adult Education, 1966.

Tinbergen, Jan, and H.C. Bos: "The Global Demand for Higher and Secondary Education in the Underdeveloped Countries in the Next Decade," in OECD, *Conference on Economic Growth and Investment in Education*, 1962.

Toronto Education Center Library: *Aspects of Illiteracy*, Board of Education for the City of Toronto, 1962.

Trouton, Ruth: *Peasant Renaissance in Yugoslavia 1900–1950: A Study of the Development of the Yugoslav Peasant Society as Affected by Education*, London, Routledge and Kegan Paul Ltd., 1952.

Tumin, Melvin, and Arnold Feldman: *Social Class and Social Change in Puerto Rico,* Princeton, Princeton University Press, 1961.

Turnbull, William W.: "From Goals to Results in Education," in George Z.F. Bereday: *Essays on World Education,* New York, Oxford University Press, 1969, pp. 195–209.

Turner, J.D.: "The Structure of the Educational System in Predominantly Rural Countries," in J.D. Turner and A.P. Hunter (Eds.): *Educational Development in Predominantly Rural Countries,* Proceedings of a seminar held at the University of Botswana, Lesotho and Swaziland, Roma, Lesotho, 1968.

Ulich, Mary Ewen: *Patterns of Adult Education,* New York, Pageant Press, 1965.

Ulmer, Curtis: *Teaching the Disadvantaged Adult,* University of Georgia and Georgia State Department of Education, December 1968.

United Nations: Population Commission. Third Session, 1948–*Report* (UN Doc. E/805) Lake Success, 1948 (mimeo).

——: United Nations Regional Community Development Conference for South and South-East Asia–*Report,* Manila, 1954 (New York, UN, 1955).

——: *The Universal Declaration of Human Rights,* New York, 1950.

——: *Seminar: Administrative Aspects of Community Development,* The Hague, 1959.

——: *World Social Situation,* New York, UN, 1961.

——: *The Growth of World Industry 1938–1961: International Analysis and Tables,* New York, UN, 1965.

——: *Demographic Yearbook, 1969,* New York, 1970.

——: *The United Nations Development Decade: Proposals for Action,* New York, UN, 1962.

——: *Pulp and Paper Prospects in Asia and the Far East,* Vol. I, Bangkok, 1962.

——: Bureau of Social Affairs: *Social Progress Through Community Development,* United Nations Bureau of Social Affairs, New York, 1955.

——: Economic and Social Council: *Principles of Community Development Social Progress Through Local Action,* Report by the Secretary General, New York, The Council, 1955.

——: *Official Records of the 24th Session, Annexes, Agenda Item 4: 20th Report of the Administrative Committee on Coordination to the Council,* Annex III, Geneva, 1957.

——: Conference on Education and Economic and Social Development in Latin America, *Final Report,* ECOSOC, UNESCO/ED/CEDES/37, Paris, March 1962.

——: *World Campaign for Universal Literacy,* New York, 1963, (E/3771).

——: *Evaluation of U.N. Technical assistance activities in the field of rural Community Development,* New York, 1963.

United Nations, Economic Commission for Africa: *Community Development in Africa; A Report of a U.N. Study Tour in Ghana, Nigeria, Tanganyika and U.A.R.,* 15 October–3 December 1960.

——: *Report on the Workshop on Planning and Administration of National Programs of Community Development,* Addis Ababa, 14–25 September 1959.

United Nations Educational, Scientific and Cultural Organization: *Fundamental Education: Common Ground for All People,* Report of a Special Committee to the Preparatory Commission of the United Nations Educational, Scientific and Cultural Organization, Paris, 1946, New York, The Macmillan Company, 1947.

——: *Fundamental Education: Description and Program,* UNESCO, Monographs on Fundamental Education, No. 1, Paris, 1949.

——: *Literacy Education: A Selected Bibliography* (UNESCO), 1950.

——: *UNESCO Seminar on Rural Adult Education for Community Action,* Mysore, India, 1949, New Delhi, Ministry of Education, 1950.

——: *The Haiti Pilot Project: Phase One,* UNESCO Monographs on Fundamental Education No. 4, Paris, 1951.

——: Meeting of Experts on the Use of Vernacular Languages, *Regional Paper on Vernacular Languages No. 4,* Paris, 1951.

——: Expert Committee on Standardization of Educational Statistics, *Report,* UNESCO, Paris, 1952.

——: *Progress of Literacy in Various Countries,* UNESCO, Paris, 1953.

——: *Men Against Ignorance,* Paris, 1953.

——: *The Use of Vernacular Languages in Education,* UNESCO Monographs on Fundamental Education No. 8, Paris, 1953.

——: *Fifteenth Report of the Administrative Committee on Coordination to the Economic and Social Council,* New York, 1953.

——: "Experiments in Fundamental Education in French African Territories," *Educational Studies and Documents* Series, No. IX, Paris, UNESCO, January 1955.

——: *Regional Meeting of Experts on the Production of Reading Materials for New Literates,* Final Report, Muru, West Pakistan, 11–18 June 1956, UNESCO/ED/146, 1956.

——: *World Literacy at Mid-Century,* UNESCO, Paris, 1957.

——: The Definition and Measurement of Literacy in *UNESCO Journal of Adult and Youth Education,* UNESCO, 1/1957.

——: *Rural Television in Japan: A Report on an Experiment in Adult Education,* Paris, UNESCO, 1960.

——: *World Conference on Adult Education,* Montreal, Canada, 21–31 August 1960, Final Report, UNESCO, ED/177, 1960.

——: *Meeting of Experts on the Access of Girls and Women to Education in Rural Areas in Asia, Final Report,* Paris, 8 July 1962.

——: International Committee of Experts on Literacy, *Report,* UNESCO, Paris, 1962.

——: *Report of Meeting of Ministers of Education of Asian Member States Participating in the Karachi Plan,* UNESCO, Tokyo, 1962.

——: *World Campaign for Universal Literacy: Request Addressed to UNESCO by the General Assembly of the United Nations at its 16th Session,* Paris, 10 October 1962.

——: *Resolutions of the 12th General Conference,* (Provisional), Paris, 12 January 1963.

United Nations Educational, Scientific and Cultural Organization: *World Campaign for Universal Literacy,* New York, United Nations, ECOSOC E/3771, 1963.

——: *Document on World Campaign for Universal Literacy,* UNESCO, Paris, PRG/3, 1963.

——: *World Literacy Program,* Paris, September 4, 1964 (BC/PRG/4).

——: *13th General Conference: Addendum and Corrigendum to Proposed Program and Budget for 1965–1966,* Paris, 4 September 1964 (13C/5).

——: *International Committee of Experts on Literacy,* Paris, 1–10 April 1964, Final Report, UNESCO/ED/204, Paris, May 1964.

——: *Conference of African States on the Development of Education in Africa, Final Report,* Addis Ababa, 15–25 May 1964.

——: *Final Report of the Regional Conference on the Planning and Organization of Literacy Programs in Africa,* (Abidjan, Ivory Coast, 9–14 March 1964). UNESCO/ED/203, Paris, 25 May 1964.

——: *Regional Conference on the Planning and Organization of Literacy Programs in the Arab States*– Final Report, Alexandria, 10–18 October 1964. UNESCO/ED/212 Paris, 14 May 1915.

——: *Statistics of Illiteracy,* UNESCO, Minedlit/5, Paris, 1965.

——: World Conference of Ministers of Education on the Eradication of Illiteracy, *Final Report,* Teheran, 1965.

——: *Literacy as a Factor in Development,* Minedlit/3, Paris, 1965.

——: *Cours sur la Planification et l'Administration des Programmes d'alphabetisation,* Rapport Général, Dakar, Groupe régional de planification de l'éducation (UNESCO), 1966.

——: *Literacy: Three Pilot Projects,* Paris, 1966.

——: *Regional Conference on the Planning and Organization of Literacy Programs in Latin America and the Caribbean,* Caracas, 30 May–4 June 1966, Final Report, UNESCO/ED/224, Paris, 4 October 1966.

——: *International Committee of Experts on Literacy, Second Session,* Paris, 29 November–8 December 1965, Final Report, UNESCO/ED/220, Paris, 16 March 1966.

——: *Guide for the Preparation of Pilot Experimental Work Oriented Literacy Projects,* UNESCO, Paris, April 1967.

——: *International Consultative Liason Committee for Literacy, First Session,* Paris, 5-9 June 1967, Final Report, UNESCO/ED/229, Paris, 18 July 1967.

——: *UNESCO and the Eradication of Illiteracy or the Metamorphosis of Fundamental Education,* Paris, 20 October 1967.

——: *78th Session of the Executive Board,* "Cooperation with the United Nations Development Program (UNDP)" *Annexes,* UNESCO 78 Ex/14 Annexes, Paris, 26 April 1968, (Annex 1 – Ethiopia-Work-Oriented Adult Literacy Project), pp. 4–5.

——: *International Advisory Committee for Out-of-School Education, UNESCO House,* 18–26 March 1968, UNESCO ED/C.C. OUT-ED. 68/12, Paris, 5 August 1968.

——: *The Position as Regards Functional Literacy Pilot Projects,* UNESCO, 15C/52, Paris, September 12, 1968.

——: *Meeting of Experts on Research in Literacy,* UNESCO House, 8–12 July 1968, "Suggestions for Research in Adult Literacy," UNESCO, ED/MD/5, Paris, 4 December 1968.

——: *International Consultative Liaison Committee for Literacy,* Second Session, Paris, 3–6 September 1968; Final Report, UNESCO, ED/MD/6, Paris, 27 December 1968.

——: *Round Table of Bankers, Economists and Financiers on Literacy,* Rome, 11–13 February 1969; Final Report, UNESCO, ED/BEFLIT/69/3, ED/LS-47/1, Paris, 17 March 1969.

——: *Meeting on the Experimental Work Literacy Program, Working Paper, Experimental Functional Literacy Projects,* Paris, 13 November 1969.

——: *Literacy 1967–1969,* UNESCO, Paris, 1970.

——: *The Concept of Functional Literacy and its Application,* Round Table, Turin, 22–24 April 1970 (mimeo).

——: *List of Functional Literacy Programmes-Iran,* Document 2-Misc. SN. 31, UNESCO Workshop on Functional Literacy, Addis Ababa, 7 May 1970.

——: *Progress Made Since December 1969 and Present Situation,* Third Meeting of the Panel for the Evaluation of Experimental Literacy Projects, Paris, 20 August 1970.

——: *Equality of Access of Women to Literacy,* Comparative Study, UNESCO, ED/MD/14, Paris, 31 August 1970.

——: *Long-term Outline Plan for 1971–1976,* Presented by the Director General, UNESCO, 16C/4, Paris, September 1970.

——: "A Functional Literacy Experiment in an Industrial Environment," Supplement to *Literacy–A Newsletter,* UNESCO, 1970.

——: "Functional Literacy Experiments in Iran," Supplement to *Literacy–A Newsletter,* UNESCO, 1970.

——: "Functional Literacy Materials for Cotton Growing," Supplement to *Literacy–A Newsletter,* UNESCO, 1970.

——: *The Teaching of Reading (a collection of statements from various countries),* UNESCO publication 113, n.d.

——: International Bureau of Education, *Facilities for Education in Rural Areas,* Geneva, Publication No. 192, 1958.

—— and International Bureau of Education: *Literacy and Education for Adults,* Geneva, Publication No. 266, 1964.

——: *Literacy and Education for Adults: Supplement 1965,* Geneva, Publication No. 278, 1965.

United Nations Population Commission: *Report of the Third Session,* 10–15 May 1948, Lake Success, 1948.

——: *Fourth Session–1949 Report,* (UN Doc. E/1313), Lake Success, 1949 (mimeo).

United States Office of Education: *Report of the Task Force on Planning a Nationwide Adult Right-to-Read Effort,* Washington, D.C., USOE, June 1970 (mimeo).

U.S.S.R.: *The Abolition of Adult Illiteracy in the U.S.S.R. (1917–1940),* UNESCO Journal of Fundamental and Adult Education, XI, 3, 1959.

Valderrama, Fernando: *La Alfabetización en la Educación de Adultos* (Quito: Casa de la Cultura Ecuatoriana), 1963.

Verner, Coolie: *Adult Education,* Washington, D.C., Center for Applied Research on Education, Inc., 1964.

Versluys, J.D.N.: "Functional Literacy in Rural Areas," in *Prospects in Education,* No. 2, 1969.

Vygotsky, L.S.: *Thought and Language,* edited and translated by E. Hanfmann and C. Vakov, Cambridge, M.I.T. Press, 1962.

Wall, W.D.: "Unconscious Resistance to Education," in John W. Hanson and Cole S. Brumbeck (Eds.), *Education and the Development of Nations,* New York, Holt, Rinehart and Winston, 1966.

Weingrod, Alex: *Reluctant Pioneers: Village Development in Israel,* Ithaca, Cornell University Press, 1966.

Weiner, Myron (Ed.): *Modernization: The Dynamics of Growth,* New York, Basic Books, 1966.

Weisenburg, Theodore: *Adult Intelligence,* London, Oxford University Press, 1936.

Wharton, Clifton R., Jr.: "Education and Agricultural Growth: The Role of Education in Early-Stage Agriculture," in C.A. Anderson and M.J. Bowman (Eds.), *Education and Economic Development,* Chicago, Aldine Publishing Co., 1965, pp. 202–28.

Whiting, John W.M., and Irvin L. Child: *Child Training and Personality: A Cross Cultural Study,* New Haven, Yale University Press, 1953.

Whorf, Benjamin: "The Relation of Habitual Thought and Behavior to Language," in Benjamin Whorf (Ed.): *Language, Thought and Reality,* Cambridge, M.I.T. Press, 1956.

Wickert, Frederick R. (Ed.): *Readings in African Psychology From French Language Sources,* East Lansing, African Studies Center, Michigan State University, 1967.

Widstrand, Carl Gosta (Ed.): *Development and Adult Education in Africa,* The Scandinavian Institute of African Studies, Uppsala, 1965.

Wientge, K.M., and P.H. DuBois: *Factors Associated with the Achievement of Adult Students,* St. Louis, School of Continuing Education Research Publications, Washington University, 1964.

Willems, Emilio: "Protestantism as a Factor of Culture Change in Brazil," in *Economic Development and Cultural Change,* Vol. 3, No. 4, July 1955, pp. 321–33.

Wood, Freddie (Ed.): *The Evaluation of Functional Literacy Projects,* UNESCO Workshop, London, 3–22 August 1969, University of London, Institute of Education (mimeo), 1969.

Wood, Kenneth A.: "Student Motivation," in *Scottish Adult Education,* No. 48, September 1968, pp. 23–28.

Woodruff, C.: "Nutritional Aspects of Metabolism Growth and Development," in the *Journal of the American Medical Association,* Vol. 196, 1966.

World Confederation of Organizations of the Teaching Profession: *Survey of the Status of Teaching Professions in Africa,* Washington, D.C., 1964.

World Health Organization (WHO): *Deprivation of Maternal Care: A Re-Assessment of its Effects,* Public Health Papers 14, World Health Organization, Geneva, 1962.

———: *Malnutrition and Disease,* Geneva, WHO, Freedom From Hunger Campaign Basic Study 12, 1963.

Wright, Peter C.: *Literacy and Custom in a Ladino Peasant Community,* Ed.D. Thesis, Michigan University, 1967.

———, Thomas A. Rich, and Edmund E. Allen: *The Impact of a Literacy Program in a Guatemalan Ladino Peasant Community,* Tampa, University of South Florida, 1967 (mimeo).

Yale University Institute of Human Relations: Studies in Attitude and Communication: *Attitude Organization and Change,* New Haven, Yale University Press, 1961 (3 vols.).

Zahn, Jane: "Some Adult Attitudes Affecting Learning: Powerlessness, Conflicting Needs and Role Transition," in *Adult Education,* Vol. 19, No. 2, Winter 1969, pp. 91–97.

Zammit-Tabona, V.: "The Health Aspects of Development," in Richard Symonds (Ed.), *International Targets for Development,* New York, Harper & Row, 1970.

Zelditch, Morris, Jr.: "Role Differentiation in the Nuclear Family: A Comparative Study," in Talcott Parsons and Robert F. Bales: *Family, Socialization and Interaction Process,* New York, The Free Press, 1955.

Zinovyev, M., and A. Pleshakova: *How Illiteracy Was Wiped Out in the U.S.S.R.,* Moscow: Progress Publishers, n.d.

Zitmus, Colin S.: *Adult Education in France,* Oxford, Pergamon Press, 1967.

Index

About the Author

David Harman received the B.A. in History and Middle East Studies from the Hebrew University of Jerusalem and the Ed.M. and the Ed.D. in Educational Planning from the Graduate School of Education, Harvard University. He is Lecturer in Education and Director of the Center for Pre-Academic Studies at the Hebrew University of Jerusalem. Dr. Harman has directed the Israel Literacy Campaign and has helped plan an educational reform program in that country; he has also planned and developed a program of adult functional education for family life planning which is in progress in rural areas of Thailand. He has served as advisor and consultant to many adult and community education programs in various countries, including the Adult Basic Education program in the United States. Dr. Harman taught at Harvard University's Graduate School of Education and has participated as lecturer and resource person at many workshops and seminars on different aspects of non-formal education. He is the author of several articles and a monograph entitled *Functional Education for Family Life Planning: Program Design.*